TAMING THE BUREAUCRACY

Taming the Bureaucracy

MUSCLES, PRAYERS, AND OTHER STRATEGIES

WILLIAM T. GORMLEY, JR.

Princeton University Press

Princeton, New Jersey

COPYRIGHT © 1989 BY PRINCETON UNIVERSITY PRESS
PUBLISHED BY PRINCETON UNIVERSITY PRESS,
41 WILLIAM STREET, PRINCETON, NEW JERSEY 08540
IN THE UNITED KINGDOM: PRINCETON UNIVERSITY PRESS,
GUILDFORD, SURREY

LIBRARY OF CONGRESS CATALOGING-IN-PUBLICATION DATA
GORMLEY, WILLIAM T., 1950–
TAMING THE BUREAUCRACY.
BIBLIOGRAPHY: P.
INCLUDES INDEX.
1. BUREAUCRACY—UNITED STATES. 2. ADMINISTRATIVE AGENCIES—UNITED
STATES. 3. UNITED STATES—EXECUTIVE DEPARTMENTS. I. TITLE.
JK421.G645 1989 353'.01 88–28916
ISBN 0–691–07806–8

PUBLICATION OF THIS BOOK HAS BEEN AIDED BY THE
WHITNEY DARROW FUND OF PRINCETON UNIVERSITY PRESS

THIS BOOK HAS BEEN COMPOSED IN LINOTRON BASKERVILLE

CLOTHBOUND EDITIONS OF PRINCETON UNIVERSITY PRESS BOOKS
ARE PRINTED ON ACID-FREE PAPER, AND BINDING MATERIALS ARE
CHOSEN FOR STRENGTH AND DURABILITY. PAPERBACKS,
ALTHOUGH SATISFACTORY FOR PERSONAL COLLECTIONS,
ARE NOT USUALLY SUITABLE FOR LIBRARY REBINDING

PRINTED IN THE UNITED STATES OF AMERICA BY
PRINCETON UNIVERSITY PRESS, PRINCETON, NEW JERSEY

To
NANCY PFENNING AND SUE HOGAN

CONTENTS

TABLES

ABBREVIATIONS

ADA	Americans for Democratic Action
AFDC	Aid to Families with Dependent Children
APA	Administrative Procedure Act
BEOGs	Basic Educational Opportunity Grants
BOB	Bureau of the Budget
CAB	Civil Aeronautics Board
CBO	Congressional Budget Office
CDBG	Community Development Block Grant
CEA	Council of Economic Advisers
CETA	Comprehensive Employment and Training Act
CIA	Central Intelligence Agency
COWPS	Council on Wage and Price Stability
CPSC	Consumer Product Safety Commission
CUB	Citizens Utilities Board
DEA	Drug Enforcement Agency
DOD	Department of Defense
DOE	Department of Energy
DOL	Department of Labor
DOT	Department of Transportation
EDF	Environmental Defense Fund
EIS	Environmental Impact Statement
EPA	Environmental Protection Agency
FAA	Federal Aviation Administration
FBI	Federal Bureau of Investigation
FCC	Federal Communications Commission
FDA	Food and Drug Administration
FEA	Federal Energy Administration
FERC	Federal Energy Regulatory Commission
FMC	Federal Maritime Commission
FPC	Federal Power Commission
FTC	Federal Trade Commission
GAO	General Accounting Office

LIST OF ABBREVIATIONS

GRS   General Revenue Sharing

HCFA   Health Care Financing Administration

HEW   Health, Education and Welfare

HHS   Health and Human Services

HUD   Housing and Urban Development

INS   Immigration and Naturalization Service

MBO   Management by Objectives

MHSA   Mine Health and Safety Administration

MSPB   Merit Systems Protection Board

NASA   National Aeronautics and Space Administration

NEPA   National Environmental Policy Act

NIH   National Institutes of Health

NLRB   National Labor Relations Board

NOAA   National Oceanic and Atmospheric Administration

NRC   Nuclear Regulatory Commission

NRDC   Natural Resources Defense Council

NSA   National Security Agency

OAL   Office of Administrative Law

OE   Office of Education

OMB   Office of Management and Budget

OPEC   Organization of Petroleum Exporting Countries

OPM   Office of Personnel Management

OSHA   Occupational Safety and Health Administration

OSM   Office of Surface Mining

PHS   Public Health Service

PPBS   Planning, Programming and Budgeting Systems

PUCS   Public Utility Commissions

PURPA   Public Utility Regulatory Policies Act

RARG   Regulatory Analysis Review Group

RIFS   Reductions in Force

SCS   Soil Conservation Service

SEC   Securities and Exchange Commission

SEPAS   State Environmental Policy Acts

SES   Senior Executive Service

SSA   Social Security Administration

SSS   Selective Service System

UMTA Urban Mass Transit Administration
UNC   University of North Carolina
USDA U.S. Department of Agriculture
ZBB   Zero-Based Budgeting

ACKNOWLEDGMENTS

I wrote this book in the friendly confines of Pittsburgh, where I first learned to think about politics. An Andrew Mellon Postdoctoral Fellowship enabled me to write without distraction for a year. I am grateful to the University of Pittsburgh Faculty of Arts and Sciences for their financial support and to members of the University of Pittsburgh Political Science Department for their collegiality. The Graduate School of the University of Wisconsin also provided timely financial support.

A number of friends and colleagues have helped to set me straight as I wrote this book. Bert Rockman, Guy Peters, Samuel P. Hays, Ken Meier, Charles Anderson, Murray Edelman, John Witte, Bill Dunn, James Q. Wilson, and two anonymous reviewers offered sage advice on the enterprise as a whole. Morris Ogul, Graham Wilson, Dick Merelman, Bob Navazio, Jim Gosling, Tony Walters, Alberta Sbragia, Bill Keefe, Mike Margolis, Barry Rabe, Jim Christoph, Colin Campbell, and others offered constructive suggestions on individual chapters. I am especially grateful to Bob McTiernan for helping me rethink the role of the federal courts. His persistent kibitzing has finally paid off.

I have covered a lot of ground in this book, much of it familiar to my long-suffering students. They, too, deserve thanks for their comments and questions as I developed the central themes over a period of time. Debi Hegerfeld of the La Follette Institute also merits special thanks for typing numerous drafts and getting them in the mail on time.

I have enjoyed a good relationship with Princeton University Press and its able staff. Wendy Wong, Gail Ullman, and Sandy Thatcher helped steer the manuscript through the approval process and beyond. Cynthia Perwin Halpern proved a judicious copy editor, and Beth Gianfagna kept the book on schedule. Eric Rohmann persuaded me to tinker around with the original title; Peter Eisinger and Alice Honeywell helped me wade through two dozen alternatives.

I wrote most of this book in the neighborhood where I grew up, surrounded by warm and friendly people who took an equal interest in the progress of my book and my garden. I would like to thank them for their thoughtfulness and support. Finally, I would like to thank my sisters, Nancy and Sue, for helping me remember that there is more to life than just muscles and prayers.

TAMING THE BUREAUCRACY

CHAPTER ONE

A Framework for Analysis

The American bureaucracy is beleaguered and besieged. Its critics, from one end of the political spectrum to the other, are being ap- plauded for their vigilance and concern. Citizens who criticize the bureaucracy are given a respectful hearing and media coverage. Politicians who criticize the bureaucracy are elected and reelected. Scholars who criticize the bureaucracy are awarded the Nobel Prize. The bureaucracy's critics have prospered because they are right on a number of counts. The bureaucracy has become enor- mously powerful, and that power is especially troublesome in a de- mocracy. The bureaucracy spends a great deal of our money, and taxpayers are becoming frugal. The bureaucracy makes frequent blunders, and those mistakes have tragic consequences for many of us.

Unfortunately, the bureaucracy's critics are equally capable of making blunders. Impatient and self-righteous, they have reversed the usual sequence of target practice. Instead of "Ready, aim, fire!" their motto has been "Ready, fire, aim!" Casualties have run high. Nor are bureaucrats the only victims. In many instances, reforms have ensured that citizens are doubly victimized—first by the bu- reaucracy and then by the bureau-bashers.

Bureau-Bashing as a Solution

All of us are now familiar with bureaucratic pathologies. These include: (1) clientelism—agencies defer to clientele groups, dem- onstrating favoritism that runs contrary to the public interest; (2) incrementalism—agencies resist change and tolerate only modest departures from the status quo; (3) arbitrariness—agencies dem- onstrate arbitrary and capricious behavior in their handling of in- dividual cases; (4) imperialism—agencies seek to expand their re- sources without regard to cost constraints; and (5) parochialism— agencies miss the "big picture" by focusing narrowly on a limited set of purposes and goals.

In response to these failings, politicians, judges, journalists, and scholars have unleashed a withering barrage of antibureaucratic

3

rhetoric. The bureaucracy has been blamed for a wide variety of social ills, ranging from the decline of the family to the erosion of civil liberties to the disintegration of our foreign policy to the decline in our economy. But the bureaucracy's critics have moved well beyond rhetoric. As Huntington (1981) has pointed out, the 1960s and 1970s were years of remarkable reform. Although Huntington misreads the reformist mood in certain respects,[1] he argues correctly that we have realigned our political institutions. It is my view that "bureau-bashing" has been the central focus of that institutional realignment. At a time when we could agree on little else, we agreed that the bureaucracy must be controlled.

Efforts to control the bureaucracy have dominated the institutional reform agenda at both the federal and state levels.[2] Chief executives have championed administrative reorganization, civil service reform, new relationships between different levels of government, and policymaking through executive orders. Legislators have opted for clearer statutes, oversight, annual appropriations, legislative vetoes (acts invalidating administrative rules or regulations), and sunset laws (acts requiring the expiration of an agency or program on a fixed date). Judges have expanded the concept of procedural due process to include new property rights; they have insisted on "hybrid rulemaking" procedures that increase the formality of bureaucratic hearings; and they have invoked a strict standard of judicial review known as the "hard look" doctrine. In some instances, judges have taken over state bureaucracies, such as prisons and homes for the mentally retarded. New methods of interest representation have also developed. Ombudsmen now represent individual consumers who run afoul of the bureaucracy, while proxy advocates represent consumers as a class in policy disputes within the bureaucracy. Freedom of information statutes guarantee access to bureaucratic records, and sunshine laws require bureaucrats to hold open meetings. The New Federalism,

1. Huntington's analysis is flawed in several respects. First, he blurs the distinction between the 1960s and the 1970s, despite sharp differences in the values (participatory democracy versus representative democracy), approaches (substantive reform versus institutional reform), and targets (social norms versus bureaucratic behavior) of reformers during the two decades. Second, he characterizes recent reforms as reaffirmations of traditional values (liberty, equality, individualism, and popular control of government), despite considerable emphasis on a newer set of values (accountability, responsiveness, efficiency, and effectiveness). Third, he fails to identify bureaucratic control as the central preoccupation of recent reformers.

2. At the local level, there seems to be a greater emphasis on bypassing the bureaucracy altogether through privatization.

aimed at the federal bureaucracy, has given way to controls aimed at state bureaucracies. These include partial preemptions (the federal government establishes minimum standards that all state bureaucracies must uphold); crossover sanctions (the federal government threatens a reduction in one agency's funding if another agency fails to comply with the law); cross-cutting requirements (the federal government stipulates certain requirements, such as nondiscrimination, for all state agencies that receive federal funds); and direct orders (the federal government insists that state agencies do something or refrain from doing something). Even policy analysis has been turned against the bureaucracy. Planning, Programming, and Budgeting Systems (PPBS) required agencies to group proposed expenditures according to programs rather than traditional categories, such as personnel and supplies; zero-based budgeting (ZBB) instructs agencies to reject last year's appropriation as the starting point for this year's budget exercise; environmental impact statements require agencies to specify the effects of proposed actions on the environment; and cost-benefit orders call upon agencies to choose policies that minimize costs and maximize benefits.

Unfortunately, many of these controls have backfired. Bureau-bashing, a response to the "first generation" of bureaucratic pathologies, has created a "second generation" of bureaucratic pathologies as vexing as the first. These pathologies include: (1) beancounting—agencies that focus on outputs, not outcomes, in order to generate statistics that create the illusion of progress; (2) proceduralism—agencies that adopt uniform procedures in order to rebut charges of arbitrariness and unfairness; (3) avoidance—agencies that escape restrictions by avoiding actions that raise suspicions, even when those actions seem appropriate; (4) particularism—agencies that deviate from the general rules to benefit particular people, organizations, cities, or legislative districts; and (5) defeatism—agencies that abandon public interest goals in the face of tight controls and painful insults. It would be bad enough if we substituted one set of problems for another. In many instances, however, we have created new problems without solving the old ones.

Bureau-bashing illustrates a great deal that is wrong with our approach to institutional reform. We begin with sensible premises and lurch hastily toward questionable conclusions. We pursue vaguely defined procedural values (accountability or responsiveness) without attending to their long-run implications and unin-

5

tended consequences. We value quick fixes more than slow cures. We value action more than thought. We value headlines more than trend lines. We prefer morality plays to the tedium of rational discussion. Finally, we focus more on problems than on solutions. In this way we virtually guarantee that old problems will not be solved and that new problems will emerge.

This is a book about solutions to the bureaucracy problem. More specifically, it is a book about solutions that steer a middle course between bureaucratic independence and bureaucratic abolition. One premise of the book is that we need to live with the bureaucracy, though not necessarily with every bureaucracy that exists today. Deregulation may be appropriate in some instances, such as transportation and communications, where the marketplace offers the promise of real competition on a durable basis. Privatization may be appropriate in cases where the government may purchase vital services from a number of reliable, capable suppliers (e.g., garbage pick-up and job training services). Yet the bureaucracy is indispensable in a modern society. We cannot eliminate the Department of Defense (DOD) simply because of cost overruns. We cannot eliminate public utility commissions because they approve higher rates than we wish to pay. We cannot abolish police departments because the police occasionally run slipshod over our civil liberties. If neither the private sector nor another government agency can do better, then the question becomes: how can we best control the bureaucracy to improve its performance? In answering that question, it is not enough to invoke such values as accountability, responsiveness, efficiency, and effectiveness. Rather, we must think strategically, employing an approach that is purposive, comparative, and contextual.

Although much has been written about specific solutions to the bureaucracy problem, we lack analytical constructs that might enable us to transform concrete findings into abstract lessons. We also lack the habit of comparing different solutions to the same institutional problem, such as runaway spending. Instead we prefer to focus on one reform at a time. Finally, we pay little attention to political and organizational conditions that might help us to differentiate between appropriate and inappropriate reforms. The aim of this book is to generate insight into the consequences of reform by appraising alternative reform strategies. This book is at once a bureaucratic impact statement, an exercise in institutional policy analysis, and a plea for greater civility in interinstitutional relations. A political system in which public officials are routinely "bashed" by other public officials is not likely to serve as a model for our youth. Instead it is likely to generate discontents as worrisome as the original problems that fueled the fires of reform.

Bureaucracy and Its Discontents

Although existing bureaucratic pathologies are numerous, two features of modern bureaucracies explain much of our distress: bureaucratic discretion and bureaucratic authority. Together they constitute the twin pillars of the administrative state from which many pathologies flow. The two elements are of course interrelated. Bureaucratic discretion would be more tolerable if the bureaucracy had less authority; bureaucratic authority would be more tolerable if the bureaucracy had less discretion. However, each problem is also discrete. To some critics concerned about authority, the bureaucracy has no business intruding into private affairs, regardless of the bureaucracy's relationship to its sovereigns; to others who are concerned about discretion, even a nonintrusive bureaucracy should be circumscribed by legislators, the chief executive, and by judges.

Prior to the twentieth century, neither bureaucratic discretion nor bureaucratic authority was much of an issue in the United States. In James Q. Wilson's words (1978: 76), "Some agencies wielding discretionary authority existed, but they either dealt with groups whose liberties were not of much concern (the Indian Office) or their exercise of discretion was minutely scrutinized by Congress (the Land Office, the Pension Office, the Customs Office)." The Progressive Movement and the New Deal changed all of that, though they did so in different ways. The Progressives, who regarded the bureaucracy as an antidote to partisan politics and to dangerous concentrations of corporate power, aggressively promoted bureaucratic autonomy. First, they established independent regulatory commissions (e.g., public utility commissions and railroad commissions), which were deliberately structured to minimize political control by chief executives. Second, they nurtured and institutionalized a strong civil service based on the merit system to protect the bureaucracy from both chief executives and party bosses. Third, they installed city managers at the local level in an effort to remove technical, managerial questions from the political arena. Fourth, they stressed the distinction between politics and administration as the philosophical basis for bureaucratic discretion. The bureaucracy's experts, they argued, should be free

7

to perform technical tasks undistracted and unencumbered by political burdens (Wilson, 1887). Independent agencies, relying on their expertise, would in their opinion promote efficiency, good government, and the common good.

Like the Progressives, the New Dealers created several independent regulatory commissions, including the Securities and Exchange Commission (SEC), the Federal Communications Commission (FCC), the Federal Maritime Commission (FMC), the National Labor Relations Board (NLRB), and the Civil Aeronautics Board (CAB). Unlike the Progressives, however, the New Dealers also created a wide variety of agencies that reported directly to the president (the Works Progress Administration, the Public Works Administration, the National Recovery Administration, the Office of Price Administration, and so forth). In addition, they sharply reduced the proportion of federal employees protected by the civil service from 80 percent to 60 percent. After two years in office, Franklin Roosevelt had established sixty new agencies with one hundred thousand new jobs, all exempt from civil service procedures (Van Riper, 1958: 320).

Despite some overlap in approaches, the New Dealers seemed more interested in bureaucratic power than in bureaucratic autonomy. From their vantage point a strong bureaucracy was an indispensable tool of strong executive leadership. To promote that vision they supported several reforms and practices. First, they endorsed broad delegations of authority by the legislative branch to the executive branch, as a means of coping with various national emergencies. Second, they supported the use of executive orders to ensure that presidential policies would be swiftly implemented by the bureaucracy. Third, they counseled judicial acceptance of both legislative delegations of authority and of executive branch decisions. Indeed, in one celebrated case (*Humphrey's Executor v. U.S.*, 1935), President Roosevelt urged the courts to allow him to replace a Federal Trade Commission (FTC) commissioner who had incurred his wrath. Although the Supreme Court ultimately refused to allow that, the case suggested that the Roosevelt administration's commitment to bureaucratic independence was very weak indeed.

Many New Deal bureaucracies, tightly controlled by the White House, differed considerably from the independent agencies of the Progressive era. This reflected both Roosevelt's style and the mood of the times. Economic recovery and the war effort, it seemed, required strong central control of a growing bureaucratic establishment. With the end of the war and the death of Roosevelt, however, the White House's grip on the bureaucracy relaxed. As domestic and foreign crises receded, the federal bureaucracy became more independent of its sovereigns. The president delegated considerable authority to subcabinet officers and White House aides. The Congress delegated considerable authority to the executive branch and to congressional committees. The courts adopted a posture of deference toward both Congress and the executive branch. The result at the federal level was a prolonged period of neglect during which "semi-sovereign" bureaucracies enjoyed the privileges of discretion without the burdens of accountability. The principal manifestation of this independence was the rise of "iron triangles"—clusters of like-minded congressional subcommittee members, executive bureau officials, and clientele groups. Sometimes known as subgovernments, iron triangles were subject to few external constraints by the president, the Congress, or the courts. A related development was agency "capture," where special interest groups dictated terms to regulatory agencies that were supposed to be regulating them in the public interest. Despite occasional criticism from academics (Huntington, 1952; Bernstein, 1955), this pattern aroused little controversy, because those most affected were reasonably content.

The process was roughly similar at the state level, although the courts occasionally checked state bureaucracies and state legislatures by invoking the "nondelegation" doctrine or the "substantive due process" doctrine. The former insisted on a modicum of statutory specificity to legitimate bureaucratic power; the latter rejected overly intrusive economic regulation when it seemed to undermine competition. Despite occasional judicial reminders that something was askew, state legislatures continued to delegate considerable authority to state agencies. Indeed, state bureaucracies were probably more autonomous than their federal counterparts throughout most of the twentieth century. Weak governors, limited in their appointment powers, presided over a fragmented executive branch in many states. The low visibility of state politics and the low expertise of state legislative bodies contributed to the enlargement of administrative discretion.

The age of semi-sovereign bureaucracies might have persisted were it not for the presidency of Lyndon Johnson. By announcing a war on poverty and an end to racial discrimination, the Johnson administration invited both controversy and disappointment. Social service bureaucracies and the Justice Department aroused considerable resentment, and not just in the South. It was easier to justify bureaucratic power at a time when the bureaucracy sought to rescue the entire nation from the throes of the depression; it was more difficult to justify bureaucratic intervention on behalf of disadvantaged members of society. The Johnson administration's pursuit of an elusive victory in the jungles of Vietnam made matters worse by exposing the moral obtuseness and the logistical weaknesses of the military, DOD, the State Department, and the Selective Service System (SSS). By the end of the Johnson years, the bureaucracy was seen not only as powerful but as arrogant and intrusive, inefficient and ineffective.

Other developments contributed to the bureaucracy's growing image problem and to demands for stronger controls. These included: (1) a participation explosion—the emergence of many public interest groups committed to environmental protection, consumer protection, open government and other broad goals; (2) inflation—deepening frustration over the costs of government and growing awareness of the impact of government spending on wageearners and taxpayers; (3) Watergate and its aftermath—the erosion of public confidence in the executive branch (and in government as a whole); (4) divided government—a growing tendency for the legislative and executive branches to be controlled by different political parties; (5) the professionalization of legislatures— this reduced the expertise gap between legislative bodies and the bureaucracy; (6) investigative reporting—eye-opening accounts of bureaucratic abuse, waste, fraud and corruption; and (7) evaluation research—scholarly studies questioning the effectiveness of government programs and the bureaucracy's capacity for satisfactory policy implementation.

Disappointed and infuriated by the bureaucracy, reformers sought to restrict both bureaucratic discretion and authority. Subgovernments were broken up, enlarged, or exposed to public scrutiny. Laws were written with fewer loopholes and with greater clarity and precision. Public hearings multiplied. Budget constraints became more significant. Traditional personnel controls, which granted chief executives somewhat more discretion in appointments, yielded to more comprehensive efforts at control, such as the Carter administration's Senior Executive Service (SES). Judicial review, focusing on agency procedures, became less deferential and judges imposed requirements not specified in the federal Administrative Procedure Act (APA) or its state counterparts. Moreover, this was the tip of a very large iceberg.

Not content with traditional controls, some economists and public choice theorists proposed more radical remedies, including privatization (especially at the local level) and deregulation (especially at the federal level). These reforms redrew the lines between the public and private sectors and shifted important tasks from bureaucracies to private firms. In most instances, however, reformers sought to reduce bureaucratic discretion without significantly reducing the scope of government. Most reforms were Madisonian in character, relying on "checks and balances" to limit the discretion of particular bureaucracies. Yet these reforms, alike in their emphasis on taming the bureaucracy but not abandoning it, differed considerably in the degree of discretion they afforded the bureaucracy. The least restrictive were *catalytic controls*, which relied on complaints to induce change. More restrictive were *hortatory controls*, which resorted to pressure, combining complaints with the threat of coercion. The most restrictive were *coercive controls*, which relied on force, actual or perceived, to secure bureaucratic compliance and cooperation.

These controls may be viewed, in Hood's (1983) terms, as "tools of government." Yet in contrast to the tools discussed by Hood (nodality, treasure, authority, organization), they are tools by which government officials control other government officials, either directly or through surrogates. Such controls are less visible and less controversial than controls aimed at citizens or at private firms. However, they are no less important, as they determine which bureaucratic pathologies we will conquer and which will persist.

Muscles and Prayers

The choice between coercive controls and catalytic controls (or muscles and prayers) is as fateful as the choice between semi-sov-

TABLE 1.1
Strategic Responses to the Bureaucracy Problem

	Distribution of Power			
	Semi-Sovereign Bureaucracies	*Checks and Balances*		*Market Forces*
	Neglect, Deference	Catalytic Controls	Hortatory Controls	Coercive Controls	Privatization, Deregulation
Strategic Responses	very high bureaucratic discretion	fairly high bureaucratic discretion		fairly low bureaucratic discretion	very low bureaucratic discretion

11

ereign bureaucracies and market forces. Coercive controls and catalytic controls involve different players, values, opportunities, dangers, and conceptions of the role of bureaucracy in government.
These differences, routinely ignored by public officials and by
many scholars, are nevertheless striking enough to tilt a delicate
balance, to promote functional or dysfunctional behavior, to determine success or failure. As a result, we need to think carefully before choosing a particular type of control.

Coercive controls (muscles) reduce bureaucratic discretion without reducing bureaucratic vulnerability to criticism. These kinds of
controls, rooted in a hierarchical model of government, are solution-forcing and highly restrictive. Examples include legislative vetoes, which invalidate administrative rules or regulations; sweeping court injunctions, which mandate changes in bureaucratic
behavior; nondiscretionary executive orders, which tell bureaucrats exactly what to do; and technology-forcing statutes, which require agencies to insist that private firms use the best available
technology by a certain date. Coercive controls are legally and politically irresistible because they are tightly worded and unambiguous; however, they do not take the bureaucracy off the hook.
They leave the bureaucracy with little room to maneuver and few
opportunities to be creative, but they do not absolve the bureaucracy of responsibility if programs fail or if clients complain. It is
no wonder that bureaucrats resent these controls. Few of us like to
be blamed for actions over which our control is limited at best.

In contrast, catalytic controls (prayers) strike a different balance
between bureaucratic discretion and permeability. Catalytic controls require the bureaucracy to act but do not predetermine the
nature of the bureaucracy's response. They require the bureaucracy to address a problem, but they do not specify a mandatory
solution. Catalytic controls are attention-grabbing, action-forcing
and energizing. They seek to raise the bureaucracy's consciousness
by forcing bureaucrats to take certain ideas, problems and interests
seriously. Examples include ombudsmen, proxy advocates, environmental impact statements, and agenda-setting statutes, such as
the Public Utility Regulatory Policies Act (PURPA), which required
state public utility commissions to "consider and determine" the
merits of various rate structure reforms. In all of these cases, bureaucrats must explain themselves to an attentive and demanding
audience but may improvise and experiment if they wish.

Hortatory controls fall somewhere in between coercive controls
and catalytic controls. They are catalytic controls with "bite," coer-

TABLE 1.2

Alternative Checks on the Bureaucracy: A Comparison of Ideal Types

	Catalytic Controls	Hortatory Controls	Coercive Controls
Principal focus	agendas, alternatives	incentives, disincentives	commands, bans
Key players	citizens, interest groups, journalists	federal officials, political executives, legislative staffers	legislators, judges, chief executives
Source of power	ideas, publicity	threats, promises	authority, discipline
Bureaucratic options	diverse	somewhat limited	severely limited
Key values	responsiveness, effectiveness	cooperation, accommodation	accountability, compliance
Inspirational models	pluralist model, expertise model	exchange model, bargaining model	formalist model, judicial review model
Opportunities	flexibility, creativity, innovation	compromise, progress, trust	speed, coherence, predictability
Dangers	opportunism, symbolic politics, demagoguery	brinkmanship, logrolling, instability	formalism, legalism, micromanagement
Examples	proxy advocacy, environmental impact statements, freedom-of-information acts, agenda-setting statutes	intergovernmental bargaining, a senior executive service, inspectors general, legislative audits	legislative vetoes, executive orders (nondiscretionary), court injunctions (structural), solution-forcing statutes

cive controls with an "escape hatch." A typical hortatory control involves the threat of coercion, as when an interest group threatens to go to court if an agency fails to adopt a satisfactory rule.[3] Another hortatory control involves the use of financial incentives to alter bureaucratic behavior, as when the Congress authorizes a

---

3. The credibility of that threat and the severity of the threatened outcome determine whether a control is catalytic, hortatory, or coercive. As a threat becomes more credible and the threatened outcome more severe, a hortatory control comes to resemble a coercive control. As a threat becomes less credible and the threatened outcome less severe, a hortatory control comes to resemble a catalytic control.

federal agency to withhold funds from states that fail to enforce the law or to perform satisfactorily. A third hortatory control involves a legislative audit (e.g., by the General Accounting Office) that results in immediate embarrassment and that could eventually generate serious repercussions. A. M. Rosenthal (1986: 50) has defined pressure as complaint accompanied by a threat. Hortatory controls involve pressure in precisely that sense.

Coercive controls are muscular in that they substitute force for reason—not physical force in most instances but political or legal force. Coercive controls rely upon intimidation to secure specific results. In contrast, catalytic controls are prayerful in their reliance on an earnest entreaty by persons who acknowledge their need for help. Catalytic controls are prayers in this secular sense and not in some other sense of the word. However, like all prayers, they express both faith and hope. Also, like all prayers they may or may not be heeded.

Muscles and prayers differ most fundamentally in the degree of coercion they employ. Coercion manifests itself as much through content and style as through source and form. A court order may or may not be coercive, depending on what the judge chooses to say. An executive order may or may not be coercive, depending on whether the chief executive insists on a procedure, an explanation, a decision rule, or a decision. Despite these ambiguities, it is possible to specify certain factors that help to differentiate coercive from catalytic controls.

As a general rule, controls from above (instituted by judges or politicians) are more coercive than controls from below (instituted by citizens or interest groups). Studies of bureaucratic attitudes confirm this. According to Abney and Lauth (1985), local administrators fear interventions by city council members much more than they fear interventions by interest groups. The former, it seems, have less respect for such norms as objectivity and impartiality than the latter do. Similarly, municipal administrators prefer contacts by citizens to contacts by elected officials (Greene, 1982). Based on experience, they have found that citizens can be persuaded to obey the law, while elected officials expect bureaucrats to bend the law.

As a general rule, substantive controls are more coercive than procedural controls. A court injunction requiring a state agency to provide specified services or to abandon an established policy is more restrictive than a court order requiring a public hearing or cross-examination opportunities. An executive order requiring

14

civil servants to take a drug test is more restrictive than an executive order requiring agencies to adopt a particular budgeting technique. This is not to say that procedural controls are never coercive. In some instances the connection between a particular procedure and a particular outcome is so close that a given procedure will have predictable substantive consequences. In most instances, however, substantive commands reduce bureaucratic discretion more thoroughly than procedural requirements do.

Finally, as a general rule, controls established by one person are more coercive than controls established by many persons. This is both surprising and disturbing, because it suggests that a single legislative "freelancer" may be able to exercise more influence over the bureaucracy than the legislature as a whole. An individual legislator's views are often clearer than those of the legislature as a whole; in addition, an individual legislator's interest in a particular dispute is often greater than that of the legislature as a whole. This enhances the influence of individual policy entrepreneurs, who may or may not speak for the full legislature. From the bureaucracy's standpoint, a warm legislator is often more intimidating than a cold statute.

When we opt for catalytic controls or coercive controls, we are, intentionally or not, making a statement about the models of bureaucracy we prefer. Frug (1984) has argued that four models dominate our thinking: (1) a formalist model—the bureaucracy is a rationalized, disciplined mechanism for implementing the wishes of its creators; (2) an expertise model—bureaucratic discretion enables expert professionals to be creative, flexible and effective; (3) a judicial review model—the bureaucracy must be subject to the rule of law through careful judicial scrutiny; and (4) a market-pluralist model—legitimacy flows from the operation of political or market mechanisms within bureaucratic structures. In general, catalytic controls are compatible with the expertise and pluralist models because they require the bureaucracy to apply its expertise to challenges or problems identified by pressure groups. In contrast, coercive controls are compatible with formalist and judicial review models because they expect the bureaucracy to follow orders from the chief executive, the legislature, or the courts. It is fair to say that neither catalytic controls nor coercive controls are compatible with a market model or a democratic model. If we were to pursue these models, we would probably opt to end bureaucracy, to reduce its size, alter its responsibilities, or decentralize it to facilitate public control.

15

Muscles and prayers have different advantages and disadvantages. Catalytic controls promote flexibility, creativity, and imagination; coercive controls promote speed, coherence, and predictability. Catalytic controls may be too weak; coercive controls may be too strong. Because they stress the role of an agency's sovereigns, coercive controls tend to promote accountability or fidelity to narrow operational goals, as specified by bureaucratic overseers. As a result, muscles and prayers are subject to different pathologies. As Nonet (1980) has warned, accountability, though desirable, may lead us down the road to formalism and legalism. In contrast, responsiveness may result in demagoguery and opportunism if bureaucrats simply capitulate to powerful constituencies. We must make these choices with considerable care.

A Normative Model of Control

Despite advantages and disadvantages, prayers are normally superior to muscles. This is true for several reasons. First, prayers are action-forcing but not solution-forcing. They require the bureaucracy to address a problem but they do not predetermine the bureaucracy's response. Thus, they preserve the bureaucracy's capacity to apply expertise to difficult problems. Second, prayers stress persuasion and appeals to the common good. Prayers seek to change behavior by means of reminders of our obligations to other members of the community. Thus they are rooted in some conception of the public interest. Third, prayers preserve bureaucratic morale and self-respect. In contrast to muscles, they treat bureaucrats with dignity and they assume that bureaucrats are capable of behaving with wisdom, fortitude, and good sense. This expression of potential confidence is important for all bureaucrats but especially for "street-level" bureaucrats (Lipsky, 1980), who, suffering from status anxiety, may try to compensate in dysfunctional ways if their anxiety is reinforced by coercive controls. Fourth, prayers encourage flexibility at the enforcement stage. According to Wildavsky (1979: 33), rigidity is the single most troublesome characteristic of bureaucracies. Yet muscles often promote the very rigidity that supposedly generates the need for such controls in the first place. In many instances, bureaucrats will behave rigidly if their sovereigns behave rigidly toward them. For all these reasons, the burden of proof should be on those who advocate muscles rather than prayers.

Of course, I have only established that muscles are disappointing, not that prayers are better. Catalytic controls have their critics as well. Citizen intervenors are often unrepresentative of society as a whole, and their conceptions of the public interest may be seriously flawed. Bureaucratic intervenors are part of the same "establishment" that they purport to challenge. Journalistic observers, armed with agency documents, indulge in exaggeration and oversimplification. These, at any rate, are frequent objections to specific catalytic controls, including public hearings, proxy advocacy, and freedom-of-information statutes.

By far the most common objection to catalytic controls is that they are ineffective, that they are ritualistic exercises in symbolic politics. If religion is the opium of the people, are prayers the gestures that legitimize ill-advised administrative policies and practices? Do prayers involve the spinning of wheels but no real movement? Do they contribute to false consciousness? Do they represent the triumph of process over substance? Do they substitute bureaucratic autonomy for bureaucratic discretion?

In certain situations, specified below, my answer would be yes. But the premise that catalytic controls are generically weak is, I think, incorrect. Consider public hearings, often derided as exercises in symbolic politics (Arnstein, 1969; Checkoway, 1981). In fact, a number of studies confirm that public hearings make a significant difference. In environmental policy, for example, they have resulted in substantial gains for citizens concerned about air pollution, water pollution, and coastal zone management (Jones, 1975; Godschalk and Stiftel, 1981; Rosener, 1982).

Proxy advocates and ombudsmen have also won significant concessions from bureaucrats, including public utility regulators and public health officials. As a result of the efforts of proxy advocates, numerous state public utility commissions have revised their rate structures to promote energy conservation (Gormley, 1983). As a result of the efforts of ombudsmen, state agencies have adopted a wide variety of policy and process innovations. In Hawaii, for example, the Health Department, the Labor Department, and the Transportation Department have accepted numerous reforms after reasonably amicable negotiations with the state ombudsman (Hill, 1983).

Environmental impact statements and economic impact statements have also had substantial policy consequences. The former have changed the habits of such crusty agencies as the Army Corps of Engineers and the U.S. Forest Service (Mazmanian and Nienaber, 1979; Taylor, 1984). Furthermore, they have encouraged agencies to hire highly skilled professionals with diverse points of view. Economic impact statements have also had substantial effects on agencies' consideration of alternatives and their attentiveness to cost considerations. In Illinois, for example, economic impact statements have resulted in a relaxation of noise standards for forging plants, saving $3 million without changing health impacts (Croke and Herlevsen, 1982).

In order to understand these successes, it is important to recognize that many bureaucrats see themselves as public servants and as promoters of the public interest. Indeed, according to Schmidt and Posner (1986), high-ranking federal executives are much more interested in effectiveness, leadership, and productivity than in organizational stability, budget stability, or organizational growth. It is easy enough to think of executives who do not fit this sanguine view. Nevertheless, for those who do, catalytic controls may actually be welcome because they enable bureaucrats to pursue their statutory missions more effectively.

It is also important to recognize that catalytic controls have usually been sanctioned by elected public officials. Indeed, it is appropriate to think of catalytic controls as oversight through other means. Thus, McCubbins and Schwartz (1984) distinguish between "police-patrol" oversight (centralized, direct, proactive) and "fire-alarm" oversight (decentralized, indirect, reactive). From their perspective, fire-alarm oversight (e.g., opportunities for citizens to report problems) is preferable to police-patrol oversight (e.g., requirements that legislators identify and remedy problems), because it saves legislators time and benefits them politically. From my perspective, the key advantage of fire-alarm oversight is that it requires bureaucratic action while preserving a substantial degree of bureaucratic discretion. It also reduces the temptation for bureaucrats to engage in subversion, sabotage, circumvention, and deception.

These findings and observations confirm that catalytic controls can work. They do not however tell us when they will work. Nor do they tell us what type of control is best in a given set of circumstances. In some situations, coercive controls are needed either in lieu of or in addition to catalytic controls. In other situations, hortatory controls may be preferable. Given the special dangers of coercive controls, it is important to give them special attention. A critical task is to specify the circumstances under which coercive controls are needed (and ultimately to specify the form that coercive controls should take).

In recent years, a number of analysts have attempted to identify those controls likely to improve bureaucratic performance. The most popular analytic approaches, stripped to their essentials, include the following: cure-alls (a single solution); the golden mean (a balanced solution); and issue-sensitive strategies (a discriminating solution). Unfortunately, none of these approaches is satisfactory.

To some analysts, the solution to the bureaucracy problem lies in a single reform, adopted across the board. Thus, Lowi (1979) has called for statutory specificity to curb bureaucratic discretion and to reduce bureaucratic power. DeMuth (1980) has recommended cost-benefit analysis to ensure that agencies adopt highly efficient rules. Leventhal (1974) and Garland (1985) have urged strong judicial review (the "hard look" doctrine) to ensure reasoned decision making and fidelity to legislative intent.

Each of these remedies has much to commend it. Cost-benefit analysis makes a great deal of sense when several large public works projects are being considered by the same agency. Statutory specificity makes sense when a consensus exists that significant progress must be made in a short period of time. The hard look doctrine makes sense when legislative intent is clear, when issues are not overwhelmingly complex, and when an agency demonstrates a flagrant disregard for evidentiary requirements. Unfortunately, cure-alls ignore these important questions of context. Moreover, they fail to explain why we continue to be dissatisfied with bureaucratic performance, despite more specific statutes, more cost-benefit analysis, and more "hard looks."

A second approach, the golden mean strategy, posits a bureaucratic ideal-type, characterized by administrative efficiency and pluralist democracy (Yates, 1982). This approach attempts to reconcile the views of Max Weber with those of James Madison by following the advice of Ben Franklin—everything in moderation. Thus, if a bureaucracy is highly centralized, specialized, and professionalized, the solution is to introduce a strong dose of pluralist politics into it. If a bureaucracy is decentralized, permeable, and adaptive, the solution is to introduce greater administrative efficiency, e.g., through administrative reorganization or a quality assurance system.

Mashaw (1985) makes a similar argument in his provocative analysis of welfare bureaucracies. According to Mashaw, we cannot choose between fairness and efficiency, between individual rights and social welfare, between law and economics. Therefore the solution is to combine diverse values (such as appropriateness, competence, and dignity) in a hybrid model. Similarly, Nonet (1980: 295–96) argues that all purposive institutions should contain elements of positivism (the rule of law), pragmatism (appeal to reason), and pluralism (interest representation).

There is much to be said for this sensitivity to competing values. Yet it is not clear that competing values can best be pursued through multiple controls.[4] Moreover, there may be some bureaucracies that should emphasize justice regardless of efficiency (police departments); others that should strive for accuracy without regard to consequences (the Bureau of the Census). Perhaps some agencies should pursue neither administrative efficiency nor pluralist democracy (the Federal Bureau of Investigation, the SEC); perhaps others should be less accountable than most need to be (the Central Intelligence Agency, the Federal Reserve Board). In short, it is by no means clear that every bureaucracy in our system of government should strike the same balance between competing values, nor is it clear that the same values are pertinent in all issue areas.

A third strategy, the issue characteristics approach, is more promising. Depending on levels of issue certainty and stability, we may pursue different models of bureaucratic decision making. If stability and certainty are relatively high, a synoptic (or comprehensive problem-solving) model makes sense; if stability and certainty are relatively low, an incrementalist (or limited change) model is probably preferable (Diver, 1981). This strategy moves us away from a mythical golden mean and toward the more complex, varied world of highly differentiated bureaucracies.

Walcott and Hult (1986) have developed a similar theme in arguing for diverse bureaucratic governance structures, depending on preferences about possible outcomes and beliefs about causation. Their framework builds on the work of Thompson (1967), who suggested years ago that we need to take controversy and uncertainty into account in designing organizations. Moreover, Walcott and Hult recognize that the synoptic model and the incrementalist model are not the only choices that lie before us. Collegial models, decentralized models, and adjudicatory models are also worth considering.

4. Both Mashaw and Yates seem to recognize this in different ways; yet the logic of their approach leads inexorably to a proliferation of controls in pursuit of diverse values.

Yet even this third approach is wanting, because it completely ignores bureaucratic characteristics as constraints. In order to decide when coercion is necessary (or when a given organizational model is appropriate), we need to consider not only issue characteristics (or problem characteristics) but also bureaucratic characteristics (or organizational characteristics). Ultimately, then, we need a fourth approach, which I shall call an integrative approach—one that takes both issue characteristics and bureaucratic characteristics into account in specifying the need for coercive controls.

To my knowledge, only Gruber (1987) has developed an integrative model of this sort with an eye toward specifying appropriate contexts for different forms of bureaucratic control. I find Gruber's model appealing and am happy to acknowledge similarities in our approaches. For example, Gruber and I both emphasize the importance of conflict and complexity; we also agree that the choice between loose and tight constraints is crucial. In three respects, however, my approach differs from Gruber's. First, my data base consists of a large number of reforms at different levels of government and in diverse policy arenas. Second, I draw a sharp distinction between control by citizens (normally catalytic) and control by elected officials (normally coercive). I also introduce a third category (hortatory controls). Finally, I analyze both democratic (interest representation, executive management, legislative oversight) and nondemocratic controls (judicial review, policy analysis, regulatory federalism) as strategic options. The former rely upon citizens or politicians to check bureaucrats; the latter depend upon judges or other bureaucrats.

In Table 1.3, I develop the initial outlines of an integrative approach that encompasses both issue characteristics (complexity, conflict) and bureaucratic characteristics (skill, support). By *complexity*, I mean the amount of specialized knowledge necessary to resolve uncertainties about the consequences of action.[5] By *conflict*,

5. My definition of complexity differs somewhat from others found in the literature. Weiss (1982) blurs the distinction between complexity and conflict by including the number of conflicting values as a facet of complexity. To preserve the integrity of conflict as a separate variable, I reject that approach. Cohen (1984) blurs the distinction between the beginning and the end of the search process by defining complexity as the degree of uncertainty that exists. In fact, uncertainty depends not only on issue characteristics (intrinsic difficulty) but also on bureaucratic characteristics (such as professionalism). As I see it, complexity is a function of the issues; it may or may not be accompanied by a thorough search process. If it is, uncertainty is likely to be reduced.

21

TABLE 1.3

Coercive Controls of Bureaucracy: A Normative Model

	Issue Characteristics			
	Low Complexity, Low Conflict	*Low Complexity, High Conflict*	*High Complexity, Low Conflict*	*High Complexity, High Conflict*
Bureaucratic Characteristics				
High skill, high support	Coercion is unnecessary and distracting		Coercion is unnecessary and risky	
High skill, low support	motivation is key problem (try positive incentives)	COERCION IS JUSTIFIABLE (but should be used as last resort)	skepticism is key problem (try informational strategies)	COERCION IS JUSTIFIABLE (but should be limited in scope)
Low skill, high support	coercion as electioneering (particularism may result)	coercion as game (bureaucracy is not real target)	suboptimization due to resource constraints (try informational or personnel strategies)	
Low skill, low support	corruption is key problem (try publicity)	COERCION IS NECESSARY (but beware of overkill)	obsolescence is key problem (try retraining)	COERCION IS NECESSARY (but focus on outcomes, not outputs)

I mean disagreement over values (goals), institutions (actors), or operations (techniques). By *support*, I mean bureaucrats' philosophical commitment to legitimate goals (as reflected in both agreement and enthusiasm).[6] By *skill*, I mean the level of specialized education or training found within the bureaucracy.

In singling out several contextual variables for early attention (complexity, conflict, support, skill), I do not mean to imply that other variables are unimportant. In the pages that follow, I discuss a wide variety of issue characteristics and bureaucratic character-

6. It is important to define support more narrowly than conflict, so that the one is not simply a pale reflection of the other. This distinction helps to remind us that a breakdown of consensus is not always worrisome. What is essential is bureaucratic commitment to legitimate goals and that is what I mean by support. Bureaucratic skepticism toward particular means or techniques does not necessarily signal low support and may in fact be desirable, especially when issue complexity and bureaucratic skill are both high.

istics. In addition to conflict and complexity, I consider whether an issue is high or low in visibility; whether it is perennial, ephemeral, or cyclical; whether it is relatively discrete or intertwined with other issues. In addition to dimensions of skill and support, I consider whether a bureaucracy is large or small, centralized or decentralized, young or old, punitive or supportive.

Nevertheless, I would argue that conflict, complexity, skill, and support are especially important because they help us to choose between muscles and prayers. Thus, coercion is justifiable when conflict is high and bureaucratic support is low. Under other circumstances, coercion is risky, distracting, counterproductive, or otherwise questionable.

If bureaucratic skill and support are both high, key preconditions for successful implementation are already in place. Under such circumstances, coercion is distracting at best, dangerous at worst. Depending on the situation, coercion may trigger a pointless paper chase, bureaucratic resentment, or the triumph of politics over expertise. The latter is especially troubling when complexity is high, because the bureaucracy's masters may not know what they are doing.

The dynamics are a bit different when skill is high but support is low. If conflict is low, bureaucratic support may be manipulable through new information or positive incentives. Low support is unlikely to mean fierce opposition. If conflict is high, coercion may be justifiable. However, if skill and complexity are both high, skeptical bureaucrats may be right and impatient overseers may be wrong. If low support poses a threat to minority rights, there may be no alternative to coercion. In other cases, however, coercion should be used only as a last resort.

Coercion is usually misguided when bureaucratic support is high, even when bureaucratic skill is low. It is often possible to upgrade bureaucratic skills without resorting to coercion. Alternatively, low skill may be accepted as a temporary fact of life. Clear directives, information-sharing, and technical support can overcome the limitations of a bureaucracy with limited skill. Hortatory control strategies may be sufficient to upgrade bureaucratic skills—not instantly perhaps but in a timely manner.

When skill and support are both low, the case for coercion is strongest. This is especially true when conflict is high. Under these circumstances, low support reflects willful intransigence rather than mild indifference or skepticism. Yet even here it is important to reject the notion that any form of coercion will do. Coercive instruments should be selected with care to avoid overkill or dysfunctional behavior.

The choice of a particular coercive form is as important as the initial decision to opt for a coercive control. With that in mind, the following guidelines may be useful. First, muscles should be *legitimate*—open, broad-based, constitutional, and legal. It is of course desirable that prayers be legitimate as well, but that is less necessary, because the bureaucracy can deflect illegitimate prayers. Second, muscles should be *selective*, not instituted across the board. If coercive controls are to be applied, they should be limited in scope. They should be tailor-made reforms, not generic reforms. Third, muscles should be *scalable*, so that the intensity of the instrument may be adjusted through smooth increments. A dimmer switch is a good example of a "scalable" control (Hood, 1983: 146). Fourth, muscles should be *reversible*. If coercive controls prove dysfunctional, it is important that they can be stopped or overhauled. Finally, muscles should be *enforceable*. It makes little sense to require (or prohibit) behavior that cannot be monitored or to threaten sanctions that cannot be imposed. If coercive controls are nonenforceable, they simply encourage resentment, sabotage, or both.

From Ideal Types to Grim Realities

The actual application of controls to bureaucracies in recent years suggests a crazy-quilt pattern that departs significantly from these groundrules. The only discernible principle has been that of George Washington Plunkitt: "I seen my opportunities and I took 'em." Legislators, chief executives, and judges, seeing their opportunities, frequently applied coercive controls to federal and state bureaucracies. In some instances, hortatory controls evolved into coercive controls; in others, impatient overseers reached for the sledgehammer before trying reason or persuasion.

Table 1.4 cites examples of coercive controls applied against the backdrop of different issue characteristics and different bureaucratic characteristics. This is not a definitive list of coercive controls. Many more examples will be cited. Nor is this a random sample of coercive controls. Indeed, it is difficult to imagine how a random sample of controls, coercive or otherwise, might be drawn. Nevertheless, these examples help to capture the range of coercive controls applied to bureaucracies since bureau-bashing became popular around 1970.

In an ideal world, coercive controls would be clustered in those

TABLE 1.4

Coercive Controls of Bureaucracy: A Descriptive Model

	Issue Characteristics			
	Low Complexity, Low Conflict	*Low Complexity, High Conflict*	*High Complexity, Low Conflict*	*High Complexity, High Conflict*
Bureaucratic Characteristics				
High skill, high support	Regulatory federalism, child support, Pa.	Executive order, drug tests; Executive order, lie detector tests; *Goldberg v. Kelly*, state agencies, welfare rights	Congressional oversight, aspartame, FDA; Pork barrel politics, Army Corps of Engineers; Congressional oversight, artificial heart research, NIH	Hard look doctrine, formaldehyde, CPSC; Legislative language, forced scrubbing, EPA; OMB disapproval, EPA asbestos rule
High skill, low support		Regulatory federalism, aff. action, UNC; Quality control, AFDC; Legis. veto, used car rule, FTC; Admn. presidency		Regulatory federalism, Ohio EPA; Quality control, SSA; Legis. veto, natural gas pricing, FERC; Congressional oversight, Gorsuch EPA
Low skill, high support	Pork barrel politics, state highway depts.	*Finney v. Arkansas* Board of Corrections, prison reform, Ark.	Regulatory federalism, Wis. Home for the Developmentally Disabled	*Wyatt v. Stickney*, mental health reform, Alabama
Low skill, low support		*James v. Wallace*, prison reform, Ala.; *U.S. v. Brignoni-Ponce*, abuses, INS; Regulatory federalism, 55 m.p.h., Ariz.		Regulatory federalism, strip mining, Okla.; *FERC v. Mississippi*, utility rate reform; Regulatory federalism, San Diego Co. Mental Health Facility

four cells where conflict is high and bureaucratic support is low. Yet that does not appear to be the case. In fact, what is most striking, as demonstrated in this table, is that coercive controls have been largely unrelated to issue characteristics and bureaucratic characteristics. High complexity has not inhibited judges and legislators from imposing coercive controls on environmental protection agencies, energy regulatory agencies, and mental health facilities. High skill does not protect bureaucracies from coercive controls involving welfare policy, consumer protection policy, and foreign policy. High support does not shield state bureaucracies from intrusive federal court orders, nor does it protect federal agencies from drug tests and lie detector tests. Judging from this table, the only variable that has had a consistent impact is conflict.

What does Table 1.4 tell us about the bureaucracy's overseers? It reveals that they have a keen eye for conflict, and that they are most likely to resort to bureau-bashing when conflict is high. However, it also suggests that the bureaucracy's overseers fail to distinguish between "low-game" conflict (Lynn, 1987: 59–64) and other kinds of conflicts.[7] Thus, the Congress immersed itself in low-game questions (micromanagement) when it insisted through legislative committee reports that all coal-burning power plants should be forced to use scrubbers (Ackerman and Hassler, 1981). Judge Frank Johnson got embroiled in low-game questions when he required Alabama's mental health facilities to hire a specified number of psychologists and other trained personnel (Yarbrough, 1981). President Reagan participated in low-game disputes when he instructed federal agencies to handle drug problems through mandatory urine testing.

This initial glimpse of our bureaucratic control network also suggests considerable hubris by legislators and judges in addressing highly complex issues. Thus, in *Gulf South Insulation v. CPSC* (1983), the U.S. Court of Appeals overturned a decision banning urea-formaldehyde foam insulation because it disagreed with the methodology employed by the Consumer Product Safety Commis-

7. Lynn (1987) argues persuasively that policy conflicts arise at different levels of the political game. Thus, high-game conflicts involve fundamental questions (is there a role for government? what social values ought to be pursued?); middle-game conflicts involve important institutional questions (who will have responsibility? how shall resources be allocated?); low-game conflicts involve highly technical, practical, operational questions (how will programs be organized and administered? how should programs be fine-tuned?). Using Lynn's terminology, I would argue that high-game conflicts generally warrant greater reliance on coercive controls.

sion (not enough rats in laboratory studies; too much attention to problem homes in household studies). With equal bravado, the House of Representatives overturned a carefully considered natural gas pricing rule adopted by the Federal Energy Regulatory Commission (FERC) after lengthy hearings and testimony from over five hundred parties (Craig, 1983: 122–35). Admittedly, Congress has a good deal of expertise at its disposal, largely as a result of the expansion of congressional staffs. However, the problem with coercive controls in relation to highly complex issue areas is not merely the inadequacy of political and judicial expertise but rather the remoteness of the possibility that experts in any branch of government can fashion a detailed rule appropriate for all occasions. This problem is compounded when the federal government attempts to fashion rules appropriate for all fifty states. Thus, the U.S. Environmental Protection Agency's rules on hazardous waste resulted in a bizarre situation in Minnesota, where a lime sludge pile could not be removed from a highway site, could not be used for waste-water treatment, and could not be used to clean an electric utility company's smokestack emissions because it was officially classified as a hazardous waste, even though tests showed that the lime was not corrosive (Black, 1985).

Another disturbing pattern highlighted by Table 1.4 is a striking inattention to bureaucratic characteristics. The bureaucracy's overseers seem virtually oblivious to the characteristics of the bureaucracies they are trying to regulate. This is highly ironic, since bureaucracies themselves are often accused of a similar indifference in their dealings with regulated firms. Thus, according to Bardach and Kagan (1982), regulatory bureaucracies often fail to distinguish between responsible firms (good apples) and irresponsible firms (bad apples). This results in the unreflective application of stringent procedures, inflexible inspection schedules, and burdensome paperwork requirements to responsible and irresponsible firms alike. This is not only inefficient but it also reduces private sector incentives to behave responsibly. Yet precisely the same phenomenon is apparent in the relationship of politicians and judges to bureaucrats (and in the relationship of federal bureaucrats to state bureaucracies).

Coercive controls are not reserved for bureaucracies low in skill or low in support. Rather, they are applied with little regard for bureaucratic characteristics. Consider, for example, congressional intervention to reshape the heart research priorities of the National Institutes of Health (NIH). Following a careful analysis of

27

technical problems and financial considerations, the NIH concluded that the quest for a total artificial heart would be less fruitful than other heart research. Senator Edward Kennedy, chair of the Senate committee that oversees NIH, and Senator Orrin Hatch, the ranking Republican on the same committee, threatened dire consequences unless NIH reversed itself. Contractors in Kennedy's home state of Massachusetts and Hatch's home state of Utah stood to gain from the artificial heart research, which would cost $22.6 million over six years. Despite an unfavorable ratio of benefits to costs, NIH decided that it would be "prudent" to reinstate the program (Boffey, 1988). Coercive controls are not applied across the board. One can think of bureaucracies (the Federal Reserve Board, state insurance commissions, state banking commissions) that are subject to few coercive controls. However, it is difficult to escape the conclusion that coercive controls are being applied for political reasons and not because issue characteristics and bureaucratic characteristics warrant such strong remedies.

A final problem with coercive controls in the real world is that they are poorly designed. Coercive controls, if applied, ought to be legitimate, selective, reversible, enforceable, and scalable. Unfortunately, few coercive controls embody these characteristics. Legislative oversight often lacks legitimacy because of the gap between the collective will and a single legislator's policy preferences. For example, every time Senator Howard Metzenbaum resurrects the "aspartame" dispute and requires the Food and Drug Administration (FDA) to produce more reams of paperwork on this beverage additive, he is speaking for himself. Other legislators exploit legislative oversight to speak for their constituents, as when a member of the Armed Services Committee puts pressure on the Defense Department to award a defense contract to a firm from his or her district or state. A key problem with the massive drug tests ordered by President Reagan, aside from their fallibility, is that they are not very selective. If aimed at Federal Aviation Administration (FAA) employees with poor performance records or poor health records, drug tests might be more acceptable (and less costly). A serious drawback of the legislative veto—still being applied by Congress despite an adverse Supreme Court ruling—is that it is not scalable. When a legislative body considers a legislative veto, it has two crude options: yes or no. A better rule is unlikely to result from the application of such a blunt instrument. A key problem with many court decisions is that they are not enforceable. Thus, when Judge Frank Johnson insisted that prison cells in Alabama be sixty square feet, he was issuing an order that for practical reasons could not be implemented or enforced. Finally, Office of Management and Budget (OMB) review of agency rules under the Reagan administration could not be reversed, because OMB's critiques of proposed rules could not be challenged in court.[8] Indeed, much of OMB's feedback on proposed agency rules is not even made public. When OMB rejects an agency rule, it is difficult to know whether OMB's cost-benefit review was technically faulty, a smokescreen for political choices, or both.

In short, there are two serious problems with coercive controls as they have been applied in recent years. First, they are applied in many instances where they are inappropriate, given the levels of complexity, conflict, skill, or support in the bureaucracy to which they apply. Second, they are not designed to take legitimacy, selectivity, scalability, enforceability, and reversibility into account. In our zeal to control errant bureaucracies, we have paid little attention to issue characteristics, bureaucratic characteristics, and the characteristics of controls themselves. We have resorted to muscles when prayers would suffice, and we have not designed coercive controls with sufficient care.

Conclusion

The proliferation of bureau-bashing reforms in recent years was an understandable response to specific bureaucratic pathologies (clientelism, incrementalism, arbitrariness, imperialism, parochialism) and to the broader problems of bureaucratic discretion and authority. Institutional realignments may revitalize a political system, and there is reason to believe that bureaucratic control was necessary. The application of Madisonian logic (checks and balances) to the bureaucracy problem is fully consistent with our cultural heritage. Nevertheless, it should be recalled that the great debates in Philadelphia in 1787 focused less on the concept of checks and balances than on the specific tools through which that concept could best be realized (bicameralism, advice and consent, and so forth). As we extend checks and balances to a fourth branch of government, the bureaucracy, we need to think again about those and other tools.

8. Several members of Congress challenged OMB's regulatory review efforts in court but received little encouragement from the U.S. Court of Appeals (D.C. Circuit). See *Public Citizen Health Research Group v. Rowland* (1986).

In our efforts to control the bureaucracy, we have relied too heavily on muscles rather than prayers. Restless and impatient, we have opted for coercive controls when catalytic controls would do the job. Coercive controls promote speed, consistency, and accountability, but they undermine flexibility, creativity, and responsiveness. They generate new bureaucratic pathologies (beancounting, proceduralism, avoidance, particularism, and defeatism) without eradicating old ones. Far from ending bureaucratic rigidity, they guarantee that the bureaucracy will be more rigid than before.

Admittedly, there is a place for coercive controls. When issues are high in conflict and bureaucratic support is low, coercive controls are justifiable. Thus federal judges have no choice but to invoke coercive controls when state prisons or state school systems demonstrate a flagrant disregard for constitutional rights. Similarly, a strong dose of regulatory federalism is warranted when state bureaucracies are unable or unwilling to pursue important federal goals, such as environmental protection, energy conservation, and error reduction in social welfare programs.

Unfortunately, however, we seldom take issue characteristics and bureaucratic characteristics into account in deciding when to apply coercive controls. This results in numerous mismatches—controls that make little sense because they underestimate bureaucratic skill or issue complexity or because they confuse a "low-game" conflict with a "high-game" conflict. The case for coercive controls depends on a series of contingencies that are unlikely enough that the burden of proof should be on those who advocate such controls.

Moreover, the coercive controls we invoke are poorly designed. If coercive controls are to be applied, they should be legitimate, selective, scalable, reversible, and enforceable. Legislative vetoes, which bypass the chief executive and present legislators with simplistic yes-no options, violate at least two of these criteria (legitimacy and scalability). Far-reaching executive orders that use an elephant gun to shoot a squirrel violate other criteria (selectivity and reversibility). The only consistent principle that seems to operate, it seems, is seeing political opportunities and taking them.

The proliferation of bureau-bashing reforms that has taken hold in recent years poses a policy problem, but it also represents a research opportunity. There is much that we can learn from these reforms if we adopt a purposive, comparative, and contextual approach. It is not necessary to take the bureaucracy's side or to view controls from a bureaucratic perspective, but it is necessary to prepare the equivalent of a bureaucratic impact statement. It is also essential that we reject the ritualistic invocation of such words as "accountability" and "compliance" as a substitute for strategic thinking.

In evaluating bureaucratic reforms I focus deliberately on reforms that involve external control of the bureaucracy. These reforms, discussed in chapters 3–8, encompass new forms of interest representation, due process, management, policy analysis, federalism, and oversight. I do not examine reforms that transfer bureaucratic tasks to the private sector (those involving privatization and deregulation). Such reforms, though interesting, have been less widespread and less dramatic than "checks and balances" reforms.

I also focus primarily, though not exclusively, on reforms of the 1970s. I do so because of my interest in institutional realignment. When the history of the twentieth century is written, the 1960s and the 1980s will be viewed as times of shifting values and of substantive reforms. The 1960s will be recognized for their emphasis on redistribution, entitlement, and the rights of the disadvantaged (civil rights, the war on poverty, Medicare, Medicaid, and so forth); the 1980s will be recognized for their emphasis on contraction, obligation, and taxpayer preferences (supply-side economics, cutbacks in social programs, tax reform, workfare, and so forth). By contrast, the 1970s will be recognized as a time of remarkable institutional reform. Although reformers reshaped many political institutions (including legislative bodies, the presidency, and the political parties), they devoted special attention to the bureaucracy. To limit bureaucratic discretion and authority they institutionalized new and old versions of interest representation, due process, policy analysis, management, federalism, and oversight. These reforms, which peaked during the 1970s, tell us a great deal about the relative merits of muscles and prayers.

31

The 1970s: A Golden Age of Institutional Reform

The Culture of Reform

During the 1970s politicians, judges, professors, journalists, and citizens reached a remarkable consensus on what ailed the body politic. The fundamental problem with our political system was a powerful bureaucracy that was simultaneously unaccountable, unresponsive, inefficient, and ineffective. This consensus was especially noteworthy because deep, bitter divisions over substantive issues divided liberals from conservatives, Democrats from Republicans, business from labor, the young from the old. Despite these conflicts, a wide range of leaders and citizens agreed on the need to control the bureaucracy.

As Goodsell (1983) has noted, criticisms of the bureaucracy were numerous and diverse in this period. The bureaucracy was often described—in the scholarly literature and in the mass media—as inefficient, expansionist, dysfunctional, means-oriented, rigid, conservative, ineffective, irrational, insubordinate, elitist, and discriminatory. Individual bureaucrats were perceived as arrogant, slow, remote, insensitive, lazy, inhumane, petty, inept, manipulative, secretive, and callous. Although critics disagreed on which of these traits were most worrisome and which bureaucrats were most incorrigible,[1] there was virtual unanimity on the need for reform.

What forces contributed to this rare consensus on the need for institutional reform? There were in fact a number of factors:

1. *Social Movements.* The late 1960s and early 1970s catapulted two new social movements into the limelight—the consumer movement and the environmental movement.[2] These movements were broad-based and well-organized—

---

1. In general, liberals were sharply critical of economic regulatory commissions, distributive agencies, the Defense Department, and intelligence agencies. Conservatives, in contrast, were sharply critical of social regulatory agencies, redistributive agencies, and the Justice Department.

2. Later, a third movement—the taxpayers movement—would join the assault on the bureaucracy, though with different purposes in mind.

built on the backs of strong middle-class constituencies and headed by clever leaders with a zest for combat and a flair for publicity. Ironically, while these social movements generated sharp criticisms of existing bureaucracies, such as the Federal Trade Commission (FTC) and the Army Corps of Engineers, they also led to the creation of new bureaucracies, with their own peculiar discontents.

2. *New Agencies, New Regulations.* Newly created environmental protection and consumer protection agencies generated their own set of problems. Shortly after their creation, they were denounced by some as too aggressive, denounced by others as too lax. Such criticisms helped to justify strong measures taken by legislators, judges, and chief executives to bring these new bureaucracies under control—measures ranging from legislative vetoes to the "hard look doctrine" of judicial review to requirements for cost-benefit analyses accompanying new rules and regulations.

3. *Old Agencies, New Crises.* As new problems arose, old agencies, long accustomed to serenity and obscurity, found themselves overwhelmed by urgent problems and besieged by impatient critics. The energy crisis, which first erupted in 1973 with the Organization of Petroleum Exporting Countries (OPEC) oil embargo, put state public utility commissions and various federal agencies on the spot. The aging of the population and advances in medical technology contributed to rising health care costs and triggered criticism of health care agencies. The expansion of the welfare rolls—one consequence of the Great Society—led to sharp increases in welfare budgets and to new demands for quality control.

4. *Watergate.* Watergate contributed to institutional reform in various ways, both direct and indirect. To restore public confidence in government officials in the wake of Watergate, reformers advanced measures to open up the government to public scrutiny (e.g., by sunshine laws) and to prevent troublesome conflicts of interest (e.g., through restrictions on the "revolving door" between government and private industry). A leading champion of these reforms, Common Cause, found its membership bulging as the Watergate scandal worsened (McFarland, 1984: 44). Watergate also led to a sharp increase in congressional

33

oversight of the bureaucracy (Aberbach, 1979). The tele-
vised hearings of the Senate Watergate Committee and the
House Judiciary Committee proved to have great public relations benefits for legislative interlocutors. Members of
Congress—and their counterparts at the state level—began
to realize that legislative oversight was not only interesting
and important but a potential source of valuable publicity
as well.

5. *Vietnam.* The Vietnam War was blamed primarily on the
presidents who committed us to a war effort we were unable or unwilling to win. Yet the supporting cast of experts
extended deep into the bowels of several bureaucracies, including the Defense Department, the State Department,
and the military. These experts—the "best and the brightest" in Halberstam's (1972) words—supported our intervention in Vietnam and helped to keep us there long
enough for over forty-five thousand Americans to die. The
Pentagon Papers, published in 1971, implicated these experts and established a pattern of official deception that
undermined the credibility of the executive branch.
Among other things, it helped to generate support for passage of important amendments to the Freedom of Information Act in 1974. Later in the decade, memories of government deception during the Vietnam War would fuel the
congressional drive for stronger oversight of the nation's
intelligence agencies.

6. *Inflation.* The Johnson administration's gift to the American people was not only an unpopular, expensive war but
also a period of spiraling inflation that began in 1968. The
"guns and butter" philosophy of the Johnson administration in conjunction with an ill-advised tax cut in 1964 resulted in sharp increases in government spending, a growing deficit, and a period of "demand-push" inflation that
could have been avoided (Cameron, 1985). This in turn
generated support for efforts to reduce unnecessary government expenditures and (later) unnecessary regulations,
both of which were thought to aggravate the burden of inflation. For example, President Ford's executive order
11821, requiring administrative agencies to conduct cost-
benefit studies before adopting new rules, was officially un-

veiled as part of the president's WIN (Whip Inflation Now!) campaign.

7. *Ticket-Splitting.* Since the 1950s, the American people have been more and more willing to split their tickets, choosing Democratic legislators and Republican chief executives, or vice versa. This phenomenon has contributed to "divided government" at both the federal and state levels. At the federal level, the resurgence of Congressional power stemmed partly from the fact that the Democrats controlled the Congress while the Republicans controlled the White House throughout much of this period (from 1969 to 1976). At the state level, divided governments also contributed to reform. For example, states with divided governments were more likely to adopt legislative veto provisions than other states (Hamm and Robertson, 1981).

8. *Public Opinion.* Although government officials normally worry more about their own job security than about public opinion graphs concerning government institutions, many government officials were troubled by growing evidence of a public disaffection with government. Beginning in the mid-1960s, public confidence in a wide range of political institutions plummeted dramatically. Confidence in business and the mass media also declined, but not as dramatically. By the mid-1970s, only 11 percent of the American people believed that the government was responsive to the thinking of ordinary people (Lipset and Schneider, 1983: 25). Alarmed by these and other polls, reformers sought to restore public confidence in government by means of a wide range of institutional reforms.

The Progressive Legacy

In certain respects, the reforms of the 1970s paralleled those of the Progressive Era (from 1900 to 1914), often characterized as the "golden age of reform" (Hofstadter, 1955). Like the Progressives, the reformers of the 1970s placed considerable emphasis on institutional reforms—on reforming the machinery of government. Like the Progressives, the reformers of the 1970s were backed by a strong middle-class constituency. Like the Progressives, the reformers of the 1970s were goaded, needled, and often supported by a cranky, muckraking press.

Yet there were noteworthy differences between the Progressive era and the 1970s. To the Progressives, the bureaucracy was the solution to a whole fistful of problems, including corrupt party bosses, meddlesome judges, and unscrupulous businessmen. To the reformers of the 1970s, the bureaucracy itself was the problem—self-directing (but not self-correcting) organizations that seemed increasingly out of control. To the Progressives, the legislators were the villains—captured by utility companies, railroads, and corrupt party bosses. To the reformers of the 1970s, the legislators were the redeemers in the vanguard of reform. Although some historians would prefer not to characterize Progressivism as a "movement" (Filene, 1970; Buenker, 1977), Progressives were in fact united on a wide variety of substantive and procedural issues. They were at any rate cohesive enough to form their own political party, the Progressive Party, in 1912. In contrast, the reformers of the 1970s belonged to loose, fluid, shifting coalitions. Alliances were temporary, born out of expediency rather than a commitment to a shared vision of "the good society." The Progressive reformers, surrounded by such architectural geniuses as Louis Sullivan and Frank Lloyd Wright, saw themselves as political architects. As "architects," they designed sleek new institutions in pursuit of their goals—the Food and Drug Administration (FDA), the FTC, the Federal Reserve Board, public utility commissions, railroad commissions, industrial commissions, the direct primary, the initiative, the referendum, and the recall. In contrast, the reformers of the 1970s were "fixers" who found themselves repairing institutional machinery that had grown dilapidated over time. Their role model was not Frank Lloyd Wright but Mr. Goodwrench. While some new bureaucracies were created, the principal thrust of the 1970s was to overhaul the existing machinery of government. The Progressives were idealists, with a sour view of special interests but great expectations for the public at large. In contrast, the reformers of the 1970s were more pragmatic and more generally suspicious. Whereas the Progressives were willing to concentrate power in the hands of "experts" or "the people," the reformers of the 1970s, chastened by Watergate and Vietnam, were loath to concentrate power anywhere. In effect, they subscribed to Lord Acton's dictum that power corrupts and absolute power corrupts absolutely.

In this critical respect, the reformers of the 1970s had much more in common with our Founding Fathers than with the Progressives. Like our Founding Fathers, the reformers of the 1970s were strongly committed to "checks and balances," including inter-governmental checks, interbranch checks, and popular checks on government itself. They could heartily endorse Federalist No. 51's call for "auxiliary precautions" to ensure that ambition would counteract ambition (Hamilton et al., 1901: 353–58). Indeed, the 1970s may be viewed as an attempt to design a viable system of checks and balances for a political system with four branches of government, not three. The bureaucracy, finally recognized as a fourth branch of government, needed to be checked—by chief executives, legislators, judges, interest groups, and citizens. In this sense, the reform spirit of the 1970s was profoundly Madisonian.

Yet in one critical respect the reformers of the 1970s differed from the Federalists. According to the Federalists, the principal challenge that required checks and balances was control of the legislative branch, inherently the strongest branch of the government and the one to be feared the most. As Publius put it (Hamilton et al., 1901: 339–40): "In a representative republic, where the executive magistracy is carefully limited . . . and where the legislative power is exercised by an assembly, which is inspired, by a supposed influence over the people, with an intrepid confidence in its own strength . . . it is against the enterprising ambition of this department that the people ought to indulge all their jealousy and exhaust all their precautions." The reformers of the 1970s disregarded these warnings and those of Thomas Jefferson, who had observed that legislative despotism is no less oppressive than other forms of despotism (Hamilton et al., 1901: 341). Neither legislators nor other reformers of the 1970s seemed especially worried by this possibility.

Reformers and Their Values

The Progressive Movement has sometimes been characterized as a quest for direct democracy and expert management (Hofstadter, 1955; Goldman, 1952). In contrast, the reformers of the 1970s were committed to representative democracy and the management of experts. In practice, this meant that many of the reforms of the 1970s served a double duty. For example, reforms making the bureaucracy more accountable to the legislative branch or more responsive to the chief executive also enabled these overseers to manage the bureaucracy in pursuit of such goals as efficiency and effectiveness. Any reform movement that values both democracy and expertise must struggle with contradictions—some apparent,

37

some real. The Progressives, who believed in the dichotomy between politics and administration, resolved these contradictions by
calling for more democracy in policy formulation, more expertise
in policy implementation. The reformers of the 1970s took a different tack. Wherever possible, they devised reforms that simultaneously promoted accountability and efficiency, responsiveness
and effectiveness. These four values exemplified the reforms of
the 1970s in the same way that Roosevelt's four freedoms exemplified the New Deal. Although other values were invoked from
time to time—fairness, due process, flexibility, clarity, simplicity,
honesty, integrity—they were overshadowed by accountability, responsiveness, efficiency, and effectiveness.

While reformers agreed on the need for accountability, responsiveness, efficiency, and effectiveness, these words evoked different meanings for different reformers. To some, accountability
meant that bureaucrats should serve at the pleasure of the chief
executive; to others, it meant that bureaucrats should be required
to defend themselves before legislative committees. To some, responsiveness meant that bureaucrats should pursue policies desired by the general public; to others, it meant that bureaucrats
should respond to the policy shifts of politicians. To some, effectiveness meant that the bureaucracy should produce the desired
results, by whatever means; to others, it meant that the bureaucracy should faithfully execute the laws, without second-guessing
those who had drafted them. To some, efficiency meant that expenditures and regulations should be approved if their benefits
exceed the costs; to others, it meant that costs should be mini-
mized, regardless of benefit-cost ratios. Thus, to say that reformers
agreed on the need for accountability, responsiveness, efficiency,
and effectiveness is merely to say that a basis for coalition-building
existed.

The key to coalition-building during this period, as during the
Progressive Era, was effective political leadership. Yet there was a
critical difference between the two eras. During the Progressive
Age, political leaders were few in number, extremely prominent,
and easily identified: men such as Robert La Follette, Theodore
Roosevelt, Woodrow Wilson, Hiram Johnson, and Charles Evans
Hughes. Not coincidentally, they were all during their heyday
chief executives.[3] In contrast, the leaders of the 1970s were nu-

3. All five were governors at some point in their careers. Roosevelt and Wilson of
course also went on to become presidents.

merous and diverse. While some were more visible and more important than others (e.g., Nixon, Carter, Nader, Gardner, Muskie, and Jackson), it would be inaccurate to attribute the reforms of this decade to a mere handful of men. As Table 2.1 suggests, the reformers of the 1970s included chief executives and legislators, judges and professors, public interest groups and business groups. Those familiar with the reformers will also recognize Democrats and Republicans, liberals and conservatives. Virtually everyone got in on the act.

Many of the reforms of the 1970s were adopted with broad bipartisan support. For example, the Government in the Sunshine Act of 1976 was approved in the U.S. House of Representatives by a vote of 390–5. Similarly, the Civil Service Reform Act of 1978 was adopted in the House by a vote of 365–8. Yet there were partisan differences at times, as one might expect. Overall, it seemed, Democrats were somewhat more enthusiastic about responsiveness and accountability, while Republicans were somewhat more committed to efficiency and effectiveness. Thus, the proposed Consumer Protection Agency, which was to promote responsive government, triggered strong party-line voting whenever it came to a vote. On 6 November 1975, for example, the Consumer Protection Agency was overwhelmingly supported by House Democrats (188–80), overwhelmingly opposed by House Republicans (119–20). A bill placing a limit on Social Security disability awards, heralded as a stimulus to administrative efficiency, attracted different supporters and opponents. In a vote on 6 September 1979, the bill won strong Republican support in the House (108–36), while dividing Democrats right down the middle (127–126).

In general, partisan differences were most visible when the substantive consequences of institutional reform were clearest. Thus, the Consumer Protection Agency would not only make the bureaucracy more responsive to consumers but would also be a thorn in the side of the business community. In contrast, quality assurance in the Social Security disability program would not only promote administrative efficiency but might also result in the removal of eligibles from the roster of beneficiaries on a technicality. As Clausen (1973) has shown, government management issues (e.g., a Consumer Protection Agency) and social welfare issues (e.g., Social Security disability awards) often trigger party voting in Congress. Where institutional reforms had relatively clear implications for social welfare or government management, party differences were often manifested.

39

TABLE 2.1

Leading Reformers of the 1970s

CHIEF EXECUTIVES
Richard Nixon
Jimmy Carter
Gerald Brown
(*Calif.*)
Patrick Lucey
(*Wis.*)
Nelson Rockefeller
(*N.Y.*)
Brendan Byrne
(*N.J.*)
Marvin Mandel
(*Md.*)
Daniel Evans
(*Wash.*)
Ronald Reagan
(*Calif.*)
Christopher Bond
(*Mo.*)
Richard Riley
(*S.C.*)

LEGISLATORS
Henry Jackson
(*Wash.*)
Edmund Muskie
(*Maine*)
Wilbur Mills
(*Ark.*)
Russell Long
(*La.*)
Lawton Chiles
(*Fla.*)
John Moss
(*Calif.*)
Abe Ribicoff
(*Conn.*)
Warren Magnuson
(*Wash.*)
Elliott Levitas
(*Ga.*)
William Proxmire
(*Wis.*)
Frank Church
(*Idaho*)

Charles Mathias
(*Md.*)
John Anderson
(*Ill.*)
Robert Michel
(*Ill.*)

STATE LEGISLATURES
California
Wisconsin
New Jersey
New York
Colorado
Illinois
Maryland

JUDGES
Frank Johnson, Jr.
(*Fed. Dist. Ct.*)
Arthur Garrity
(*Fed. Dist. Ct.*)
J. Smith Henley
(*Fed. Dist. Ct.*)
Raymond Broderick
(*Fed. Dist. Ct.*)
Orrin Judd
(*Fed. Dist. Ct.*)
John Bartels
(*Fed. Dist. Ct.*)
Harold Leventhal
(*U.S. Ct. Apps.*)
David Bazelon
(*U.S. Ct. Apps.*)
William Brennan
(*U.S. Sup. Ct.*)
Byron White
(*U.S. Sup. Ct.*)

PUBLIC INTEREST
GROUPS
John Gardner
(*Common Cause*)
Ralph Nader
(*Public Citizen*)

Joan Claybrook
(*Congress Watch*)
Carol Foreman
(*Consumer Federation of
America*)
Environmental
Groups: NRDC,
EDF, Sierra Club

BUSINESS GROUPS
Roy Ash
(*Litton Industries*)
Irving Shapiro, Reginald
Jones, and Fletcher By-
rom
(*Business Roundtable*)
Jeff Joseph
(*U.S. Chamber of Com-
merce*)
Forest Rettgers
(*National Assn. of
Manufacturers*)
Grocery Manufacturers
of America, National
Federation of Indepen-
dent Businesses, Con-
sumer Issues Working
Group

PROFESSORS
Theodore Lowi
(*Cornell*)
Walter Heller
(*Minnesota*)
L. Keith Caldwell
(*Indiana*)
Peter Drucker
(*N.Y.U.*)
Charles Reich
(*Yale*)
Alan Campbell
(*Syracuse*)
Walter Gellhorn
(*Columbia*)
Alfred Kahn
(*Cornell*)

Many of the reforms of the 1970s redefined relationships between branches of government and between levels of government. As a result, it is not surprising to find different values being invoked by persons in different roles.[4] For example, chief executives at various levels of government stressed efficiency and effectiveness. More than other actors, they seemed interested in results, in the proverbial "bottom line." Perhaps this was because they would be judged by what the government did or did not accomplish during their tenures in office. Or perhaps it was because their tenures in office were clearly limited to four or eight years. In contrast, legislators stressed the need for bureaucrats to be accountable to their elected representatives—a position that could be used to justify virtually any form of legislative control. Often legislators seemed more interested in bureaucratic penance than in bureaucratic performance, more interested in public relations than in public policy. Their interest in outcomes was slight.

The language of interest groups was also fairly predictable. Public interest groups invoked such values as accountability, responsiveness, openness, and access (See Table 2.2). Occasionally they mentioned effectiveness, but never efficiency. To them, efficiency may have implied stinginess, insensitivity, and haste. In contrast, business groups stressed efficiency and effectiveness more than accountability and responsiveness. To them accountability and responsiveness may have conjured up visions of mass democracy. On intergovernmental relations, the lines of cleavage were also rather predictable, with governors, mayors, and state legislators expressing strong support for various forms of revenue-sharing, disagreeing only on the relative merits of states and local governments as beneficiaries of federal funds.

Yet there were surprises. Richard Nixon's strong support for the New Federalism, to be discussed further, must have puzzled observers familiar with Nixon's efforts to create an "administrative presidency." At first glance, a president seeking to gain control over bureaucratic policymaking ought not to cede authority over significant policy decisions to state and local officials, who are beyond his personal control. Congressional support for a senior executive service, which strengthened presidential leverage over the upper echelons of the civil service, also fit rather oddly with congressional admonitions against "the imperial presidency." If

4. This conclusion emerges from an analysis of speeches, legislative testimony, articles, and other sources.

TABLE 2.2

Values of Reformers

CHIEF EXECUTIVES	high ethical standards	openness
effectiveness	reduced regulatory burden	
efficiency		BUSINESS GROUPS
responsiveness	JUDGES	effectiveness
flexibility	fairness	efficiency
accountability	due process of law	coordination
performance	consistency	adaptability
inflation control	rationality	accountability
cost-effectiveness	thoroughness	flexibility
reduced regulatory burdens	completeness	responsibility
honesty	balance	consistency
integrity	reasoned decision making	
public access	reasoned discretion	PROFESSORS
	reasoned analysis	juridical democracy
LEGISLATORS	fidelity to legislative intent	the rule of law
accountability	dignity and well-being of all persons	new property rights
oversight		
responsiveness	adequate treatment	citizenship
access to information	humane treatment	responsiveness
full and true disclosure		efficiency
workable, meaningful rules	PUBLIC INTEREST GROUPS	effectiveness
flexibility	responsiveness	leadership
expeditiousness	accountability	experimentation
impartiality	access	judicial activism
competence	effectiveness	
sensitivity	self-government	
	citizen action	

the presidency was already too imperial, why promote strong executive leadership? Most surprising of all were the values invoked by federal judges, especially federal appeals court judges. Frequent references to due process, fairness, and constitutional rights were familiar enough to students of the courts. During the 1970s, however, other phrases crept into the judicial vocabulary: reasoned decision making, reasoned analysis, reasoned consideration, reasoned discretion. Judges, once advocates of administrative discretion, had become critics of administrative irrationality. Moreover, they saw themselves as stronger defenders of rigorous policy analysis than the bureaucratic experts whose professional training equipped them with the requisite analytical skills. In retrospect, it is possible to explain all of these developments by acknowledging the depth of opposition to the federal bureaucracy. At the time, however, these developments seemed surprising. Even today, they seem far from inevitable.

The Reforms

In considering the bureaucracy's place in a democratic society, scholars persistently think in terms of dichotomies. For example, Yates (1982) distinguishes between reforms that promote administrative efficiency and reforms that promote pluralist democracy. The former, according to Yates, include management and governance, while the latter include oversight and participation. Unfortunately, this dichotomy oversimplifies the struggle over government reform. For example, participation and oversight lead in very different directions, although both promote pluralist democracy. Participation is considerably less coercive than oversight; for this reason, participatory demands may be satisfied in a variety of different ways. In contrast, oversight requires fairly specific bureaucratic responses. Less obviously, management and policy analysis also lead in different directions. While promoting administrative efficiency, management may also encourage a suboptimal allocation of scarce resources. While promoting economic efficiency, policy analysis may also increase paperwork and contribute to delays.

To do justice to the reforms of the 1970s, it is necessary to think of at least six categories: (1) *interest representation*—efforts to expand the variety of interests represented in administrative proceedings; (2) *due process*—the extension of procedural safeguards to individuals, firms, or groups that participate in the administrative process; (3) *management*—the consolidation of authority within the executive branch for the sake of coordination, integration, and consistency; (4) *policy analysis*—the application of scientific methods to administrative decision making; (5) *federalism*—the allocation of responsibilities between different levels of government; and (6) *oversight*—legislative supervision and control of the bureaucracy. Within each of these categories there are further distinctions of importance—some controls are broad, while others are narrow; some controls are coercive, while others are catalytic; some controls push bureaucracies toward a "golden mean," while others stress the distinctiveness of policy arenas. There is also some overlap between categories. A General Accounting Office report on policy options illustrates both policy analysis and oversight; quality control of welfare expenditures involves both management and

43

federalism. Nevertheless, these six approaches to bureaucratic control are discrete enough and coherent enough to provide a convenient framework for analysis. In contrast to dichotomies, the six categories help to capture the diversity and richness of recent efforts to control the bureaucracy.

Interest Representation

Many of the reformers of the 1970s were dissatisfied with the balance of interests represented in administrative agency proceedings. All too often, it seemed, the "special interests" were represented by a veritable armada of lawyers in three-piece suits, while the "public interest" was poorly represented, if it was represented at all. As a Senate committee investigating the problem pointed out (U.S. Senate, 1977), the battle usually pitted David against Goliath, with Goliath the heavy favorite to win.

To adjust the balance of interests represented in administrative agency proceedings, reformers sought to open up the administrative process to the people. Toward that end, they advocated open government—"sunshine laws" to ensure public awareness of important administrative decisions and freedom of information statutes to ensure public access to important information. They also advocated participatory government. Common Cause, Public Citizen, and other citizens' groups argued that citizens should have an opportunity to be heard and that they should be heard early in the decision-making process—before irrevocable decisions were made. By the end of the decade, these efforts had transformed the administrative process at both the federal and state levels. Freedom of information statutes and sunshine laws had been adopted by Congress and by the overwhelming majority of state legislatures; public hearings were required in a wide variety of administrative proceedings at all levels of government.

Although reformers sought to democratize the administrative process, their principal model was not the Progressive ideal of direct democracy but rather a new variation on the pluralist theme of representative democracy. In a variety of issue areas and at various levels of government, they established citizen representatives on various advisory boards (federal advisory committees, local health systems agencies) and on agencies with decision-making power (state occupational licensing boards for instance). They also established counterbureaucracies in instances where citizens were unable to represent themselves. Thus, "proxy advocates" represented consumers in public utility commission proceedings, om-

TABLE 2.3

A Partial List of Bureaucratic Control Mechanisms and Reforms

INTEREST REPRESENTATION
Advisory Committees
Proxy Advocacy
Legal Services Corporation
Ombudsmen
Lay Membership, Occupational Licensing Boards and Health Systems Agencies
Intervenor Funding
Citizen Utilities Boards
Freedom of Information Acts
Open Meeting Laws

DUE PROCESS
Administrative Procedure Acts
Formal Rulemaking
Hybrid Rulemaking
Ex Parte Contact Restrictions
Goldberg v. Kelly
Goss v. Lopez
Human Rights Committees
Wyatt v. Stickney
James v. Wallace
Morales v. Turman
Halderman v. Pennhurst

MANAGEMENT
Administrative Reorganization

Interagency Councils
The Administrative Presidency
Office of Management and Budget
The Short Ballot
Cabinets and Subcabinets
Inspectors General
Paperwork Reduction
Senior Executive Service

POLICY ANALYSIS
Environmental Impact Statements
Economic Impact Statements
Management by Objectives
Zero-Based Budgeting
General Accounting Office—Program Evaluation
Legislative Audit Bureaus
The Hard Look Doctrine

FEDERALISM
General Revenue-Sharing
Special Revenue-Sharing (CETA, CDBG, etc.)
Cross-Cutting Requirements
Crossover Sanctions

Partial Preemptions
Federal Reinspections
Quality Control (AFDC)
Quality Assurance (SSA)
Low-Level Nuclear Waste Compacts
Public Utility Regulatory Policies Act

OVERSIGHT
Casework
Oversight Hearings
Appropriations Hearings
Authorization Hearings
Senate Confirmation of Exec. Appts.
Annual Authorizations
The Legislative Veto
Sunset Laws
Statutory Specificity

budsmen represented nursing home patients and other aggrieved citizens, and the Legal Services Corporation represented the poor in a wide variety of administrative proceedings involving welfare, housing, and child custody cases.

Some of the most innovative interest representation reforms were initiated by state governments. In the area of public utility regulation, for example, there emerged a Department of Public Advocate (in New Jersey), a Citizens Utilities Board (in Wisconsin), a Consumer Protection Board (in New York), and intervenor funding (in Colorado). It is interesting to note that many of the

45

states that pioneered in proxy advocacy in the 1970s—Wisconsin, California, New Jersey, New York—had been staunch supporters of independent, professional bureaucracies during the Progressive Era. This apparent contradiction can be understood by recognizing that the creation of a proxy advocacy office expresses simultaneously skepticism toward a particular bureaucracy (such as a public utility commission) but also faith in the concept of bureaucracy (resulting in the creation of a counterbureaucracy).

The leading effort to create a counterbureaucracy—the federal Consumer Protection Agency—was of course unsuccessful, despite the strong efforts of Ralph Nader and other consumer activists. A Consumer Protection Agency bill passed the House and the Senate in 1975 but was vetoed by President Ford; a Consumer Protection Agency was supported vigorously by President Carter but was rejected by Congress during the Carter years. For consumer activists, it was a catch–22 situation—if Congress was willing to support the agency, the president was not; if the president was willing to support the agency, the Congress was not. The defeat of the Consumer Protection Agency was due in large measure to the mobilization of the business community, jolted by the passage of tough health and safety legislation in the early 1970s. Their principal weapon in the struggle was the ominous specter of another large bureaucracy. As *Fortune* magazine editorialized (1977: 59), "The proposal [to create a Consumer Protection Agency] is based on the discredited idea that Washington bureaucrats know what's good for consumers better than consumers do." The Consumer Protection Agency was ultimately defeated by the same antibureaucratic sentiment that led to its proposal.

In retrospect, it is tempting to dismiss the interest representation reforms of the 1970s as an unimaginative extension of old pluralist ideas. Instead of decisively rejecting interest group liberalism, reformers sought to review it and perfect it (through incremental improvements). Yet reformers would argue that their goal was not pluralism but responsiveness. Their chosen instruments were not merely interest groups but in different instances citizens, interest groups, and counterbureaucracies. The first two of these strategies involved new twists, and the last was unprecedented. Through proxy advocacy, reformers sought to institutionalize what Wilson (1974) calls "entrepreneurial politics" or the pursuit of policies that promote distributed benefits and concentrated costs. They were seeking nothing less than a "representation revolution."

Due Process

If the watchword of interest representation reforms was respon-siveness, the watchword of due process reforms was fairness. Where property or liberty interests were at stake, reformers sought to ensure that individuals and corporations would be fairly treated by bureaucracies. Through legalistic requirements, they grafted a quasi-judicial model onto the administrative process. In this respect, due process reforms differed fundamentally from in-terest representation reforms, which in effect applied a quasi-leg-islative model to the administrative process.

The centerpiece of due process reforms was the hearing—an event of potential importance in both rulemaking (policymaking) and adjudication (enforcement). In two celebrated cases, the U.S. Supreme Court required a hearing before administrative agencies could deprive a person of property, broadly defined. Thus, in *Goldberg v. Kelly* (1970), the Court required a trial-type hearing be-fore welfare department bureaucrats could remove a person from the welfare rolls. In *Goss v. Lopez* (1975), the Court required school administrators to give students a chance to explain their side of the story before being suspended from school. Many state courts, fol-lowing the lead of the U.S. Supreme Court, became strong cham-pions of procedural due process. For example, Lufler (1982: 75–105) found that state courts were even more aggressive in defend-ing student rights against the bureaucracy than federal courts.

On a related front, U.S. Courts of Appeals moved to formalize administrative policymaking through what has become known as "hybrid rulemaking." In a series of important decisions (*Interna-tional Harvester Co. v. Ruckelshaus*, 1973; *Appalachian Power Co. v. Ruckelshaus*, 1973; *Mobil Oil Corp. v. FPC*, 1973; *Natural Resources Defense Council v. U.S. Nuclear Regulatory Commission*, 1976), U.S. Courts of Appeals struck down administrative rules that were based on relatively informal decision-making processes. A fre-quent complaint by the courts was that cross-examination and re-buttal opportunities had been denied. Nor were the courts alone in imposing tough procedural requirements on administrative agencies. In a number of statutes Congress required hybrid rule-making or even formal rulemaking[5] in administrative proceedings

5. Formal rulemaking involves a full-fledged trial-type hearing as in formal ad-judication. Hybrid rulemaking requires something more than just "notice and com-ment" opportunities but something less than all the trappings of a trial-type hear-ing.

for such agencies as the Securities and Exchange Commission (SEC), the Environmental Protection Agency (EPA), the FTC, the Federal Energy Regulatory Commission (FERC), and the Consumer Product Safety Commission (CPSC) (Verkuil, 1978). Many state legislatures also tightened the procedural screws on administrative agencies by passing tough administrative procedure acts. During the 1970s, eighteen states adopted administrative procedure acts for the first time (Renfrow et al., 1985). Many of these administrative procedure acts imposed stringent procedural requirements on administrative agencies.

The due process reforms of the early 1970s triggered a mighty backlash, led by an increasingly conservative Supreme Court. In 1976 the Supreme Court ruled that a hearing need not be held before terminating Social Security disability benefits (*Mathews v. Eldridge*). While conceding a property interest in the continued receipt of benefits, the Court nevertheless stressed the importance of such values as the conservation of scarce fiscal and administrative resources. The Court also expressed support for administrative discretion (1976: 349): "In assessing what process is due in this case, substantial weight must be given to the good-faith judgment of the individuals charged by Congress with the administration of social welfare programs that the procedures they have provided assure fair consideration of the entitlement claims of individuals." In 1978 the Supreme Court issued an even stronger opinion, rebuking lower court judges for trying to formalize administrative rulemaking by imposing procedural requirements not contained in the federal Administrative Procedure Act. In *Vermont Yankee Nuclear Power Corp. v. Natural Resources Defense Council* (1978), the Supreme Court argued that the Nuclear Regulatory Commission (NRC) was not required to provide cross-examination opportunities in nuclear safety rulemaking, contrary to the conclusions of the U.S. Court of Appeals for the District of Columbia. The Supreme Court also chided the lower court for unwarranted meddling (1978: 544): "Agencies should be free to fashion their own rules of procedure."

These strong signals from the U.S. Supreme Court seemed to put an end to judicial efforts to formalize the administrative process. However, they did not put an end to due process innovations by the courts. Instead, the late 1970s ushered in a new wave of efforts by federal district courts to achieve due process through an outright judicial takeover of recalcitrant bureaucracies. In a series of landmark rulings (*Wyatt v. Stickney*, 1971; *Newman v. Alabama*, 1972; *Pugh v. Locke* and *James v. Wallace*, 1976), Judge Frank Johnson of Alabama literally took over Alabama's prisons and mental hospitals. Confronted by irrefutable evidence of inhumane conditions and inadequate care, Johnson issued detailed requirements for nutrition and personal hygiene; he also required educational programs and additional staff, citing the Fourteenth Amendment as justification (Yarbrough, 1982). To ensure that his orders were carried out, Johnson appointed human rights committees to serve as his "eyes and ears." In effect, the judge appointed himself interim manager of the state's prisons and mental hospitals.

This remarkable pattern of judicial intervention was repeated in other states and in other issue areas. In Boston, Judge Arthur Garrity took over Boston's public schools after efforts at persuasion failed to desegregate city schools. As the city's de facto school superintendent, Garrity assigned pupils, hired staff and administrators, closed and upgraded schools, and acted on spending requests (Lukas, 1985). By the time he relinquished control of the schools in 1985, Garrity had issued a total of 415 orders in the case. Meanwhile, in New York, Judges Orrin Judd and John Bartels imposed a series of detailed orders on the state's Department of Mental Hygiene after plaintiffs demonstrated scandalous conditions at Willowbrook, a Staten Island facility for the mentally retarded. Like Judge Johnson, Judges Judd and Bartels relied on a human rights committee (The Willowbrook Review Panel) to ensure that their orders were enforced (Rothman and Rothman, 1984). In short, while broad judicial interpretations of the Administrative Procedure Act seemed to have run their course by the late 1970s, broad judicial interpretations of the Fourteenth Amendment were becoming more common.

Management

In contrast to the interest representation reforms and the due process reforms of the 1970s, the management reforms were old, familiar, and unexciting. Most of them, in fact, were consistent with the letter or the spirit of Hoover Commission recommendations made some years earlier. The goal was efficient, effective government and the chosen method was a strong chief executive in a hierarchical setting. It was a model long supported by leading students of public administration (Willoughby, 1923; Gulick, 1937).

Perhaps the most familiar of the management reforms was administrative reorganization. Long touted as a remedy for inefficiency, administrative reorganization promised coordination, integration, economy, and effectiveness. Most state governments

49

reorganized themselves during this period, with eighteen states undergoing major reorganization efforts (Meier, 1980; Council of State Governments, 1978: 105–15). At the federal level, Richard Nixon's attempts to create four superdepartments (Natural Resources, Human Resources, Community Development, Economic Affairs) were stymied, but Jimmy Carter was successful in creating two new departments—the Department of Energy and the Department of Education. Reorganization efforts were greeted more often by yawns than by determined opposition. To some observers, including Ralph Nader, administrative reorganization was an exercise in "box shuffling" that did little harm but that ignored real problems and real solutions (Cameron, 1977). Nevertheless, there was no denying that reorganization strengthened the potential leverage of chief executives over their bureaucracies.

While reorganizing the executive branch to facilitate gubernatorial control, many states also shortened their ballots in pursuit of the same goal. Thus from 1970 to 1980, twenty-two states opted for shorter ballots, providing for gubernatorial appointment of such officials as the insurance commissioner, the state treasurer, the superintendent of public instruction, the secretary of agriculture, and so forth. In some states (Maryland, Minnesota, New York, North Carolina, Washington), the number of separately elected executive officials was reduced significantly during this decade (Council of State Governments, 1980: 182–83; 1970: 146–47). In taking these measures, state governments embraced a reform long advocated by the Progressives, who had been strong supporters of the short ballot in their day.

A handful of states took a more innovative step to control the bureaucracy, establishing a senior executive service consisting of high-level civil servants who could be promoted or demoted by the governor to maximize his or her policy goals. Senior executive service members had less job security than other civil servants—they could not be fired from the government but could be fired from their jobs—but they were eligible for cash awards for meritorious performance. Among the states adopting this system were California, Wisconsin, Minnesota, Oregon, and Iowa (Hamilton and Biggart, 1984: 121–46). These state systems served as models for the federal government's senior executive service, established by Congress in 1978 with the full support of the Carter administration.

Although the federal government followed the lead of state governments in some areas of management, the federal government also took two important steps entirely on its own. First, Richard

Nixon transformed the Bureau of the Budget (BOB) into the Office of Management and Budget (OMB). This action, one of the most significant reforms of the decade, vested enormous power in a single agency. The same agency that determined the fate of agency budget requests would also control reorganization efforts, management practices, bureaucratic policy analysis, and legislative proposals. OMB was destined to become the president's most powerful weapon against the bureaucracy. Although it included fewer than six hundred employees, OMB was widely feared throughout the executive branch.

A second step undertaken by the federal government was the establishment of inspectors general in large departments that spend large amounts of money (the Defense Department, the Department of Health, Education, and Welfare) and eventually in all cabinet-level departments. The principal purpose of this reform was to promote efficiency and to save taxpayers money. A secondary purpose was to free the General Accounting Office (GAO) of auditing responsibilities that seemed less and less glamorous in comparison to its new responsibilities in policy analysis and program evaluation. Not surprisingly, the GAO strongly supported these steps.

The management reforms of the 1970s were the most familiar and the least imaginative of the bureau-bashing reforms of the 1970s. They invoked familiar values (efficiency, effectiveness) and familiar means (administrative reorganization, clear lines of authority). Yet in one respect they were truly stunning. To concentrate authority in the hands of the chief executive was an old solution to problems of inefficiency, but it was a surprising solution in the wake of Vietnam and Watergate. That the reformers of the 1970s were willing to grant considerable authority to the president despite the abuses of the Johnson and Nixon years was eloquent testimony to the depths of disenchantment with the bureaucracy. If aversion to the imperial presidency was great, aversion to the imperial bureaucracy was even greater.

Policy Analysis

For years, the bureaucracy's strongest defense against external encroachment was its technical expertise. By defining policy problems in technical terms and by citing impressive professional credentials, the bureaucracy was able to fend off challenges from legislators, chief executives, judges, interest groups, and citizens. When reformers hit upon the idea of using policy analysis to control the bureaucracy, they took the bureaucracy by surprise. It was as if parishioners told their minister how to interpret scripture. Rationality, a symbol as important to bureaucratic authority as faith is to religious authority, would no longer shield the bureaucracy from external attack.

The most imaginative of the policy analysis controls was the environmental impact statement (EIS), institutionalized through the National Environmental Policy Act (NEPA), signed into law in January 1970. Proposed by Professor L. Keith Caldwell of Indiana University and supported by such powerful legislators as Henry (Scoop) Jackson and Edmund Muskie, the EIS was an "action-forcing" mechanism aimed at getting nonenvironmental agencies to take environmental protection seriously. It did so by requiring agencies to prepare an environmental impact statement for all major federal actions and by authorizing private citizens or groups to take an agency to court to secure compliance. Following the enactment of NEPA, many states also required environmental impact statements. Some of the state statutes were even stronger than NEPA. For example, Connecticut required agencies to consider both primary and secondary environmental impacts, while Montana, Wisconsin, and New York required agencies to consider measures to mitigate environmental damage (Pearlman, 1977).

A logical successor to the environmental impact statement was the economic impact assessment, also known in various incarnations as the inflation impact statement or the regulatory impact analysis. In a sense, the economic impact assessment was the mirror image of the environmental impact statement. While the latter required nonenvironmental agencies to take environmental impacts into account, the former required health and safety agencies to take nonenvironmental impacts into account. Both saw policy analysis as a tool for promoting balance between health and safety on the one hand, economy and efficiency on the other. Beginning in 1971, Richard Nixon required health and safety agencies to conduct "quality-of-life" reviews, assessing the costs of proposed rules and other initiatives. Subsequently, Presidents Ford, Carter, and Reagan extended this requirement to all agencies under the president's control (independent regulatory commissions were excluded) and strengthened the role of OMB in enforcing the order. Several states also adopted economic impact assessment requirements of various kinds (Brickman, 1979). In some instances (in Wisconsin and Montana), these requirements were piggybacked onto environmental impact statements. In others (Illinois, Florida,

Washington, Maryland), separate economic impact statements were to be prepared.

Although impact statements had important consequences for agency budgets and government priorities, they did not attempt to rationalize priority-setting and budget-making across the board. In contrast, management-by-objectives (MBO), introduced by the Nixon administration, and zero-based budgeting (ZBB), introduced by the Carter administration, were more ambitious attempts to clarify and achieve objectives and to compare programs systematically. Zero-based budgeting, originally adopted by Georgia during Jimmy Carter's tenure as governor, proved popular with many states that were struggling to balance their budgets. Management-by-objectives was less popular at the state level, but some governors such as Christopher (Kit) Bond of Missouri were willing to give it a try.

As is well known, both MBO and ZBB have been short-lived. In contrast, other efforts to promote policy analysis have been more enduring. One of the most important of these was the transformation of the GAO from a penny-pinching scold into a powerful champion of effectiveness and efficiency. The GAO, a sleepy auditing agency dominated by accountants, acquired a new lease on life in 1970 when Congress at the urging of the comptroller general authorized a major GAO commitment to program evaluation and policy analysis. Pleased by the initial results, Congress encouraged further steps in this direction in the Congressional Budget and Impoundment Control Act of 1974. Without abandoning its interest in ferreting out fraud and abuse, the GAO began to look at weak enforcement records, missed deadlines, and other evidence of noncompliance with congressional intent. At around the same time, many state legislatures established legislative evaluation units or placed greater emphasis on program evaluation within existing units (Kraft, 1981). By hiring policy analysts and other professionals with impressive technical skills, state legislative evaluation agencies like the GAO were able to invoke such values as objectivity and expertise.

The GAO and its state counterparts relied on publicity and access to politicians to put pressure on administrative agencies, but they lacked the authority to impose their vision of rationality on the bureaucracy. In contrast, the courts, suddenly reversing a long period of deference to administrative expertise, were able to act authoritatively to overturn important administrative agency actions, ranging from licensing to ratemaking to rulemaking. Beginning in

53

1969 in two landmark opinions (*Pikes Peak Broadcasting Co. v. FCC* and *WAIT Radio v. FCC*), federal appeals courts began to insist on "reasoned analysis" and "reasoned explanation" in administrative agency decisions. This approach became known as the "hard look" doctrine, a phrase coined by Judge Harold Leventhal of the U.S. Circuit Court of Appeals (D.C. Circuit), who argued that judges must assure themselves that agencies have taken a "hard look" at relevant evidence and alternatives (*Greater Boston TV Corp v. FCC*, 1970). In invoking the hard look doctrine, Leventhal and other federal judges found themselves questioning a wide range of technical judgments made by agency administrators.[6] While the trend toward judicial insistence on well-reasoned agency opinion was most pronounced at the federal level, there was reason to believe that some state courts also found the hard look doctrine appealing. For example, Frank (1978) found that state supreme courts in California and Michigan reversed nearly as many administrative agency decisions as they affirmed between 1970 and 1974. The long era of judicial deference to administrative expertise, it seemed, was over.

Federalism

As Kingdon (1984) has observed, solutions are as likely to chase problems as problems are to chase solutions. Revenue-sharing is a good example of a solution that chased a problem. Polsby (1985) would call it "an incubated innovation." Originally proposed by Representative Melvin Laird in 1958, the idea was kept alive in the 1960s by Walter Heller, professor of economics at the University of Minnesota and chairman of the Council of Economic Advisers under Presidents Kennedy and Johnson. The Great Society, however, relied heavily on the federal bureaucracy to put a quick end to poverty and inequality. Revenue-sharing, which would rob the federal bureaucracy of much of its power, was incompatible with the premises of the Great Society. Yet as enthusiasm for the Great Society and the federal bureaucracy waned, revenue-sharing began to attract powerful supporters. The most important of these was the greatest reformer of the 1970s and the most controversial figure of our time, Richard Nixon.

6. In *U.S. v. Nova Scotia Food Products Corp.* (1977), for example, the U.S. Circuit Court of Appeals (2nd Circuit) disputed the Food and Drug Administration's ruling that hot-process smoked fish must be heated for no less than thirty minutes at no less than 180 degrees Fahrenheit in water containing no less than 3.5 percent salt.

Nixon, a student of government as well as of politics, supported revenue-sharing with his heart and soul. He characterized revenue-sharing as "the New American Revolution" and fought vigorously for it, even as he lost interest in other initiatives, such as welfare reform. The genius of revenue-sharing, according to Nixon's point of view, was that it bypassed the federal bureaucracy, perceived to be dominated by Nixon's enemies.[7] Nixon's enthusiasm for revenue-sharing was directly related to his animus toward the federal bureaucracy. As Nixon put it in a public statement (Nixon, 1972: 1535): "The American people are fed up with government that doesn't deliver. . . . Under this program [revenue-sharing], instead of spending so much time trying to please distant bureaucrats in Washington—so the money will keep coming in—State and local officials can concentrate on pleasing the people—so the money can do more good."

In his fight for revenue-sharing, Nixon found strong allies at the state and local levels. The National Governors Association, the U.S. Conference of Mayors, and other state and local lobbies made strong sales pitches on Capitol Hill. Governor Nelson Rockefeller of New York (1971: 800) raised the specter of a wave of bankruptcies if the federal government did not assist state and local governments. Liberal and conservative members of Congress also warmed to the idea of revenue-sharing, though for different reasons. Liberals saw it as an alternative to imprudent tax cuts; conservatives saw it as an alternative to wasteful spending by federal bureaucrats. With such a formidable coalition behind it, general revenue-sharing became law in 1972. Over the next two years, special revenue-sharing programs such as the Comprehensive Employment and Training Act (CETA) and the Community Development Block Grant program (CDBG) also became law.

However, support for the "New American Revolution" unraveled almost as quickly as it had developed. This was especially true in relation to the CETA program, rocked by reports of widespread fraud and abuse. Congressman Jim Corman's support for CETA is said to have evaporated during an airplane conversation with a well-paid Los Angeles engineer whose salary was generously augmented by CETA (Baumer and Van Horn, 1985: 131). Highly critical reports by the General Accounting Office added fuel to the fire. By 1978, CETA was in trouble. While supporting the extension

7. As Aberbach and Rockman (1976) have shown, Nixon's perceptions were correct!

of the CETA program, President Carter (1978: 393) proposed tighter eligibility standards to ensure "a rational, efficient and targeted structural and countercyclical employment program." Congress agreed, also supporting amendments limiting CETA wages to ten thousand dollars annually. Within a few years, CETA's supporters in Washington, D.C., were calling for greater efficiency and effectiveness, talking less and less about responsiveness and grassroots accountability.

Nor was the CETA extension the only indicator of a new mood. Alarmed by sharp increases in welfare awards and disability payments by state officials,[8] Congress took steps to reduce these awards by state bureaucracies by means of such measures as quality control and quality assurance. In 1979 Congress required the federal Social Security Administration (SSA) to review at least 65 percent of state disability awards—a dramatic increase from the 5 percent review figure mandated in 1972. In the same year, Congress required the federal Department of Health and Human Services (HHS) to impose sanctions on states whose welfare departments failed to reduce error rates by specified amounts.

If there was a conservative revolution afoot, it was not apparent in other areas such as health and safety. While tightening eligibility standards for various welfare programs, Congress simultaneously authorized federal regulatory agencies to impose tough restrictions on state environmental protection, health, transportation, and education agencies. By the late 1970s, state bureaucracies found themselves subject to a wide variety of cross-cutting requirements, crossover sanctions, direct orders, and partial preemptions. The New Federalism, with its emphasis on state and local discretion, had given way to regulatory federalism, with its emphasis on federal control. Yet this sharp reversal obscured a certain consistency—during the 1970s, intergovernmental relations reflected an antibureaucratic mood. Throughout this period, bureaucracy was perceived to be the central problem. What changed was the perception of which bureaucracies posed the greatest threat, federal, state or local.

Oversight

The federalism reforms of the 1970s, like the due process reforms discussed earlier, consisted of zigs and zags. Although the bureau-

8. For example, the costs of the Social Security disability insurance program quadrupled from 1970 to 1978, rising to $13 billion per year.

cracy remained the central target of reformers, the specific values to be maximized varied over time—from responsiveness to effectiveness, from fairness to efficiency. In contrast, the oversight reforms of the 1970s were much more consistent. From the beginning to the end of the decade, legislators sought to make the bureaucracy more accountable to the legislative branch (and to individual legislators). From an outsider's perspective, there is a world of difference between accountability to the legislature as a whole and accountability to a single legislator, with an axe to grind. From an insider's perspective, however, this distinction must not have seemed all that great. Legislators seldom asked whether accountability to individual legislators served the public interest better than bureaucratic discretion. Or perhaps they asked the question but decided that 535 despots were ultimately less worrisome than a despotic bureaucracy.

The most ubiquitous form of legislative control during this decade was the legislative hearing. The number of congressional oversight hearings increased sharply during the 1970s (Aberbach, 1979). In the 91st Congress (1969–1970), for example, the House held oversight hearings on thirty-five separate subjects, while the Senate held twenty-seven. By the 94th Congress (1975–1976), the House was holding one hundred eighteen oversight hearings, the Senate sixty-seven. Nor was the oversight hearing the only form of committee supervision. Through appropriations hearings and authorization hearings, members of Congress also exercised oversight in various ways. In some instances, members of Congress used casework as a form of oversight (Ogul, 1976; Johannes, 1979).

The same pattern appeared in state governments, where oversight increased sharply (Rosenthal, 1983). Approximately two-thirds of the states also experimented with a new form of legislative control—the sunset law. Originally proposed by William O. Douglas, the idea was popularized by Theodore Lowi (1969), who recommended "tenure-of-statutes" acts automatically terminating agencies or programs unless the legislature acts affirmatively to continue them. Led by Colorado, state legislatures rushed to adopt sunset laws, confident that they would promote accountability and hopeful that they might bring an end to agencies or programs that had outlived their usefulness.

Many states also adopted legislative veto measures, providing for legislative review of administrative rules and regulations either before or after their adoption by the bureaucracy. Similarly, the Congress appended legislative veto provisions to a wide variety of bills, encompassing foreign policy, energy policy, environmental policy, education policy, consumer protection, and immigration and naturalization. Although the congressional veto was not new (it dated back to 1932), its use increased by leaps and bounds during the 1970s. Approximately three-fourths of all congressional veto provisions enacted into law from 1935 to 1985 were enacted in the 1970s (Cooper, 1985: 7). The specifics of legislative vetoes varied from committee vetoes to one-house vetoes to two-house vetoes. In practice, however, virtually all legislative veto provisions were committee vetoes in the sense that committees were free to threaten a legislative veto—a threat that was almost never carried out but that strengthened the bargaining power of committee members and their staffs.

There were, it should be noted, occasional attempts to secure accountability to the legislature as a whole. This was most evident in environmental legislation approved by Congress and the states—clean air statutes, clean water statutes, coastal zone management laws, and so forth. These statutes were remarkably detailed and specific. They contained clear standards, specific deadlines, and detailed instructions to bureaucrats. In effect, these statutes did precisely what Lowi (1969) had called for in *The End of Liberalism*—they attempted to reestablish the "rule of law."

With the exception of statutory specificity, however, most of the oversight reforms of the 1970s provided in effect for bureaucratic accountability to a particular committee, a particular committee chair, or a particular legislator. The usual pattern involved accusations, threats, apologies, and promises. Legislators, angered by reports of abuses, delays, or noncompliance, threatened to pass laws severely limiting the bureaucracy's discretion or cutting the bureaucracy's budget. Bureaucrats, chastened and afraid, vowed to do better. After the dust settled, two or three legislators took an active interest in the agency's policies. These legislators were, in Bardach's (1980) words, "fixers," who monitored compliance with legislative requirements and who intervened when programs seemed to be getting off track.

We have grown so accustomed to this pattern that it is important to recognize it for what it was—a sharp break with the philosophy of the Progressive Era and a significant adaptation of the Madisonian principle of checks and balances to the new realities of a fourth branch of government. The new political system that was beginning to emerge was one involving more or less continuous interactions between key legislators and bureaucrats on important policy issues. Many of these encounters were sufficiently unpleasant for bureaucrats that they could not be described as evidence of "cozy iron triangles." There is nothing cozy about a legislative oversight hearing, with cameras rolling and legislators doing their best to find a bureaucrat's jugular vein. Yet this friction obscured an important fact—accountability was being defined less in institutional terms than in personal terms. Bureaucrats were being held accountable to individual legislators who saw themselves as ferrets and fixers. To the extent that such legislators spoke for the general public, this meant an increase in accountability and responsiveness. To the extent that they spoke only for themselves or for their constituents, it meant the triumph of a new form of representative government in which legislative freelancers were the ultimate arbiters of the public good.

Conclusion

We sometimes view the 1970s as a sleepy interlude between the turbulent radicalism of the 1960s and the purposive conservatism of the 1980s—analogous perhaps to the 1920s or the 1950s, when we paused to catch our collective breath. But the 1970s like the Progressive Era was a golden age of institutional reform. Without convening a constitutional convention, reformers rewrote our "living constitution" in the 1970s. In essence, they adapted the Madisonian strategy of "checks and balances" to the new realities of a bureaucracy that had become a fourth branch of government. Ambitious legislators and chief executives and judges and interest groups would counteract ambitious bureaucrats. New auxiliary precautions would be adopted. The Progressive faith in bureaucratic experts and ordinary citizens would be renounced. Instead of direct democracy and expert management, we would have representative democracy and the management of experts.

The impetus for these reforms was pervasive dissatisfaction with the bureaucracy. According to critics, the bureaucracy was inefficient, ineffective, unaccountable, and unresponsive. These charges helped to structure the specifics of the reform movement. In pursuit of accountability and responsiveness, reformers institutionalized interest representation, oversight, and the new federalism. In pursuit of effectiveness and efficiency, reformers institutionalized management, policy analysis, and regulatory federalism. Judges, marching to a somewhat different drumbeat, pursued fairness and

59

humanitarian values through due process reforms. The result was a massive assault on the bureaucracy.

Some of the reforms of the 1970s were old and familiar. Administrative reorganization was a shopworn remedy, often used as an antidote for inefficiency. Notice and comment requirements had become routine since the passage of the federal Administrative Procedure Act in 1946. Audits by the GAO dated back to 1921. Partial preemptions were popular solutions to demands for power-sharing between the federal government and the states. Legislative casework and legislative oversight were familiar responses to daily constituency complaints and occasional bureaucratic scandals.

But many of the reforms of the 1970s were fresh and innovative. The creation of counterbureaucracies, such as proxy advocacy and ombudsman offices, marked a new strategy for securing interest representation. The emergence of judges as managers and the development of the "hard look" doctrine signaled a new era of judicial assertiveness in both constitutional law and administrative law. Environmental impact statements and economic impact assessments converted policy analysis from a bureaucratic shield into a weapon available to numerous participants in the policymaking process. The creation of OMB and a senior executive service facilitated and legitimized the pursuit of an "administrative presidency." The transfer of large sums of money to state and local governments, with few strings attached, marked an abrupt departure from the era of categorical grants.

There was even a certain freshness to legislative controls over the bureaucracy. While most of these control strategies were familiar enough (oversight, legislative vetoes, statutory specificity), their cumulative effect was to establish the legislative branch as the most powerful force in the bureaucracy's external environment. Together these reforms opened up new possibilities for legislators as freelancers, fixers, and ferrets. Legislators in the new regime would police a bureaucracy that had failed to police itself. Moreover, bureaucracies previously thought immune to meaningful legislative control would be brought under the legislature's ambit. Independent regulatory commissions such as the FTC would be subject to strong oversight and occasional legislative vetoes. Agencies that had operated behind a cloak of secrecy for many years, e.g., the Federal Bureau of Investigation (FBI) and the Central Intelligence Agency (CIA), would also be brought under legislative control through various reporting requirements and more stringent oversight.

In retrospect, there is reason to believe that reformers went too far. Instead of selective controls, they seemed to prefer generic controls. Instead of catalytic controls, they often chose coercive controls. In their rush to secure responsiveness, accountability, effectiveness, and efficiency, they forgot about flexibility, creativity, and innovation. In their rush to prove that the bureaucracy was manageable, they ignored the dangers of micromanagement. Yet there is no denying that they effected a profound transformation of our system of government—one whose reverberations are still being felt.

Interest Representation

Of all the institutional changes of the 1970s, interest representation reforms best fit the ideal type of "catalytic controls." By giving broad, diffuse interests access to vital information and a voice in the administrative process, reformers ensured a more balanced system of interest representation. In effect, they institutionalized what Wilson (1974) calls "entrepreneurial politics" or the pursuit of policies that provide widely distributed benefits and narrowly concentrated costs. Yet they also protected the bureaucracy from overly specific directives. While interest representation compels a bureaucratic response to a vexing problem, it does not predetermine what that response will be. In contrast to many reforms, interest representation requires the bureaucracy to be responsive without requiring the bureaucracy to abandon common sense.

The leading interest representation reforms of the 1970s included freedom of information statutes, sunshine laws, requirements for public hearings, public funding for public intervenors, and provisions for surrogate representation through ombudsmen and proxy advocates. These reforms were not unprecedented. During the 1960s attempts had been made to provide for citizen participation in the administrative process. However, the interest representation reforms of the 1960s suffered from several fatal flaws, which will be discussed. By learning from the mistakes of the previous decade, reformers in the 1970s fashioned interest representation reforms that were effective without being destructive.

The Legacy of the 1960s

During the 1960s a number of reforms were adopted in an effort to improve representation for poor people, and especially racial minorities, in local government decision making. These reforms included community action agencies, model cities programs, legal aid societies, civilian review boards, and decentralized school boards. Although these programs differed in a variety of ways, they typically sought to promote citizen participation, decentralization, and community control. In most instances, their targets included local bureaucracies that were perceived to be unresponsive to the needs of the poor and minorities (welfare departments, school boards, police departments). They were alike in still another respect: for the most part, they were unsuccessful, unpopular, or both. A decade later, only legal aid societies and model cities programs would be judged as successes, and qualified successes at that.

Of all the interest representation reforms of the 1960s, the most ill-fated and the most widely criticized were the community action agencies. As provided in the Economic Opportunity Act of 1964, these agencies, usually new nonprofit organizations, were to be the linchpins of the War on Poverty. Their role, as envisioned by the architects of the War on Poverty, was to coordinate federal, state, and local antipoverty services and to secure the cooperation of public and private agencies in a frontal assault on poverty. However, within a very short time, community action agencies became more interested in organizing the poor (and in some instances distributing favors to friends and neighbors) than in coordinating antipoverty services. In addition, they became embroiled in bitter power struggles with local elected officials that they were ill-equipped to win. These power struggles so poisoned the atmosphere that community action agencies soon found themselves bereft of powerful supporters. Although it was not until the Nixon administration that they were effectively dismantled, their credibility was permanently destroyed well before the final *coup de grace*.

Community action agencies were not completely unsuccessful. Even Daniel Moynihan (1969), a forceful critic of community action agencies, concedes that they helped to sharpen the skills of a generation of black urban leaders. Other scholars share this assessment (Peterson and Greenstone, 1977). Also, community action agencies achieved tangible successes in some cities. In New York, for example, where community action agencies were well-organized, well-financed, and relatively autonomous, they were successful in achieving substantive results for the poor (Peterson, 1970).

In most cities, however, community action agencies failed, and they failed spectacularly. Peterson (1970) concedes that community action agencies were ineffective in Chicago, where mayoral control over neighborhood council appointments ensured that the poor's representatives would be timid and pliable. In Philadelphia, they were moderately effective at first, as illustrated by a successful attempt to revise a planned parenthood proposal. However, as Philadelphia's community action agencies channeled their efforts

63

toward particularistic goals (patronage for friends and neighbors) rather than universalistic goals (improved services for the poor), their effectiveness waned. In other cities, where community action agencies usurped the functions of established bureaucracies, they encountered fierce antagonism and resistance (Sundquist, 1969).

School decentralization experiments, inaugurated in the late 1960s and early 1970s, paralleled the experience of community action agencies in many respects. In Chicago, little more than token decentralization was achieved because of the combined opposition of Mayor Richard Daley, the school board staff, and a majority of school board members (Peterson, 1976). In Los Angeles, Rochester, and other cities, meaningful decentralization never occurred (Cibulka, 1975). In two cities, New York and Detroit, school decentralization resulted in shared political resources and shared authoritative decision making (Cibulka, 1975). However, New York paid a high price for school decentralization—racial polarization, three teacher's strikes, and, quite possibly, an acceleration of white flight to the suburbs.

Community action agencies and school decentralization experiments, though troubled, were at least successful in some instances. The same cannot be said of civilian review boards, aimed at identifying, punishing, and deterring police abuse and brutality. During the 1960s civilian review boards existed in several U.S. cities, including New York, Philadelphia, Minneapolis, Rochester, and York, Pennsylvania. These experiments in citizen control of street-level bureaucrats were extremely unpopular with the police and often unpopular with the community as well. Thus, New York City's five-month-old civilian review board was overwhelmingly opposed and abolished in a 1966 referendum. The longest civilian review board experiment was Philadelphia's, which lasted approximately eight years (Philadelphia's civilian review board existed for eleven years but it functioned for eight years as a result of an adverse court decision by a common pleas court judge). According to one careful study (Halpern, 1974), Philadelphia's civilian review board was both less popular and less effective than internal review by police officers themselves.[1] The police saw civilian review as a

1. Throughout the history of Philadelphia's civilian review board, only 5 percent of all civilian complaints resulted in recommendations for punishment, and no complaint ever resulted in a recommendation for dismissal from the force. In contrast, 95 percent of the investigations conducted by the Philadelphia Police Board of Inquiry in 1970 resulted in some form of disciplinary action and 40 percent resulted in dismissal (Halpern, 1974). Even if one concedes that citizens are more

threat to their growing sense of professionalism, while the public saw it as a threat to law and order. To both, other alternatives seemed more appealing.

Not all of the interest representation reforms of the 1960s were unmitigated disasters. The model cities program, which sought to coordinate an assault on urban slums, managed to combine meaningful citizen participation and impressive urban planning. In many instances, innovative programs were recommended and developed by city residents themselves (Sundquist, 1969). Legal aid societies, which sought simultaneously to promote interest representation and due process for the poor, also secured some tangible victories. As Hollingsworth (1977) has noted, administrative agencies gradually came to consult legal services attorneys before altering or initiating rules and regulations. According to Hollingsworth (1977: 309), such informal consultations "helped to avoid later conflicts and in some cases led to agency practices initially more suitable for the poor."

Still, it is difficult to resist the conclusion that the interest representation reforms of the 1960s were largely unsuccessful. Their legacy included frustrated citizens, angry politicians, and demoralized bureaucrats. It was not simply that these programs ruffled the feathers of the rich and powerful but that bonds of trust between the poor and their most important allies, especially allies within the bureaucracy, were frayed to the breaking point. In the process, the War on Poverty, citizen participation, and street-level bureaucracies were all discredited. The costs of these forms of social experimentation were high indeed.

There were several reasons for the failures of the interest representation reforms of the 1960s. First, almost all of the reforms were aimed at improving representation for poor people generally and for blacks in particular. At times in our history, including the 1960s, the disadvantaged have been frustrated enough and powerful enough to threaten the social order. At such times, their demands must be satisfied in some fashion—through symbolic or substantive concessions (Piven and Cloward, 1971, 1977). In the long run, however, the poor constitute a very weak constituency with little staying power. As soon as the threat to social order subsides, political support for the poor is likely to evaporate. Thus

likely to file complaints with a civilian review board, the evidence suggests that civilian review boards are relatively weak.

reforms designed to improve representation for underprivileged members of society are not easily sustained.

Second, many of the reforms of this period placed greater emphasis on formal representation (the election of representatives by the poor) and descriptive representation (participation by the poor) than on substantive representation (tangible results for the poor). As Peterson (1970) has shown in his study of community action agencies, formal representation and descriptive representation often became substitutes for substantive representation. Indeed, in Philadelphia the principal consequences of formal representation and descriptive representation seem to have been particularism, pork barrel politics, and a preoccupation with patronage, all of which precluded substantive representation. The Congress's insistence that one-third of all community action agency board members be poor contributed to this preoccupation with formal and descriptive representation. While this may have promoted greater political equality, it may also have stymied efforts to promote greater economic equality.

Third, few of the reforms of the 1960s recognized the importance of expertise and experience as prerequisites to successful interest representation. Many of the directors and employees of community action agencies were so lacking in expertise and experience that they quickly lost the respect of bureaucrats whose cooperation was essential if they were to succeed. This was also a key reason for the opposition of police associations to civilian review boards. Legal aid societies, staffed by attorneys, possessed considerable expertise, which helps to account for their greater success. Yet, legal aid society attorneys often lacked experience (because the program was new and because turnover was high), which handicapped their efforts.

Fourth, the reforms of the 1960s focused on local bureaucracies, which are often immune to interest representation efforts. Many local bureaucrats have limited technical skills, which reduces their ability to solve problems, even if they genuinely wish to do so. Moreover, local governments depend on other levels of government for considerable financial support. This reduces the discretion of local bureaucrats, who may be legally or politically bound to behave in certain ways. Effective interest representation in local politics, though not impossible, is highly problematical.

A final problem with many of the reforms of the 1960s was that they threatened the bureaucracy unnecessarily. According to Moynihan (1969), a key problem with the War on Poverty was its reliance on newly created counterbureaucracies, as was the case with community action agencies. Counterbureaucracies can be a threat to existing bureaucracies, which may regard them with disdain, alarm, or both. Yet, the real problem was with the role these counterbureaucracies chose to play. There is an enormous difference between a counterbureaucracy that functions as a gadfly and one that functions as a usurper. The former will be perceived by existing bureaucracies as a nuisance, the latter as a mortal threat. In fact, community action agencies usurped the roles of employment agencies and welfare agencies in such a way that resistance was inevitable (Sundquist, 1969). In the process, they earned the enmity of the personnel whose practices they were supposedly trying to improve, people who, in their own minds at least, were committed to helping the poor.

As the 1970s began, the limitations of the interest representation reforms of the 1960s had become painfully apparent to many scholars, citizen activists, and government officials. Moreover, new issues were beginning to emerge that promised to displace the issues of civil rights and poverty. Scholars noted that much was wrong with state and federal bureaucracies (McConnell, 1966; Lowi, 1969). Regulatory agencies at all levels of government were especially inviting targets (Kohlmeier, 1969). Moreover, new social movements were emerging that appealed to broad, diffuse constituencies, e.g., the environmental movement and the consumer movement. The reformers of the 1970s with different concerns and constituencies than the reformers of the 1960s tried a variety of new approaches. In addition they seemed to have learned something from the mistakes of the previous decade.

The interest representation reforms of the 1970s differed from those of the 1960s in several crucial respects: (1) they attempted to represent broad, diffuse interests (consumers, environmentalists, taxpayers) rather than just the underprivileged; (2) they appealed to relatively powerful and relatively numerous middle-class constituents rather than to smaller, less powerful poor constituents; (3) they placed greater emphasis on representation, less emphasis on democracy; (4) they shifted attention from formal representation and descriptive representation to substantive representation (to tangible results); (5) they devoted greater attention to regulatory agencies, not just social service agencies; (6) they focused on problems at all levels of government, including state and federal bureaucracies that might be more easily controlled than local bureaucracies; and (7) they stressed the importance of expertise and responsible, constructive dissent, in the hope that this would avoid the backlash that followed many of the reforms of the 1960s. There were, to be sure, some exceptions, such as health systems agencies (HSAs) and lay representation on occupational licensing boards.[2] By and large, however, the interest representation reforms of the 1970s constituted a sharp break with the past.

The interest representation reforms of the 1960s had paid homage to such goals as citizen participation, decentralization, and community control. In contrast, the interest representation reforms of the 1970s were more practical and less utopian. The reformers of the 1970s were guided less by Rousseau than by Madison, less by Alinsky than by Dewey. They proposed to work within the existing political system rather than to create a new society. As a result, their goals often seemed prosaic and mundane: knowledge, hearings, resources, and surrogates. These do not seem like the building blocks of a revolution. Yet, during the 1970s a representation revolution did in fact occur.

Knowledge

It has long been recognized that democratic government depends on a well-informed citizenry. As Madison (1953) put it: "A popular government without popular information, or the means of acquiring it, is but a Prologue to a farce or a tragedy; or perhaps both." Yet, when citizens or citizens' groups requested information from administrative agencies, they were often rebuffed on the grounds that the request was burdensome or that they had no need to know. In 1966 Congress took a significant step to remedy that problem by passing the Freedom of Information Act. The central aim of the act was to make disclosure of information to the public the rule, not the exception. In effect, the Freedom of Information

2. In the National Health Planning and Resources Development Act of 1974, Congress called upon local governments to establish HSAs to identify local health priorities and review institutional proposals for capital expenditures. By requiring that HSAs be "broadly representative of the social, economic, linguistic, and racial populations . . . of the area," Congress placed too much faith in descriptive representation (Morone, 1981; Morone and Marmor, 1981). Congress also ignored the difficulties that part-time agency members would face when trying to represent consumer interests in highly complex, technical issue areas. The same expertise gap problem surfaced in occupational licensing when states required consumer representation on part-time occupational licensing boards (Thain and Haydock, 1983).

Act shifted the burden of proof from citizens to bureaucrats, who would have to show why information should not be released.

Although the Freedom of Information Act of 1966 was a useful first step toward greater public access to administrative records, it was plagued by multiple implementation problems. Many agencies took months to respond to citizen requests and charged high fees for the information sought. The overclassification of documents, especially by the Defense Department, the Federal Bureau of Investigation (FBI), and the Central Intelligence Agency (CIA), continued. Journalists, who were expected to be among the primary users of the act, were intimidated by long delays and court costs (Archibald, 1979; Relyea, 1981).

Disappointed by the implementation of the act, Congress adopted a number of major amendments to it in 1974. They required agencies to respond to information requests within ten working days, imposed penalties on bureaucrats for the arbitrary or capricious withholding of information, and stipulated that "reasonably segregable" portions of agency documents should be released. They limited user costs to search and copying fees and provided the option of a fee waiver when that was deemed "in the public interest" by the agency. To discourage the denial of reasonable requests, they authorized the courts to assess court costs and attorney fees if the government lost a Freedom of Information Act decision on appeal. They also provided for in camera review of documents withheld by the agency (including classified documents) by the federal courts to determine if these documents had been improperly withheld.

The amendments of 1974 went a long way toward promoting public access to agency documents, and the Freedom of Information Act has been widely praised by public intervenors (Lynch, 1977; Nader, 1981). Yet, the Freedom of Information Act has also been criticized on several grounds. First, some critics have argued that the act was overly expensive to administer. Scalia (1982) contended that the act was "the Taj Mahal of the Doctrine of Unanticipated Consequences, the Sistine Chapel of Cost-Benefit Analysis Ignored." More specifically, the Justice Department estimated that the Freedom of Information Act cost $47.8 million per year to administer (Relyea, 1981). In the eyes of many executive branch officials, this was too much. Second, critics argued that the Freedom of Information Act was used primarily by corporations, not by citizens. For example, the commissioner of the Food and Drug Administration (FDA) estimated that approximately 90 percent of all Freedom of Information Act requests to his agency were attempts at "industrial espionage," e.g., Squibb asking for documents concerning Upjohn (Lardner, 1976). Finally, critics have contended that agencies continued to drag their feet in responding to information requests despite the 1974 amendments. The CIA and the FBI were frequently cited as being among the more recalcitrant government agencies in this regard (U.S. Senate Subcommittee, 1980). In short, the Freedom of Information Act was said to cost the government a lot of time and money without providing commensurate benefits to the general public.

These criticisms, though accurate enough, were far from compelling. First, the costs of administering the Freedom of Information Act do not seem exorbitant when one compares them to the costs of bureaucratic public relations offices or the costs incurred by taxpayers when members of Congress furnish baby booklets to their constituents. Ralph Nader (1981: 320) has suggested another analogy worth considering: "The amount of money which the Federal Government claims it spends each year to administer the Freedom of Information Act is roughly half the amount of money which the Defense Department spends on marching bands." With all deference to John Philip Sousa, the country's vital interests are probably better served by the Freedom of Information Act than by occasional performances of "The Thunderer." Second, it is true that corporations use the Freedom of Information Act more often than citizens, journalists, and public interest groups. Nevertheless, direct public use of the Freedom of Information Act is substantial. Moreover, the public may benefit from some disclosures effected by corporations. Whatever Squibb's motives in requesting information about Upjohn, the public interest is served if this leads to disclosures of faulty testing procedures, harmful side effects, and so forth. Third, the extent of compliance by administrative agencies does seem to vary from agency to agency. This is true, incidentally, not only at the federal level but also at the state and local levels where analogous statutes often apply (Robbin, 1984; Gordon and Heinz, 1979). At certain agencies (e.g., the FBI, the CIA), nondisclosure remains a serious problem. At most agencies, however, denials of information requests are relatively rare. For example, the FDA received twenty-two thousand Freedom of Information requests in 1976 and denied only 309 of them (Sherick, 1978). Moreover, it is important to remember that many denials—those by mental health or social service agencies, for instance—serve a legitimate purpose and protect other important values, such as the right to privacy (Robbin, 1984).

What exactly has the Freedom of Information Act accomplished? The following is a partial list of information that has been made public under the act (Nader, 1981):

1. inspection reports from the U.S. Department of Agriculture (USDA) on the wholesomeness (or lack thereof) of meat;

2. test data submitted to the FDA by drug manufacturers showing that certain drugs shown to cause cancer in animal tests have been used on humans;

3. Nuclear Regulatory Commission (NRC) records on the adequacy of programs to safeguard nuclear powerplants from the diversion and theft of plutonium and other nuclear materials;

4. reports of widespread fatalities and injuries caused by defective autos that the government refused to recall;

5. reports on drug testing of inmates of Iowa state penitentiaries;

6. an unpublished Public Health Service (PHS) study showing a high death rate from leukemia among Utah residents exposed to fallout from atomic bomb testing between 1950 and 1964;

7. an NRC plant safety rating that found that ten of the fifty plants surveyed were in the "below average" category; and

8. a report prepared by the Consumer Product Safety Commission (CPSC) on the potential hazards of aluminum wiring.

Some of the most secretive government agencies have been forced to justify highly questionable behavior as a result of disclosures forced by the Freedom of Information Act. Thus, the CIA's experiments in thought-control drugs were disclosed as a result of the act, as were CIA files on possible assassinations of foreign leaders (Weaver, 1977). FBI counterintelligence activities against "radical" organizations—activities that may have undermined the civil liberties of group members—were also made public through the Freedom of Information Act (Sherick, 1978: 75). These counterintelligence activities included wiretaps of Martin Luther King, Jr., and other prominent civil rights leaders.

71

Have these disclosures improved the performance of the bureaucracy? Have they improved the quality of public intervention in the administrative process? Have they made a difference for public policy? These questions are difficult to answer, and indeed the literature contains no systematic attempt to answer them. However, case studies suggest that the Freedom of Information Act has been used to good advantage by citizens and citizens' groups. For example, Rex Power, arrested for speeding despite the fact that he had been driving under the speed limit, resolved to investigate police radar equipment. At the Federal Communications Commission (FCC), where he cited the Freedom of Information Act to gain access to agency documents, he discovered that most police departments were operating such equipment without FCC licenses (contrary to federal law) and that some radar equipment had not been properly inspected prior to use (Sherick, 1978: 79–81). His disclosures embarrassed both the FCC and local police departments and led to prompt reforms. To cite another example, records showing the extent and severity of the incidence of defective steel-belted radial tires led to a nationwide recall of over ten million tires (Nader, 1981). Those persons whose lives were saved as a result are among the beneficiaries of the Freedom of Information Act.

In contrast to the Freedom of Information Act, which embraces all federal agencies, the Government in the Sunshine Act of 1976 applies to a narrower band of federal agencies, namely, collegial bodies composed of two or more members. Historically, collegial bodies have included some of the least visible but most important agencies in the bureaucracy—regulatory bodies shielded from public view by their structural independence and by the complexity of their subject matter. By requiring collegial bodies to open their meetings, legislative reformers hoped to promote open decision making and greater public confidence in government. By specifying ten categories of exempt information that could be considered in closed meetings—e.g., national defense and foreign policy, personnel rules and practices, trade secrets, accusations of criminal conduct, information generated in the regulation of financial institutions—reformers hoped to preserve the confidentiality of highly delicate discussions.

Although the Government in the Sunshine Act appears innocuous enough, it has been criticized on several grounds. First, critics contend that it permits the disclosure of information that might invade privacy, damage national security, or disrupt financial markets. Second, critics argue that it inhibits spirited debate, thereby damaging the collegial dialogue that is so important to a multi-member body. Third, critics charge that it gives special interests an extra advantage, because their representatives are most likely to attend open meetings.

These are serious charges, but they are overdrawn. First, the Government in the Sunshine Act expressly provides for a number of specific exemptions. As a result most meetings of financial regulatory bodies, such as the Federal Reserve Board, and the Federal Deposit Insurance Corporation (FDIC), are still held behind closed doors. Adjudicatory proceedings, personnel deliberations, and discussions of pending litigation are also closed. Moreover, these exemptions have been upheld by the courts (Welborn et al., 1984: 10–35). Second, it does appear that debate at open meetings is less lively and less spontaneous than debate at closed meetings. Furthermore, many commissioners or board members now make up their minds before meetings rather than afterward (Welborn et al., 1984: 64–65). However, another way of putting this is that members prepare better for open meetings (Welborn et al., 1984: 50). Surely that is not an unwelcome result! Nor does the quality of commission decisions seem to have suffered. Indeed, many observers believe that the quality of commission decisions has improved as a result of sunshine laws (Welborn et al., 1984: 72). The fact that independent regulatory commissions have been exceptionally innovative in recent years (Pertschuk, 1982; Derthick and Quirk, 1985) lends support to that conclusion, although it does not confirm it. Finally, as for the beneficiaries, many observers agree that "particularistic interests" benefit from the Government in the Sunshine Act, but they add that journalists and public interest groups benefit more (Welborn et al., 1984: 57). One explanation for this may be that open meetings are especially valuable to organizations that rotate their employees from one "beat" to another (news organizations) and to organizations that have high turnovers (public interest groups). Open meetings enable new recruits to familiarize themselves with administrative practices, policies, and personalities. By shortening the orientation process, they help to reduce the advantages of those trade associations that can afford to keep seasoned veterans in place for many years.

There is no question that sunshine laws have disrupted old routines and habits. As a result, agency officials accustomed to the status quo are less enthusiastic about sunshine laws than others are. However, it is generally conceded that open meetings have significantly increased the amount of information available to attentive publics (Welborn et al., 1984: 54). Moreover, much of that information is more comprehensible than ever, as various agencies have attempted to make their proceedings understandable to laypersons in attendance (e.g., by publishing special brochures). There is no guarantee, of course, that open meetings will result in broader, more effective citizen participation in the administrative process. Like other catalytic controls, sunshine laws provide opportunities, not certainties. However, by affording journalists more frequent glimpses of the decision making process of powerful commissions, such as the Federal Reserve Board, sunshine laws offer valuable insights to attentive publics. In doing so they help to equalize informational resources when participation occurs, as at public hearings.

Public Hearings

The public hearing was not invented in the 1970s. For many years, public hearings have been required at all levels of government and for a wide variety of issue areas. Although public hearings are not new, their number and use increased sharply during the 1970s when numerous provisions for public participation were written into federal law (Rosenbaum, 1978). In addition to mandating public participation opportunities in federal administrative proceedings, Congress insisted that state and local governments provide for public participation when administering federal programs. Even when Congress did not explicitly require a public hearing, administrative agencies often responded to vague public participation clauses by institutionalizing the public hearing as a key element (in some instances, the only element) of a citizen participation program.

The public hearing has been derided by some scholars as an empty ritual, a public relations exercise aimed at assuaging aroused publics without seriously addressing their underlying needs (Arnstein, 1969; Checkoway, 1979). Among the most common criticisms of public hearings are the following: (1) hearings are often held at inconvenient times and inaccessible places; (2) the communications process seldom provides for meaningful interaction between participants and decisionmakers; (3) participants are not representative of the public at large; and (4) hearings do not really change the minds of decisionmakers.

Evaluations of public hearings in intergovernmental programs suggest that there is some truth to these criticisms. A careful study of public hearings in General Revenue Sharing (GRS) programs revealed the minimal influence of citizen participants on budget allocation decisions (Cole and Caputo, 1984). A federal requirement for public participation in employment and training programs—through manpower planning councils—did little to promote meaningful citizen participation, because most manpower planning councils were dominated by service providers (Van Horn, 1979). Public hearings on Community Development Block Grant (CDBG) spending decisions do seem to have facilitated effective citizen involvement by new participants in the political process (Van Horn, 1979: 112). However, few would argue that these citizen participants were representative of the community at large.

In retrospect, one wonders whether public hearings had a fair chance under the revenue-sharing programs of the 1970s. As Van Horn (1979) has noted, public participation requirements tended to be vague and ambiguous. Congressional legislation failed to specify who should participate, when, and under what circumstances. Also, federal agencies, preoccupied with other problems, took very little interest in monitoring and enforcing citizen participation requirements. Finally, the acute financial problems of many local governments seem to have magnified the influence of local politicians and diminished the influence of citizens. Under more auspicious circumstances, citizen participation in revenue-sharing programs might have been more successful.

In fact, research on public hearings on environmental issues indicates quite clearly that public hearings can have a significant impact on administrative decision making. For example, Rosener (1982) analyzed 1,816 public hearings conducted by three California coastal commissions between April 1973 and December 1975 in an effort to assess the effectiveness of public hearings. She found that the commissions were more likely to deny a permit request by a developer when citizen opposition to the development surfaced (see Table 3.1). Moreover, this relationship persisted after controling for staff recommendations. Using the same data base but different methods, Mazmanian and Sabatier (1980) reached similar conclusions.

In a study of public hearings on state water quality planning in North Carolina between December 1976 and July 1979, Godschalk and Stiftel (1981) also found evidence of effective citizen participation. Of seventy-six specific recommendations considered by state authorities, fifty were either chosen or deleted in accordance with participant opinion, eleven were chosen or deleted despite

75

TABLE 3.1

Relationship between Citizen Participation
and California Coastal Commission Decisions

	Commission Decision		
	Decision to Approve	Decision to Deny	
Presence or Absence of Citizen Opposition			
No opposition	89% (987)	11% (127)	66% (1,114)
One or more groups in opposition	66% (387)	34% (197)	34% (584)
	81% (1,374)	19% (324)	N = 1,698

SOURCE: Judy B. Rosener, "Making Bureaucrats Responsive," *Public Administration Review*, Vol. 42, No. 4 (July–August 1982), p. 342. Reprinted with permission from *Public Administration Review*, © 1982 by the American Society for Public Administration, 1120 G St., N.W., Suite 500, Washington, D.C. All rights reserved.
Level of Association: phi = .27
Level of Signifance: $p < 0.0001$

participant opposition, and fifteen showed no clear implications. As a result of citizen participation, the State of North Carolina modified its original water quality plans, especially those concerning on-site wastewater disposal, construction, and mining.

Numerous case studies also attest to the effectiveness of public hearings on environmental issues. Thus Caldwell et al. (1976) cite many examples of successful citizen participation in environmental disputes, including effective presentations and demonstrations at public hearings. A good case in point would be a successful effort by the Berkshire Natural Resources Council and an affiliated group, Save Scenic Monterey, to dissuade the Massachusetts Department of Public Works from building a bypass to Route 23 through the scenic Berkshire hills. Mazmanian and Nienaber (1979) also cite examples of successful citizen participation in public hearings held by the U.S. Army Corps of Engineers. In some instances, citizens managed to torpedo plans for new construction projects. For example, citizen opposition to a levee construction project on the Missouri River near St. Louis helped convince the corps to scuttle the project. In other instances, e.g., flood control on the Wildcat and San Pablo Creeks near San Francisco, public hearings enabled citizens to express community support for one of several flood control alternatives proposed by the corps. The result was a corps decision to pursue channel improvements with trails and recreational facilities rather than other approaches, such as a multipurpose reservoir. The Wildcat and San Pablo Creeks case nicely illustrates the fact that citizens and bureaucrats can work together (through public hearings and other formats) to distinguish between desirable and undesirable policy alternatives.

It is no accident that much of the literature attesting to the virtues of public hearings involves environmental policymaking. As I have argued elsewhere (Gormley, 1986), environmental issues involve certain special conditions that facilitate successful citizen participation—high issue salience, strong public support, well-organized citizens' groups, and, in many instances, sympathetic administrative officials. The public hearing is no panacea. When citizens are uninterested or uninformed or deeply divided, public hearings may be of limited value. A public hearing on banking issues is unlikely to draw a crowd; a public hearing on abortion is unlikely to resolve much. The utility of public hearings may also depend on the political culture. In "moralistic" political cultures, where citizen participation is considered normal and desirable (Elazar, 1966), public hearings are likely to be more effective than in "traditionalistic" political cultures, where politics is regarded as the special province of a governing elite. Most importantly, public hearings make sense as part of a well-integrated interest representation strategy rather than as the sole outlet for concerned citizens. As Mazmanian and Nienaber have argued (1979: 125, 147), public hearings are most effective when combined with less formal and more narrowly focused devices, such as workshops, seminars, citizen committees, and brochures outlining alternative solutions to difficult problems. Public hearings can make a difference when circumstances are propitious and when other participation strategies are also employed. One catalytic control is not always enough.

Resources

Without significant financial resources, it is extremely difficult for citizens' groups to take advantage of the Freedom of Information Act, sunshine laws, public hearings requirements, and other reforms aimed at opening up the administrative process to the public. Yet, citizens' groups often lack the resources to conduct research, hire an attorney, and present expert testimony—all important if citizen participation is to be meaningful and effective (Gellhorn, 1972; Cramton, 1972). This problem, always serious, became acute in the 1970s as foundation funds, previously available to some citizens' groups, became increasingly scarce.

In 1975 Congress decided to deal with the problems at one discredited agency, the Federal Trade Commission (FTC), by means of a novel approach known as intervenor funding. Under the Magnuson-Moss FTC Improvement Act, which was aimed at reinvigorating an agency that had grown lax over the years, Congress empowered the FTC to reimburse intervenors (groups or individuals) for the costs of their participation in agency rulemaking proceedings under the following circumstances:

1. the interest to be articulated would not otherwise be represented;

2. the representation of that interest was necessary for a fair determination of the proceeding; and

3. the group or individual represented lacked the financial resources to pay for the cost of participation.

The program provided for the FTC at its discretion to disburse approximately five hundred thousand dollars per year.

The FTC, under new leadership, was enthusiastic about intervenor funding and committed to making the program work. This was true in 1975 when the program began, and especially true in 1977 when consumer advocate Michael Pertschuk took over as chairman of the FTC. Despite this enthusiasm, or perhaps because of it, the FTC was an inauspicious choice for an intervenor funding experiment. Charged by Congress with the task of protecting consumers as vigorously as possible against anticompetitive practices and unfair or deceptive advertising, the FTC initiated rulemaking proceedings aimed at the funeral industry, the used car industry, the cereal industry, the broadcasting industry, the eyeglass industry, the hearing aid industry, and a host of others. The initial rules proposed by the FTC were far from radical—they relied heavily on the disclosure of information to consumers so that they could make intelligent choices in the marketplace—but they were tough, direct, and extremely unpopular with industries that had grown accustomed to a lethargic FTC. Before long a howl of protests had emerged from affected industries, which lobbied Congress to rein in an agency alternatively described as a "national nanny" and a "rogue elephant."

The FTC, having failed to anticipate how quickly Congress could sour on aggressive regulation, made several strategic decisions in implementing the intervenor funding program that added fuel to the fire. Instead of distributing funds to a diverse group of poorly funded organizations from across the country, the agency opted instead to fund a relatively small number of organizations, almost half of which were located in Washington, D.C., or in California. America's heartland was largely ignored. Moreover, 65 percent of all the funds went to only eight groups (Boyer, 1981). The FTC's logic was understandable enough: well-established organizations with proven track records were good bets to participate effectively in agency proceedings. Yet, in stressing experience and expertise, the FTC left itself open to congressional criticism that it was allocating a disproportionate share of funds to a small cluster of "insider" organizations. The agency was also criticized for funding only groups that supported the agency's initial point of view, as specified in proposed rules. At least two studies have concluded that this latter charge was incorrect. The Administrative Conference (1980: 46773) found "many significant differences between the positions of the reimbursed participants and the Commission staff." Similarly, Mayer and Scammon (1983) found that only 27.3 percent of the funded witnesses agreed with the rule initially proposed by the FTC. Nevertheless, the perception of favoritism in funding decisions was widespread on Capitol Hill, where it reinforced the arguments of industry lobbyists.

These criticisms of the FTC's intervenor funding program obscured an important fact: the program actually worked. This conclusion emerges from a major study sponsored by the Administrative Conference (Boyer, 1981), from a modest questionnaire survey of funded witnesses (Mayer and Scammon, 1983), and from the comments of agency officials. First, the program made possible a better balance of viewpoints in FTC rulemaking proceedings. Although industry witnesses still outnumbered consumer witnesses by a substantial margin (Pertschuk, 1979), the program resulted in an increased proportion of consumer witnesses, government official witnesses, and expert witnesses (Boyer, 1981: 116). Moreover, funded participants handled themselves in a professional manner and made constructive contributions to agency proceedings. For example, Boyer (1981: 128) has noted that funded consumer group attorneys "frequently developed lines of questioning that had not been fully explored in agency staff examination of the witness."

The policy impacts of the FTC's intervenor funding program are difficult to gauge because many of the rulemaking proceedings initiated by the agency during this period were halted or otherwise disrupted by an angry Congress (Pertschuk, 1982). Nevertheless, the evidence suggests that intervenor funding did make a difference. A case in point is the FTC's eyeglass rule, which invalidated bans on price advertising of ophthalmic goods and services. The Americans for Democratic Action (ADA), with funding from the FTC, argued that services should be included in the final rule. The ADA prevailed over the FTC staff, which wanted to limit the rule to the sale of goods.

The ADA also lent strong support to the staff's view that eye examiners should be required to give the patient a copy of his or her prescription. This view also prevailed. Of course, this was only one proceeding. However, the overall picture appears to be much the same. Commenting on intervenor funding, Chairman Pertschuk (1979) observed: "As an individual commissioner, I know that I have benefited enormously from the clash of advocacy." Other commissioners agree with Pertschuk (Boyer, 1981), as do the intervenors themselves. Thus, seventeen of thirty-one funded applicants say that their influence was great or moderate (Mayer and Scammon, 1983). Overall, the policy impacts of the FTC intervenors funding program were noticeable and in some instances considerable, despite inauspicious circumstances.

Eventually, the FTC's intervenor funding program was terminated when President Reagan's appointees declined to continue it. Other federal intervenor funding programs—at the Environmental Protection Agency (EPA), CPSC, National Oceanic and Atmospheric Administration (NOAA), Department of Transportation (DOT), FDA, and USDA—also appear to have been phased out by the Reagan administration. However, intervenor funding programs at the state level continue to exist. For example, several states have established intervenor funding programs for citizens' groups that participate in utility regulatory proceedings. Most of these programs, like the FTC's program, are administered by the regulatory agency itself. Not surprisingly, some of the same criticisms that plagued the FTC have also arisen at the state level. For example, the Wisconsin intervenor funding program has been criticized on the grounds that 60 percent of the total funding has gone to a single citizens' group (Trubek and Hickey, 1985). This raises the question of whether the regulatory agency ought to be making funding decisions. Even if this does not result in favoritism, it does result in the appearance of favoritism, which undermines the credibility of a fragile program. For this reason, Michigan's approach to intervenor funding seems superior. Under the Michigan plan, adopted in 1982, a five-person Utility Consumer Protection Board, independent of the state Public Service Commission, administers a Utility Consumer Representation Fund (Gormley, 1983). Although the Michigan intervenor funding program has not been thoroughly studied, it appears even more likely to succeed and to survive than programs that depend on the regulatory agency to make reimbursement decisions.

Intervenor funding is no panacea. It probably makes sense only in salient issue areas, where concerned citizens' groups are already active, though underrepresented. It also probably makes sense only in states with favorable political cultures, where citizen participation in the administrative process is accepted as a natural and desirable form of political involvement. It is doubtful that an intervenor funding program for environmental regulation would get very far in Mississippi and doubtful that an intervenor funding program for banking regulation would work anywhere, given the low salience of banking issues. Nevertheless, in certain issue areas and in certain states, intervenor funding can improve the quality of citizen participation in the administrative process.

Surrogates

It is not always possible to rely on citizens' groups to achieve a better balance of views in administrative policymaking. First of all, some issue areas, though important, fail to excite or arouse citizens' groups. When issues are low in salience, citizens may not know enough to be concerned. Even if group leaders recognize the importance of the less salient issues, they may prefer to emphasize more salient issues to attract better media attention, public support, and membership contributions. Second, some issues are so complex that citizens' groups lack the expertise to address them effectively. While intervenor funding can solve this problem, intervenor funding programs are vulnerable to cutbacks by politicians, to capricious implementation by bureaucrats, or both. As a result, they are not terribly reliable. Finally, citizens' groups have a very short life span, and that limits their effectiveness in certain issue areas. While some administrative controversies are quickly resolved, many last far longer than the citizens' groups that wish to influence their outcome. Citizens' groups are simply not durable enough to offer sustained, persistent intervention in many policy arenas.

Aware of these limitations, reformers in the 1970s turned increasingly to citizen surrogates to improve the quality of public representation in administrative decision making. These surrogates included legal aid societies, little city halls, ombudsmen, consumer protection boards, assistant attorneys general, and public intervenors of various descriptions. Most of these institutional arrangements preserved a vital role for citizens as initiators of action, as consultants, as advisors, or as overseers. However, with the exception of legal aid societies and citizens' utilities boards, they all relied on government bureaucracies with advocacy responsibilities to control government bureaucracies with policymaking responsibilities on behalf of citizens. This constituted a marked departure from previous approaches. To the Progressives, bureaucracy was the solution. To the reformers of the 1960s, bureaucracy was the problem. To the reformers of the 1970s, bureaucracy was both the problem and the solution.

Exemplifying the transition from the 1960s to the 1970s were legal aid societies. Like many interest representation reforms of the 1960s, legal aid societies were explicitly charged with representing the poor. Also, legal aid attorneys, though funded primarily by the government, were not government officials. Nevertheless, legal aid societies relied on citizen surrogates rather than on citizens themselves to improve the quality of public representation in administrative and judicial proceedings. In this respect legal aid societies reflected the thinking of the 1970s as much as that of the preceding decade.

According to most accounts, the performance of legal aid societies improved considerably over time (Hollingsworth, 1977). The orientation of legal aid societies also changed over time (Handler et al., 1978). While the focus of legal aid societies remained the representation of individual clients, legal aid societies attempted to do more to represent the poor as a whole by devoting more resources to law reform. Although law reform proved to be more controversial than constituent services, many legal aid attorneys won the respect and confidence of key bureaucrats. As Hollingsworth (1977) has noted, agency officials often consulted with legal services attorneys before altering or initiating rules or regulations. According to Johnson (1978), legal aid attorneys were especially effective at working with welfare agencies and public housing authorities.

If legal aid societies bridged the thinking of two decades, ombudsman offices more closely reflected the premise that government bureaucrats can help citizens in their dealings with other government bureaucrats. In contrast to legal aid attorneys, ombudsmen are government officials who seek to improve relations between citizens and bureaucrats by providing information, investigating complaints, and making recommendations. American ombudsmen, in contrast to their Scandinavian counterparts, come in many different sizes and shapes. Some are appointed by the chief executive, while others are appointed by the legislature; some focus on state government, while others focus on local government; some are centralized, others are decentralized; some are broad-based (with the freedom to intervene in any issue area), while others are narrowly focused (e.g., ombudsmen who specialize in nursing home or corrections issues). The common denominator is that ombudsmen are catalytic agents who prod bureaucrats into taking corrective action.

Although some American ombudsman offices were established before 1970, most did not become fully operational until the 1970s. By the late 1970s, all fifty states had a long-term health care ombudsman, and several states had a corrections ombudsman. Broad-based ombudsmen could be found in Hawaii, Pennsylvania, Iowa, and Oregon (at the state level), and in such cities as Honolulu, Chicago, Boston, New York, Detroit, Atlanta, Houston, San Antonio, Columbus, and Hartford.

Like legal aid societies, ombudsmen have had to choose between client representation and class representation, between service responsiveness and policy responsiveness. A number of studies confirm that ombudsmen have focused their energies on client representation, on the assumption that they have an obligation to assist individual citizens who come forward with a complaint about a particular bureaucracy or a particular bureaucrat. By all accounts, ombudsmen perform this function effectively and to the satisfaction of their clients. Thus, the Administration on Aging (1983) found that long-term health care ombudsmen have been successful in resolving complaints received from nursing home residents, family members, and other interested parties on a wide variety of subjects, including Medicaid programs, guardianship, the power of attorney, inadequate hygiene, family problems, and theft of personal items. In fiscal year 1982, for example, the average percentage of verified complaints that were reported as resolved in twenty-five states was 85.4 percent. Case studies of broad-based ombudsman offices have also reached positive conclusions about the representation of individual clients. For example, Nordlinger (1973) found that 22 percent of Boston households had used Boston's "little city halls" by the end of its first full year of operation and that 75 percent of those who did so were fairly satisfied or very satisfied with the results. Similarly, Moore (1973) found that Honolulu's Office of Information and Complaint was prompt and effective in handling complaints and dispensing useful information to citizens.

The public policy consequences of ombudsmen have been more limited, largely because ombudsmen devote far less time to policy than to service. In a report on nineteen state health care ombudsman offices, CRC Education and Human Development (1981) found that the median time spent on administrative advocacy was a mere 5 percent. Although more time was devoted to legislative advocacy, only about 15 percent of the median effort was devoted to issue advocacy of any sort. In a comprehensive study of health care ombudsman programs in all fifty states, Monk et al. (1982) reached fairly similar conclusions. Ombudsmen were asked to rank the relative importance of six skills thought to be necessary for the successful performance of the ombudsman function. Of these six skills—complaint processing, supportive counseling, legal activism, understanding nursing home operations and procedures, sensitivity to the aging progress and to old people, and community organizing—legal activism ranked dead last. Studies of broad-based ombudsman have reached similar conclusions (Nordlinger, 1973; Moore, 1973).

There is no denying that ombudsmen have done more to promote service responsiveness than they have to promote policy responsiveness. Nevertheless, it should be noted that ombudsmen have successfully recommended changes in agency policies, practices, and procedures. To cite a mundane example, the Honolulu Office of Information and Complaint managed to preserve the beauty sleep of Honolulu residents by relaying complaints about early morning refuse collection to responsible officials and by pressing successfully for a "reasonable" pick-up time. More significantly, the Honolulu office initiated an investigation after learning that city and county ambulances took one hour and fifteen minutes to arrive at the scene of a traffic accident. As a result of the investigation, the city and county instituted a fail-safe system for dispatching its ambulances. It is probably true, as Moore asserts (1973: 67), that ombudsman offices are "geared for the prompt disposition of complaints of generally modest complexity." However, since many complaints fit that description, especially at the local level, this is no small accomplishment.

Many administrative agencies, of course, grapple with complex policy problems. Under such circumstances, neither ombudsmen nor citizens' groups are likely to provide effective representation for consumers or other broad interest groups. Recognizing this, reformers created a new kind of institution to represent citizens in highly complex but important administrative proceedings. Elsewhere, I have characterized that solution as "proxy advocacy." Proxy advocacy emerged in the 1970s as a response to sharp increases in utility rates approved by state public utility commissions (PUCs). Concerned and perplexed by these decisions, most states established offices to represent consumers as a whole (or residential consumers in particular) in PUC proceedings. In some instances, this was accomplished by creating a special unit within the attorney general's office; in other instances, an independent office was established.

In a fifty-state empirical study of proxy advocacy, I found that proxy advocates were effective participants in PUC proceedings, including those involving highly complex issues (Gormley, 1983). Proxy advocates were successful in persuading PUCs to adopt late payment penalty bans and a grace period before terminating service (see Table 3.2). Both policies helped consumers who were struggling to pay their bills on schedule. Proxy advocates have also

TABLE 3.2

Effects of Public Advocacy on Public Utility Commission Policies

	Late-payment Penalty Ban (N=51)		Grace Period before Disconnection (N=47)	
	MLE	p	Standardized b	p
Grass-roots advocacy	1.071	0.002	0.101	0.250
Proxy advocacy	0.510	0.035	0.425	0.003
Political culture	−0.680	0.007	−0.294	0.030
Regulatory resources	0.324	0.098	−0.128	0.180
Method of selection	0.500	0.044	0.081	0.315
Estimated R^2 = 0.627	−2 × log likelihood ratio = 24.46		R^2 = .241	F = 2.60

SOURCE: William T. Gormley, Jr., "Policy, Politics, and Public Utility Regulation," *American Journal of Political Science*, Vol. 27, No. 1 (February 1983), p. 99. By permission of the University of Texas Press.

NOTE: MLE = maximum likelihood estimate (standardized).

been successful in reducing rate awards by PUCs. For example, Boston Edison requested a $46 million rate increase in 1979. The state attorney general opposed any rate hike, arguing that the company's request was excessive and citing evidence to support that position. Although the Massachusetts commission did not agree fully with the attorney general's reasoning, it did cut back Boston Edison's rate hike to approximately $19 million.

These findings underscore important differences between proxy advocates and ombudsmen. In contrast to broad-based ombudsmen, proxy advocates are undaunted by complexity. Charged with a fairly specific mission, they can specialize in an issue area and develop considerable technical expertise. This enhances their effectiveness in complex policy disputes. In contrast to both broad-based and narrowly focused ombudsmen, proxy advocates are more interested in policy responsiveness than in service responsiveness. Given scarce resources, proxy advocates would rather represent consumers as a whole than individual consumers. When a service problem arises, they normally refer consumers to the administrative agency or to the company. At the same time, they try to institutionalize remedies that will prevent service problems from arising in the future or that will mitigate their impact.

Although many states have experimented with various forms of proxy advocacy, Wisconsin has pioneered in this area. In 1967, Wisconsin became the first state in the country to establish an environmental public advocate. Located in the attorney general's office, the Public Intervenor, charged with protecting "public rights" in water and other natural resources, has participated in a wide variety of environmental disputes. The office was strengthened in 1976 when the attorney general designated two full-time assistant attorneys general as public intervenors and established a citizens advisory committee to offer technical and strategic advice. According to a recent survey (Christenson, 1985), 90 percent of those who have participated in proceedings in which the Public Intervenor has also participated believe that the office has made a "significant contribution."

Another Wisconsin experiment is the Citizens Utilities Board (CUB), established in 1979. Created by the State Legislature, CUB relies exclusively on voluntary contributions solicited through the mail and through door-to-door canvassing. Initially, CUB was authorized by the state legislature to solicit contributions through occasional inserts in utility bills that utility companies were obliged to accept occasionally. However, the U.S. Supreme Court ended this practice in 1986 by declaring involuntary inserts unconstitutional.[3] At the same time, CUB decided to dissolve itself as a public group and reorganize as a private, non-stock corporation.

The impacts of CUB interventions in rate cases have yet to be firmly established. CUB claims numerous victories, while utility company executives and public utility regulators are more skeptical. However, CUB did persuade the Wisconsin Public Service Commission not to adopt local measured service for telephone customers (Jones, 1987).[4] CUB also persuaded state regulators that telephone company contracts for inside wiring maintenance were overpriced (Diamond, 1987). Impressed by these and other victories, two other states—Illinois and Oregon—have established CUBs of their own.

Conclusion

Viewed in isolation from one another, the interest representation reforms of the 1970s do not seem very spectacular. Viewed together, they are much more significant. Policymakers at all levels of government decided that neither bureaucratic government nor interest group pluralism nor direct democracy offered an adequate blueprint for the future. Instead, they borrowed pragmatically from these traditions in an effort to restore public confidence in the administrative process and in government itself. In doing so, they designed reforms that would be acceptable to the bureaucracy. This was less a concession to the bureaucracy than it was a concession to common sense. Without at least grudging bureaucratic support, interest representation reforms were likely to be evaded, undermined, or ignored.

Sensitivity to bureaucrats' concerns did not constitute a betrayal of the citizenry, since bureaucrats were not really hostile to citizen

3. The California Public Utilities Commission (PUC) had ordered Pacific Gas and Electric to insert a consumer group newsletter in its billing envelopes four times a year—a practice similar to that mandated in Wisconsin. In a 5–3 decision, the U.S. Supreme Court struck down this requirement on the grounds that it compels a utility company to associate with speech with which it disagrees. The Court majority further expressed the concern that a billing insert requirement would discourage a utility company from speaking out on public issues in the first place. Court dissenters disputed such deterrent effects and argued that consumer group access to billing envelope space is roughly analogous to public access to a private forum, such as a shopping mall, which the Court has upheld on previous occasions. For the full debate, see *Pacific Gas and Electric v. PUC* of California (1986).

4. Under local measured service, customers are charged for each local telephone call based on the time of day, the distance, and the duration of the call.

participation. According to Aberbach and Rockman (1978), who interviewed 126 high-level federal executives in 1970, most bureaucrats favored more citizen involvement in the administrative process, provided that it didn't clash with other important values such as efficiency, expertise, and accountability. While expressing support for more citizen participation, bureaucrats also voiced several fears: (1) that unrepresentative demagogues would emerge as spokespersons for underrepresented groups; (2) that citizens with no continuing stake in a program would behave irresponsibly; (3) that a more open administrative process would prove cumbersome and inefficient; and (4) that citizen participants would lack the expertise to make a useful contribution.

The interest representation reforms of the 1970s allayed many of these fears by improving the quality of citizen participation in the administrative process, by reducing the need for citizens to resort to protest or litigation, and by institutionalizing representation through proxies in issue areas where this seemed appropriate. The interest representation reforms of the 1970s promised tangible benefits for citizens, but on terms bureaucrats could accept. They enabled public intervenors to develop an impressive evidentiary record in administrative proceedings and to secure important concessions. As a result, there was less need to resort to inflammatory rhetoric or demagogic appeals to the masses. There was also less need to appeal bureaucratic decisions to judges or politicians. The interest representation reforms of the 1970s challenged and prodded the bureaucracy without frightening and alienating bureaucrats.

The interest representation reforms of the 1970s accomplished a great deal for citizens, far less for the bureaucracy. Although the bureaucracy did not actively resist these reforms, most were adopted without the bureaucracy's active support. As a result, the bureaucracy got little credit for reforms imposed from the outside. Nor did the reforms themselves receive the recognition they deserved. In part, this was the doing of public intervenors, who continued to voice dissatisfaction in order to motivate supporters and to attract financial resources. Public intervenors can't afford to be too pleased with themselves or they will put themselves out of business. More significant perhaps was the absence of one grand reform that would epitomize the new approach to interest representation in the administrative process—an approach recognized by some scholars (Stewart, 1975) but not by the press or the public at large. The federal government's refusal to establish a Consumer

Protection Agency made it difficult for observers to recognize what was happening in the 1970s. A Consumer Protection Agency would have symbolized the spirit of the 1970s in a way that large numbers of proxy advocates, ombudsmen, public hearings, and freedom of information statutes could not. Yet, these scattered reforms were probably far more significant—and far more difficult to dismantle—than a Consumer Protection Agency could have been. Although there was no palace coup in the 1970s, a representation revolution did in fact occur. By broadening and improving public intervention in administrative proceedings, reformers helped to create a more humane, more responsive, and more innovative bureaucracy. This was no small accomplishment.

Due Process

Under the Fourteenth Amendment to the Constitution, no state shall "deprive any person of life, liberty, or property without due process of law." In recent years, the due process clause has been the basis for a considerable amount of litigation on behalf of various disadvantaged constituencies, including welfare recipients, prisoners, and the mentally disabled. In addition, the spirit of due process has been invoked by business groups seeking "fair" administration through various procedural protections.

In its purest form, due process is both procedural and constitutional. It requires that certain procedures be followed by administrative agencies in order to comply with the Constitution. The usual focus of activity here is administrative adjudication, where agencies apply legislative and administrative rules to individual cases. In a variety of prison discipline, employee rights, and welfare rights cases, federal courts have required that a hearing be held before administrative agencies could deprive a person of liberty or property. In some instances, the courts have gone so far as to prescribe a full-fledged trial-type hearing.

Another form of due process is both procedural and legal. It requires that certain procedures be followed by administrative agencies in order to comply with the law. Usually, the law in question is the Administrative Procedure Act (APA) of 1946, which requires judges to decide whether agencies have acted "arbitrarily" and "capriciously" in promulgating new rules and regulations. In order to discharge this responsibility, some courts have insisted that agencies follow procedures not specifically required under the APA in order to build an evidentiary record adequate for meaningful judicial review. These cases are sometimes referred to as "hybrid rulemaking" cases because they create a new form of rulemaking that falls somewhere in between the APA's polar extremes of informal rulemaking and formal rulemaking. In many instances, the Congress itself has insisted on hybrid rulemaking. Due process, it should be remembered, is primarily, but not exclusively, the province of the courts.

A final form of due process is both substantive and constitutional.¹ It requires agencies to engage in certain substantive actions (e.g., to provide prisoners three wholesome meals a day, access to adequate shower facilities, and medical care as needed) or to end certain practices (e.g., overcrowding and understaffing). Because compliance with such directives costs money, these orders impose significant requirements on legislators as well. Indeed, in many institutional reform cases legislators have been "invisible defendants" before the court. The nominal defendants—usually agency heads—have often welcomed judicial intervention despite misgivings over the specifics.² Consequently, these cases should be viewed as efforts to change both bureaucratic practices and legislative priorities.

Although they were different in their rationales, their contents, and their focuses, the due process cases of the 1970s all sought to control the bureaucracy. Even when the bureaucracy's faults were directly traceable to legislative neglect, the bureaucracy was a compelling target. By blaming the bureaucracy, federal judges might secure more concessions from politicians than by blaming the pol-

1. Despite similar language, this form of due process should not be confused with the old doctrine of "substantive due process," out of vogue at the federal level since the mid-1930s. In the early twentieth century, federal courts invoked the substantive due process doctrine to strike down state economic legislation perceived as unduly harmful to business groups (Note, "State . . . ," 1979). Like the old substantive due process cases, the institutional reform cases of the 1970s inferred substantive rights from the Fourteenth Amendment. However, the institutional reform cases differed in several respects from the substantive due process decisions of the early twentieth century: (1) their proximate target was administrative action, not legislative action; (2) their hidden concern was legislative inaction (the failure to appropriate funds) rather than legislative action (the passage of a questionable statute); (3) they sought to protect the underprivileged, not privileged groups in society; and (4) they usually invoked other constitutional and statutory provisions above and beyond the Fourteenth Amendment.

2. In 1972 Judge Frank Johnson issued a landmark decision ordering sweeping reforms of Alabama's facilities for the mentally disabled (*Wyatt v. Stickney*). Shortly after the decision, Stonewall B. Stickney, state commissioner of mental health and principal defendant, was quoted as saying, "it's kind of exhilarating to see that the courts may get the Legislature going. It's been our experience that they'd rather spend money for highways than mental health" (Yarbrough, 1982: 397). Similarly, Robert Sarver, commissioner of corrections in Arkansas, reacted favorably to Judge J. Smith Henley's prison reform decree in *Holt v. Sarver* (1970). Sarver, a self-described prison reformer, saw court intervention as a lever to be used in obtaining funds from a reluctant State Legislature (Spiller, 1977: 93). Some judges were blunt enough to acknowledge what was going on. As Judge Henley commented in *Holt* (1970: 365), "In a sense the real Respondents are not limited to those formally before the Court but include the Governor of Arkansas, the Arkansas Legislature, and ultimately the people of the state as a whole."

iticians themselves. By judicializing the administrative process, the courts might secure both procedural fairness and substantive justice. However, these were merely hopes. In practice, due process proved to be a blunt instrument for achieving reform. By the mid-1970s, even judges began to wonder if a judicialized bureaucracy was really an improvement. By the late 1970s, a number of due process controls were on the decline.

Hybrid Rulemaking

Under the federal APA, federal administrative agencies have three obligations when they make rules: (1) Notice—Agencies must give adequate notice of the rule they propose to adopt by publishing it in the Federal Register; (2) Comment—Agencies must give interested parties an opportunity to participate in the rulemaking process through written comments, with or without an opportunity for oral presentation; and (3) Reasons—Agencies must include a concise general statement of the basis and purpose of their rule when they finally adopt it. Because these requirements are not particularly onerous and because they do not approximate a trial-type hearing, this kind of rulemaking is sometimes called informal rulemaking or notice-and-comment rulemaking.

During the 1970s eighteen state legislatures decided to follow the federal government's example by adopting administrative procedure acts of their own (Renfrow et al., 1985). While some states had done this previously, more states adopted administrative procedure acts in the 1970s than in any other decade. In most instances the provisions of state administrative procedure acts mirrored the language of the federal APA. In the case of rulemaking, states simply required notice, comment, and reasons.[3]

At the same time that states were discovering the virtues of the federal APA, the federal courts were discovering its limitations. In a series of opinions, the U.S. Court of Appeals (D.C. Circuit) insisted that administrative agencies employ rulemaking procedures above and beyond those mandated by the APA—including an oral hearing, oral argument, cross-examination of witnesses, or some combination of the above. For example, in *International Harvester Co. v. Ruckelshaus* (1973), the U.S. Court of Appeals (D.C. Circuit) overturned an Environmental Protection Agency (EPA) decision

3. In general, state notice requirements are somewhat weaker than the federal APA's, while state comment requirements are somewhat stronger.

not to suspend emission standards for light-duty vehicles for one year on the grounds that the EPA's methodology was suspect. On remand, the court instructed the EPA to give auto companies an opportunity to cross-examine witnesses to test the validity of the EPA's assumptions, methods and conclusions. Similarly, in *Walter Holm and Co. v. Hardin* (1971), the U.S. Court of Appeals (D.C. Circuit) overturned a U.S. Department of Agriculture (USDA) decision restricting the sale of small "vine ripe" tomatoes but allowing the sale of small "mature greens." On remand, the court instructed the USDA to allow cross-examination in a new hearing so that importers of the "vine ripe" tomatoes could challenge the distinction.

In these and other decisions (*Mobil Oil Corp. v. FPC*, 1973; *Appalachian Power Co. v. EPA*, 1973; *Portland Cement Assn. v. Ruckelshaus*, 1973), U.S. Courts of Appeals institutionalized what has come to be known as "hybrid rulemaking." Although the precise ingredients vary from case to case, hybrid rulemaking involves something less than a full-fledged trial-type proceeding (formal rulemaking) but something more than notice-and-comment (informal rulemaking). The courts' principal justification for hybrid rulemaking requirements is the need for an adequate record for meaningful judicial review. Informal rulemaking proceedings do not always generate a record ample enough for the courts to determine whether an agency action was arbitrary, capricious, an abuse of discretion, or otherwise not in accordance with law—an obligation imposed on the courts by the APA. Through hybrid rulemaking requirements, the courts have sought to generate a record sufficient to permit meaningful judicial review.

From the vantage point of the courts, the absence of an oral hearing was not the only drawback of notice-and-comment rulemaking. The courts were also troubled by the possibility that while one record might exist in theory, two records might exist in practice: an open record for the courts and the public to scrutinize, a secret record for agency officials and knowledgeable insiders. This possibility resulted from "*ex parte* contacts" between agency officials and interested parties following the submission of written comments in formal rulemaking proceedings. Alarmed by this practice, a U.S. Court of Appeals (D.C. Circuit) panel banned *ex parte* contacts in informal rulemaking proceedings (*Home Box Office v. FCC*, 1977). A few months later, a different panel of the same court reached a different conclusion in a similar case, noting that the federal APA banned *ex parte* contacts in formal (on-the-record) proceedings only (*Action for Children's Television v. FCC*, 1977).

Nevertheless, the second panel agreed with the first that *ex parte* contacts should be banned in informal rulemaking proceedings involving "conflicting private claims to a valuable privilege."

The courts were not alone in imposing hybrid rulemaking requirements on administrative agencies. During the 1970s the Congress also required hybrid rulemaking in a number of instances. For example, the Federal Trade Commission (FTC) Improvement Act of 1974 granted a right to a hearing with either cross-examination or the presentation of rebuttal submissions when there are "disputed issues of material fact" that must be resolved and the FTC decides such procedures to be appropriate and necessary. The Congress also required hybrid rulemaking in the Securities and Exchange Commission (SEC) Amendments of 1975, the Toxic Substances Control Act of 1976, the Department of Energy (DOE) Organization Act of 1977 and other statutes. Judging from the legislative histories of these statutes, the Congress's enthusiasm for hybrid rulemaking stemmed more from a commitment to fairness and full disclosure than from the need for tough judicial review.[4] Ironically, the Congress saw hybrid rulemaking as a form of due process, while the courts saw it as a precondition for effective oversight.

It is tempting to dismiss hybrid rulemaking requirements as harmless, potentially useful attempts to provide an extra measure of due process in rulemaking proceedings where the stakes are high and the issues are complex. More often than not, however, hybrid rulemaking requirements are neither harmless nor useful. Such requirements, whether imposed by Congress or the courts, limit the discretion of administrators on important matters of procedure without contributing noticeably to either fairness or meaningful judicial review. They substitute rigidity for flexibility, formality for informality, tedium for speed. In the process, they rob rulemaking of many of its advantages and discourage a shift from adjudication to rulemaking long advocated by scholars and judges (Davis, 1978: 448).

Hybrid rulemaking requirements blur the distinction between formal adjudication and informal rulemaking. One consequence of this is delay in issue areas where delay is already a serious problem. Oral arguments, rebuttal opportunities, and cross-examina-

4. See for example House Report 93–1606, "Consumer Product Warranties and FTC Improvements Act," 16 December 1974; House Report 94–1341, "Toxic Substances Control Act," 14 July 1976; and Senate Report 95–367, "Department of Energy Organization Act," 27 July 1977.

tion opportunities require more preparation time, more execution time, and more follow-up time than other more flexible procedures. Thus it is hardly surprising that the EPA has failed to meet deadline after deadline in adopting rules under the Resource Conservation and Recovery Act, the Toxic Substances Control Act, and other statutes that require hybrid rulemaking (Rosenbaum, 1985: 204–16). The fallout effects of such delays are worsened by the fact that state environmental agencies cannot act sensibly until the U.S. EPA has acted first. Yet when the EPA is late in meeting congressional deadlines, it often expects states to move promptly to make up for lost time.[5]

If hybrid rulemaking requirements did result in a stronger evidentiary record—an assumption made by some courts—they might be justifiable. In practice, however, hybrid rulemaking requirements have been used to forestall unwelcome administrative action rather than to ferret out useful information in the hope of making a stronger case. Williams (1975) found that parties declined to use their cross-examination opportunities in three out of four instances where the courts instructed agencies to provide such opportunities. In the fourth instance, a party cross-examined witnesses but the outcome of the case was unaffected by that. In short, some litigants have been disingenuous in claiming that their due process rights have been infringed upon by an agency's failure to provide cross-examination opportunities.

The parties who benefit from hybrid rulemaking requirements, incidentally, are usually firms and corporations that have adequate access to the legislative branch and that have used that access successfully over the years. Thus the Chrysler Corporation and the Ford Motor Corporation benefited from hybrid rulemaking requirements in *International Harvester*, while Mobil Oil benefited from such requirements in *Mobil Oil*. It is possible to argue that the public as a whole benefits from *ex parte* contact restrictions, since corporate officials are more likely than ordinary citizens to engage in such contacts. However, the "hidden record" problem is easily remedied by keeping a "log" of all *ex parte* contacts, to be included in the record submitted to the courts if the agency's rule is challenged (Note, "Due . . . ," 1979). Such an approach, as practiced by the Consumer Product Safety Commission (CPSC) for example, is

5. This has been a continuing source of frustration to state officials. Indeed, as the U.S. General Accounting Office reported (1980: ii), state environmental officials identified the late issuance of regulations by the U.S. EPA as "the greatest single obstacle to the management of their programs."

95

far less onerous than an outright ban that would deprive agencies of useful information.

Hybrid rulemaking requirements are unfortunate not only because the procedures they require do little good but also because alternative procedures might do better. For example, the EPA has experimented with inquiry conferences, where top-level agency officials quiz expert witnesses in a "rapid exchange of questions and ideas" on key questions (Williams, 1975). In some instances, the EPA administrator has actually sat in on these conferences, helping to ensure that the agency's ultimate decisionmaker has a firm grasp of the nuances of a particular controversy and reducing the distorting effects of bureaucratic filtering processes. When the courts simply remand a rule for clarification, the agency is free to opt for inquiry conferences, interrogatories, written statements of methodology or other approaches tailor-made to the problem at hand. In contrast, when the courts insist on cross-examination, the agency's hands are tied. Forced to adopt specific procedures, the agency may fail to adopt other procedures that would be more useful.

Most critics of hybrid rulemaking requirements have directed their fire at the courts, arguing explicitly or implicitly that hybrid rulemaking is legitimate when required by Congress, illegitimate when required by the courts (Wright, 1974; Byse, 1978). Yet that begs the question of hybrid rulemaking's merits. If hybrid rulemaking is undesirable, it is no more desirable when mandated by Congress than when mandated by the courts. Indeed, congressional requirements may be even more damaging, because they are usually broader in scope than court requirements. A court requirement that the EPA allow cross-examination in the context of a particular rule is less restrictive than a congressional requirement that the EPA allow cross-examination in a whole series of rulemaking proceedings.

In 1978 the U.S. Supreme Court finally put the brakes on court-ordered hybrid rulemaking. In *Vermont Yankee v. NRDC* (1978), the Court ruled that federal courts may not impose procedural requirements on administrative rulemaking above and beyond those contained in the APA. As Justice Rehnquist put it (1978: 544), "Agencies should be free to fashion their own rules of procedure." The behavior of federal courts since *Vermont Yankee* has confirmed that strong judicial review does not depend on misguided hybrid rulemaking requirements. Scholars who differ on the desirability of strong judicial review nevertheless agree that judicial review of the substance of agency rules continues to be vigorous (Shapiro, 1983; Sunstein, 1984; Garland, 1985).

Hybrid rulemaking is perhaps best described as a minor nuisance rather than as a major threat to administrative agencies. But the challenges of administrative rulemaking are formidable enough that such nuisances are decidedly unwelcome. They are especially unwelcome because they seem to have moved us in the direction of a uniform, all-purpose administrative process that makes little sense in many contexts. It is not just that due process is more important in some situations than others but also that there are more ways to achieve due process than legislators or judges have recognized. For this reason, there is much to be said for leaving the design of specific rulemaking procedures in the hands of administrative agencies once a minimum of due process has been guaranteed (as in notice, comment, and reasons). As Verkuil (1978: 288) has put it, "Good faith attempts to design procedures that respect the values of fairness, efficiency, and satisfaction should be received favorably by the courts." They should be respected by legislators as well.

Hearing Rights

In the early 1970s the U.S. Supreme Court expanded due process guarantees significantly through a broad interpretation of the Fourteenth Amendment's provision that no state shall deprive a person of life, liberty, or property without due process of law. First, the Court defined property interests to include benefits previously considered privileges rather than rights—public sector jobs, welfare payments, driver's licenses, and so forth. Second, the Court expressly affirmed that some kind of a hearing is required before a person may be deprived of property. Third, the Court ruled that an informal hearing was not always a sufficient due process safeguard, depending on the degree of potential deprivation and the likelihood of an erroneous decision.

In handing down these rulings, the Court in effect expressed profound dissatisfaction with a wide variety of bureaucracies whose fairness and accuracy had become suspect over time. These bureaucracies included welfare agencies, prisons, schools, and others. By insisting that these bureaucracies provide due process protection for new forms of property, the Court was embracing a viewpoint articulated some years earlier by Yale University Law Professor Charles Reich (1964, 1965). The Court was also cham-

97

pioning the causes of a wide variety of persons vulnerable by reason of poverty (welfare recipients), age (students), confinement (prisoners), or some other factor.

The most dramatic of the due process decisions was *Goldberg v. Kelly* (1970) in which the Court ruled that a welfare recipient is entitled to a full-fledged trial-type hearing before being deprived of welfare benefits. The Court reasoned that welfare was a property interest, that welfare recipients would be grievously harmed by a negative decision, and that an erroneous decision was altogether possible, given the multitude of facts to be considered in a single case. To ensure due process, the Court required specific notice, an opportunity to appear in person or through counsel, oral argument and oral testimony, a chance to confront and cross-examine adverse witnesses, a neutral adjudicator, and a written decision based exclusively on the hearing record, before a welfare agency could terminate a person's benefits. The Court initially said that these requirements might be waived if no facts were being disputed and only policy judgments were at stake. However, in a subsequent decision (*Yee-Litt v. Richardson*, 1973), the Court decided that the fact-policy distinction was unworkable in practice. Before terminating welfare payments, welfare agencies would have to provide the full panoply of procedural guarantees.

In a stinging dissent, Judge Hugo Black (1970: 278–79) warned his colleagues that their thinly disguised sympathy for the disadvantaged would eventually backfire: "The Court apparently feels that this decision will benefit the poor and needy. In my judgment the eventual result will be just the opposite. . . . The inevitable result of such a constitutionally imposed burden will be that the government will not put a claimant on the rolls initially until it has made an exhaustive investigation to determine his eligibility." In the short run, *Goldberg* does not appear to have had this result. In the longer run, however, *Goldberg* may well have discouraged new enrollments.[6]

Stunned by the Court's ruling, many welfare agencies evaded it as best they could. According to a study of New York City's welfare program two years after *Goldberg*, two-thirds of the notices sent to welfare claimants failed to give an adequate statement of a proposed action and the factual policy bases for it and 75 percent of

6. Although AFDC caseloads continued to climb for four years after *Goldberg v. Kelly*, they declined slightly thereafter (Bernstein, 1982: 18). By 1974 some welfare officials may have concluded that the surest way to bypass the *Goldberg* and *Yee-Litt* decisions was to avoid enrolling claimants in the first place.

appellants who requested access to their files were denied it (Mashaw, 1974: 813–14). According to a later study of all fifty states, approximately two-thirds of the states permitted the state welfare agency to terminate or reduce benefits without a hearing if questions of law but not of fact were involved (Cooper, 1980). These practices, inconsistent with the *Yee-Litt* decision, were nevertheless consistent with *Goldberg* and with HEW regulations adopted in 1973.

The intangible effects of *Goldberg* were equally troublesome, though difficult to document. According to one close observer (Mashaw, 1974), *Goldberg* poisoned the atmosphere of welfare administration, transforming dealings between social workers and welfare recipients from a supportive relationship into an adversary relationship. Prior to *Goldberg*, welfare recipients, scorned by most of society, could at least turn to professional social workers for some sympathy and respect. Following *Goldberg*, this was much less likely as welfare bureaucrats scrambled to protect themselves from potentially nasty litigation.

Goldberg v. Kelly, though important, was merely one of a series of due process rulings that transformed the relationship between administrative agencies and the persons they were supposed to be helping. In *Goss v. Lopez* (1975), the Supreme Court ruled that a student is entitled to an informal hearing before being suspended from school. This decision, like *Goldberg*, was undoubtedly well-intentioned. It sought to protect students from arbitrary and capricious behavior by teachers and principals. A school suspension could mean the temporary loss of valuable educational benefits. To the Supreme Court, this suggested that some sort of a hearing was needed before suspension.

Though less coercive than *Goldberg*, *Goss* nevertheless turned the world of school discipline upside down. One reason for this, as Lufler (1982) has pointed out, is that *Goss* was poorly understood by students and teachers alike. Two years after the Supreme Court's ruling, only one-half of the teachers and fewer than one-third of the students knew the central holding of *Goss*—that a student had the right to a hearing before a short suspension. Almost all the teachers and three-fourths of the students thought that students about to be suspended had the right to an attorney (Lufler, 1982: 127–28). Confused and apprehensive, many teachers declined to discipline their students at all. The result was disorder in the classroom to the detriment of the student body as a whole. Other teachers evaded *Goss* by ordering "in-class" suspensions not covered by the Supreme Court's decision. In doing so, these teach-

99

ers bypassed not only the federal courts but school principals as well. Ironically, this meant that school discipline, when administered, became even more arbitrary and capricious than before. School principals, who had provided a modicum of fairness in the past, were now being excluded from school discipline decisions. In short, *Goss*, like *Goldberg*, appears to have backfired.

A microscopic examination of individual due process cases such as *Goss* and *Goldberg* reveals poor implementation, unanticipated side effects, and a transformation of helping professionals into wary adversaries.[7] A broader examination of due process cases reveals a pattern of requirements so illogical that it defies description. By the end of the decade, persons might be entitled to a hearing before losing their driver's license (*Bell v. Burson*, 1971), though not before losing their job (*Board of Regents v. Roth*, 1972). Prisoners were entitled to a hearing before being disciplined (*Wolff v. McDonnell*, 1974), but students were not (*Ingraham v. Wright*, 1977). A welfare recipient was entitled to a hearing by an impartial decisionmaker (*Goldberg v. Kelly*, 1970), but a nonprobationary civil servant was not (*Arnett v. Kennedy*, 1974). Due process requirements were imposed in cases where they seemed to be inappropriate and were not imposed in cases where they seemed to be necessary.

Imagine a well-ordered society in which due process guarantees vary systematically according to the degree of harm and the seriousness of the interest at stake. Following Friendly (1975), one might argue that liberty interests are more serious than property interests. One might also argue that property interests directly involving a person's livelihood (e.g., income or employment) are more serious than property interests less central to a person's life (a driver's license, or a diploma). In such a society, greater protection would be afforded in cases where more serious interests were at stake. Formal hearings might be required before depriving a person of liberty interests, informal hearings might be required before depriving a person of necessities, and no hearing might be required in other cases. Table 4.1, which depicts the Supreme Court's leading due process decisions of the 1970s, reveals a crazy-quilt patchwork of decisions apparently unrelated to these or any other basic principles.

One reason for this disorderly jumble of cases is that the Su-

7. For evidence that prisoners' rights decisions have had equally disappointing results, see Jacobs, 1977: 105–37.

TABLE 4.1

Due Process Requirements in Administrative Adjudication:
Decisions of the U.S. Supreme Court

	Requirements		
	No Hearing	*Hearing*	*Formal Hearing*
Interests			
Property: amenities	*Dixon v. Love* (1977)	*Bell v. Burson* (1971)	
	Board of Curators of U. of Missouri v. Horowitz (1978)	*Goss v. Lopez* (1975)	
Property: necessities	*Board of Regents v. Roth* (1972)	*Perry v. Sindermann* (1972)	*Goldberg v. Kelly* (1970)
	Torres v. N.Y. State Dept. of Labor (1972)	*Arnett v. Kennedy* (1974)	*Yee-Litt v. Richardson* (1973)
	Bishop v. Wood (1976)	*Mathews v. Eldridge* (1976)	
Liberty	*Paul v. Davis* (1976)	*Wisconsin v. Constantineau* (1971)	*Morrissey v. Brewer* (1972)
	Meachum v. Fano (1976)	*Wolff v. McDonnell* (1974)	*Gagnon v. Scarpelli* (1973)
	Ingraham v. Wright (1977)		

NOTE: Requirements have been categorized according to the judgment of the U.S. Supreme Court. In contrast, interests have been categorized according to my own appraisal of the stakes. In several instances, my judgment coincides with that of dissenting judges, not the Court majority.

preme Court makes decisions based on the specific properties of an individual case rather than on its generic properties. Yet each specific decision has broad implications for generic categories of cases, unless and until another more specific case comes along. A second reason for this phenomenon is sequence. During the early 1970s the Supreme Court was more generous in granting due process rights than it was in the late 1970s. In part, this was a function of the changing composition of the court, as more conservative judges commited to judicial restraint took their place on the bench. More significantly, though, the Supreme Court in the middle and late 1970s found itself reacting to its own precedents. Having established that some kind of a hearing is required if property interests are at stake, the Supreme Court grew increasingly reluctant to identify property interests where other observers had no difficulty perceiving them, as in the firing of a full-time, tenure-track college professor (*Board of Regents v. Roth*, 1972). Rabin (1976: 76) explains the practical realities of due process precedents this way: "By equating procedural due process with a value that seems to require a right to some kind of a hearing the court has correspondingly been driven to set too high a threshold when arriving at an initial determination of whether a property interest exists." Had the *Goldberg* case come later or had the Supreme Court focused on liberty interests rather than property interests (Van Alstyne, 1977), the results might have been different.

Another problem with the due process decisions of the 1970s is that the Supreme Court's repertoire of solutions consisted exclusively of hearings in various forms. Yet in many instances other remedies are superior to hearings. In prison discipline cases, for instance, a corrections ombudsman or a prisoners' grievance committee may be better able to secure justice than a hearing requirement. In welfare cases, quality control—or a systematic reanalysis of facts and decisions in a subsample of cases—may be the best way to promote accuracy. In employment cases, arbitration may be a constructive alternative. In short, in many instances management and interest representation reforms make more sense than due process solutions.

Legislative bodies, in their wisdom, have required public hearings in numerous instances where policy is being made (administrative rulemaking proceedings). Such hearings have often served a useful purpose and have had constructive results. Moreover, such requirements are not terribly onerous, largely because administrative rulemaking, though common, is much less common than administrative adjudication. Yet if a hearing were required before every administrative action was taken, our government would come to a screeching halt. Furthermore, the evidence suggests that formal hearing requirements often backfire. The point is not that due process guarantees are never appropriate but rather that such remedies seldom need to be invoked before an agency has a chance to act. The law provides other opportunities for injured parties to recover damages retroactively if they have been treated unfairly by administrative agencies. Where irreversible harm might result from an adverse administrative determination, as in the case of a welfare termination, some kind of a hearing should be required. However, even there, other remedies such as a well-run quality assurance program may do far more to protect the interests of persons who live at the margins of society.

Judges as Managers

The due process cases heard by the Supreme Court during the 1970s differed in kind from those being heard by federal district courts during the same decade. These cases involved living conditions in state prisons and reformatories and in state schools and hospitals for the mentally ill and the mentally retarded. Many were class-action suits filed on behalf of all prisoners or mental patients in a particular state. They raised extremely troublesome questions about public policy, the separation of powers, the due process clause, and federalism (Frug, 1978). In addition, they raised questions about the ability of judges to manage prisons, homes for the mentally ill, and other public institutions.[8]

The Supreme Court's decisions on hearing rights were far-reaching in the sense that they affected relatively large numbers of people. However, they were relatively narrow in that they focused on a specific allegation (a violation of the Fourteenth Amendment), a specific administrative practice (the denial of a hearing), and a specific point in time (just before depriving a person of liberty or property). In contrast, federal district court judges found themselves handling cases concerning institutional living conditions that were much broader in scope. These cases involved allegations of multiple constitutional and statutory infractions, complaints about administrative practices, personnel, and physical facilities, and an effort to change the very fabric of daily life in state institutions.

The conditions that confronted judges in these cases were truly horrendous. In Alabama, institutions for the mentally ill had become "human warehouses." They were overcrowded, understaffed, dangerous, and unsanitary. At the Partlow State School

8. School desegregation cases have many of the same characteristics as the cases discussed here. I have declined to discuss them here for two reasons: (1) The proximate targets of school desegregation cases are school board officials, who are usually though not always elected officials; and (2) School desegregation cases are technically speaking "equal protection" cases, not "due process" cases. While both kinds of cases involve the Fourteenth Amendment, they involve different aspects of that amendment.

and Hospital, for example, several patients had died as a result of understaffing, inadequate supervision, and brutality. Promises of treatment had long since been abandoned. At the Pennhurst School and Hospital in Spring City, Pennsylvania, many patients had been badly bruised by staff or other patients; one patient had been raped by a staff member. It was common to find excrement and urine on ward floors. Indeed, routine housekeeping services were unavailable during evenings and weekends. Neither was a qualified psychologist.

Conditions in state prisons and correctional facilities were equally deplorable. At the Texas Youth Council's six schools, a regime of "brutality and repression" prevailed, marked by widespread physical abuse, the unnecessary use of tear gas, the arbitrary imposition of solitary confinement, mail censorship, and prohibitions against speaking in a foreign language. In Arkansas, the penitentiaries were so understaffed that prisoners were forced to guard other prisoners. Conditions there were "dangerous, degrading, and disgusting." In Alabama, rapes and stabbings were widespread. Food was unwholesome, and physical facilities were dilapidated. At one institution, prisoners received but one meal a day with no utensils; one toilet served two hundred prisoners. The state's prisons were, in short, "wholly unfit for human habitation."

Confronted by such conditions, federal judges responded swiftly and forcefully. In Alabama, Judge Johnson issued a decree calling for adequate medical care, regular fire inspections, and regular physical exams in the state's prisons (*Newman v. Alabama*, 1972). When conditions barely improved, he issued extremely detailed standards, including cell space requirements, hiring requirements, and a mandatory classification system for categorizing and grouping prisoners (*James v. Wallace*, 1976; *Pugh v. Locke*, 1976). In Arkansas, Judge Henley ordered tight control of inmates authorized to guard other inmates and proscribed this practice under certain circumstances (*Holt v. Sarver*, 1970). In Texas, Judge Justice ordered specific limits on the use of physical force and solitary confinement, an end to "repetitive, nonfunctional degrading" tasks, an end to censorship, and psychological tests of new employees (*Morales v. Turman*, 1973). A year later, he ordered two facilities closed (*Morales v. Turman*, 1974).

Judicial decrees in mental institution cases were equally formidable. In *Wyatt v. Stickney* (1971, 1972), Judge Johnson held that mental patients have a right to adequate and effective treatment in the least restrictive environment possible. To secure that right, he issued extremely specific treatment standards and ordered rapid

TABLE 4.2

Reforms of Corrections Institutions:
Key Federal District Court Cases

Case	Plaintiffs	Constitutional Rights	Court Decree	Instrumentality
Holt v. Sarver (1969, 1970)	Prisoners (Arkansas state penitentiary)	Eighth Amendment, Fourteenth Amendment	guidelines and suggestions—bring trusties under control, reduce overcrowding, end racial discrimination and violence; proceed with reasonable diligence; no fixed timetable	
Newman v. Alabama (1972)	Prisoners (five major prisons and other facilities in Alabama)	Eighth Amendment, Fourteenth Amendment	adequate access to medical personnel, medicine, and treatment	
Morales v. Turman (1973, 1974)	Juvenile inmates (six Texas schools for juveniles)	Eighth Amendment, Fourteenth Amendment, First Amendment, right to treatment in least restrictive environment	extremely specific requirements and prohibitions—limited use of physical force and solitary confinement, end to make-work tasks and censorship; deinstitutionalization (closure of two facilities as quickly as possible)	Ombudsman (established 1973)
James v. Wallace (1976)	Prisoners (five major prisons and other facilities in Alabama)	Eighth Amendment, Fourteenth Amendment	extremely detailed standards, including cells no smaller than 60 square feet, personal hygiene requirements, adequate staffing, inmate classification plans, meaningful jobs	Human rights committee
Palmigiano v. Garrahy (1977)	Prisoners and pre-trial detainees (Rhode Island)	Eighth Amendment, Fourteenth Amendment	fairly specific health requirements, detailed space requirements, flexible staff requirements; new facility must be built	Master

deinstitutionalization. In *Welsch v. Likins* (1974), Judge Larson prescribed improvements in the physical plant, detailed staffing requirements, and the limited use of seclusion and restraint. In *Halderman v. Pennhurst State School and Hospital* (1977), Judge Broderick ordered the gradual closing of the Pennhurst School and Hospital. In the interim, he ordered the adoption of numerous transition rules to protect patients' rights to "minimally adequate habilitation" and "freedom from harm."

To assist them in carrying out their orders, federal judges relied on various devices. Some appointed masters who served as their "eyes and ears." These masters, vested with broad authority, functioned as fact-finders, intervenors, arbitrators, advisers and enforcers (Note, " 'Mastering' . . . ," 1979). Other judges, afraid of losing control or of generating unnecessary friction, appointed a human rights committee[9] or an ombudsman. Still others simply instructed the relevant parties to report directly to them at specified intervals. Though different in certain respects, all of these devices signaled a continuing judicial interest in the implementation of their decrees. Indeed these cases exemplify what Chayes (1976) has called the "new public law litigation." As Chayes (1976: 1298) explains:

> The centerpiece of the emerging public law model is the decree. . . . The decree seeks to adjust future behavior, not to compensate for past wrong. It is deliberately fashioned rather than logically deduced from the nature of the legal harm suffered. It provides for a complex, ongoing regime of performance rather than a simple, one-shot, one-way transfer. Finally, it prolongs and deepens, rather than terminates, the court's involvement with the dispute.

There is no question that federal judges had to act in these and other related cases. By almost anyone's reckoning, constitutional rights were being flagrantly violated. Conditions in prisons and mental disability institutions were inadequate in many instances, barbaric in some cases. Politicians, responsive to more powerful constituents, had long neglected prisoners and the mentally retarded. Were it not for federal judges, prisoners and the mentally disabled would have been left to rot in conditions so inhumane that they are almost inconceivable in a civilized society.

9. In practice, human rights committees (or review panels) have proved no less intrusive and heavy-handed than masters. See, for example, Rothman and Rothman (1984: 299–352) on the Willowbrook Review Panel; and Yarbrough (1982: 389–91) on Judge Johnson's human rights committees in Alabama.

TABLE 4.3

Reforms of Mental Disability Institutions:
Key Federal District Court Cases

Case	Plaintiffs	Constitutional Rights	Court Decree	Instrumentality
Wyatt v. Stickney (1971, 1972)	Mentally ill and retarded (three hospitals in Alabama)	Fourteenth Amendment, right to adequate and effective treatment in least restrictive environment	extremely specific and detailed treatment standards, including diet and hygiene requirements, space requirements, privacy requirements, staffing ratios; deinstitutionalization	Three human rights committees (established 1972)
New York State Assoc. for Retarded Children v. Rockefeller (1973) New York State Assoc. for Retarded Children v. Carey (1975)	Mentally retarded (Willowbrook State School, Staten Island, N.Y.)	Fourteenth Amendment, Eighth Amendment, right to reasonable protection from harm	no seclusion, immediate hiring of specific numbers of personnel, immediate repair of toilets; deinstitutionalization (from 5,400 to 250 beds by 1981)	Review panel (established 1975)
Welsch v. Likins (1974) Welsch v. Dirkswager (1977)	Mentally retarded (six hospitals in Minnesota)	Fourteenth Amendment, Eighth Amendment, right to treatment	specific requirements and prohibitions including improvements in physical plants, limited use of seclusion and physical restraint, and detailed staffing requirements	Monitor (established 1977)

Judicial action was indeed necessary. However, if federal judges had to act, it is by no means clear that they acted prudently. Do the mentally retarded have a constitutional right to treatment? To minimally adequate treatment? To adequate and effective treatment? If so, what exactly do these phrases mean? Also, do they

107

TABLE 4.3 (cont.)

Case	Plaintiffs	Constitutional Rights	Court Decree	Instrumentality
Halderman v. Pennhurst (1977)	Mentally retarded (Pennhurst School & Hospital, Spring City, Penn.)	Fourteenth Amendment, Eighth Amendment, right to minimally adequate habilitation and freedom from harm	deinstitutionalization (eventual shut-down of Pennhurst); no new admissions; transition rules, including no abuse or neglect, no unnecessary medication, clean, odorless, and insect-free buildings	Special master
Wuori v. Zitnay (1978)	Mentally retarded (Pineland Center, Maine)	Eighth Amendment, Fourteenth Amendment, right to habilitation	extremely detailed standards for Pineland and for community facilities; deinstitutionalization timetable; specific staffing ratios	Master

apply equally to voluntary and involuntary admissions? To job training? Do judges go too far when they specify staff ratios for doctors, psychologists, nurses and physical therapists? When they order a facility closed despite the absence of suitable alternatives? When they impose tight deadlines on administrators who are trying to act in good faith? When they ban inmates from performing household chores? When they specify the physical dimensions of living quarters? When they prohibit new admissions to prisons or to facilities for the mentally retarded?

These are partly constitutional questions, and higher courts have begun to rule on the constitutionality of various forms of judicial intervention in institutional reform cases.[10] However, these

10. Tough institutional reform decrees have received mixed reviews on appeal. For example, the U.S. Court of Appeals (5th Circuit) upheld Judge Johnson's ruling that mental patients have a constitutional right to treatment (*Wyatt v. Aderholt*, 1974) but objected to several elements of his prison reform ruling. Specifically, the Court found no basis for Johnson's cell size requirements or his assertion that prisoners have a constitutional right to education and rehabilitation (*Newman v. Alabama*, 1977). The Court also found Johnson's human rights committee to be overly intrusive and instructed him to appoint a single monitor instead.

are also strategic questions. Even if the courts are constitutionally empowered to act forcefully in such cases, is it wise for them to act so forcefully that all vestiges of administrative discretion and legislative comity are eroded? A close look at several of the leading cases suggests that the answer is no.

Consider, for example, Judge Frank Johnson's landmark prison reform order in *James v. Wallace* (1976). Various elements of that order were hopelessly unrealistic, unnecessarily nettlesome, and surprisingly detrimental to would-be beneficiaries.

Item: Within six months, each segregation and isolation cell was to be no less than sixty square feet. No cell in Alabama met those specifications and compliance would have cost the state an estimated fifty thousand dollars per cell. Not surprisingly, the state balked. Eventually, Judge Johnson modified this order, but the original requirement convinced many politicians and opinion leaders that the judge was unreasonable and inflexible.

Item: Except for escapees and parole violators, no additional inmates were to be accepted until the prison population had been significantly reduced. The state complied with this order, which resulted in severe overcrowding in local jails. This was a problem not only for hard-pressed local governments but for inmates as well, since conditions were often worse at the local jails than in the state prisons.

Item: The state corrections board was to develop and implement an inmate classification plan and contract with the University of Alabama's Department of Psychology to aid in its implementation. The board of corrections preferred to work with professors at Auburn University, who had more practical experience in corrections matters and who worked not far from the prison itself. Moreover, the University of Alabama team had actively assisted the plaintiffs in their litigation and was viewed with suspicion. Yet Judge Johnson was insensitive to these considerations despite the implementation problems they would cause. Upset and resentful, prison of-

---

The U.S. Supreme Court has also charted a middle-of-the-road course on these issues. On the one hand, the Court has denied that mental patients have a constitutional right to "appropriate treatment in the least restrictive environment" (*Pennhurst State School and Hospital v. Halderman*, 1981). On the other hand, the Court has conceded that involuntary mental patients are entitled to reasonably safe conditions of confinement, freedom from unreasonable bodily restraints, and such minimally adequate training as reasonably might be required (*Youngberg v. Romeo*, 1982). In effect, the Supreme Court has rejected mandatory deinstitutionalization but affirmed a limited right to treatment.

ficials did their best to sabotage the work of the University of Alabama inmate classification team and little progress was made.

Confrontation over prison reform was inevitable in George Wallace's Alabama. Also, it is true that a mild order in 1972 (*Newman v. Alabama*) yielded few tangible results.[11] But Judge Johnson's order in *James v. Wallace* (1976) played into Wallace's hands. If Wallace's opposition was inevitable, the opposition of Attorney General William Baxley and the board of corrections was not. Indeed, Baxley was reluctant to appeal Johnson's order and did so only after Johnson refused to budge on the inmate classification plan (Yarbrough, 1981: 208–11). Through his intransigence, Johnson unwittingly shifted the focus of public debate from conditions in the state's prisons to the propriety of judicial "micromanagement." In the process, he forfeited the strategic high ground in this dispute. Had Johnson been more circumspect and flexible, he would not have been able to avoid all friction but he almost certainly could have reduced it. Prison reform might well have proceeded more rapidly as a result.

In relation to prison reform, there is much to be said for strategies that fall in between the polar extremes of muscles and prayers. Consider, for example, the case of *Holt v. Sarver*—a shorthand expression for a series of cases stretching over a period of several years.[12] The focus of this litigation was the Arkansas prison system—perhaps the most notorious prison system in the U.S. (Spiller, 1977: 35). Unwilling to appropriate any money to corrections (the state's prisons were sustained entirely by the meager revenues they produced), Arkansas relied primarily on a "trustie" system whereby inmates guarded other inmates. At the Cummins facility, for example, which housed one thousand inmates, there were only thirty-five civilian employees! Such a system was not only very risky (some prisoners were armed) but it also led inevitably to arbitrary punishment, violence, and abuse.

Inmates at Cummins and other facilities lived in crowded barracks where there were frequent stabbings, homosexual assaults, and drug abuse. Trusties routinely engaged in bribery, extortion, usury, the sale of jobs and personal services, and the smuggling of

11. As Judge Johnson noted in *James v. Wallace* (1976: 329), "The Court has previously ordered that the penal system provide reasonable medical care for inmates (*Newman v. Alabama*, 1972). . . . The evidence in these cases leads to the inescapable conclusion that the gross inadequacies in medical care found in that case have not been remedied."

12. *Holt v. Sarver* (1969); *Holt v. Sarver* (1970); *Holt v. Hutto* (1973); *Finney v. Arkansas Board of Corrections* (1974); and *Finney v. Hutto* (1976).

contraband. Sanitation was poor, especially in isolation cells where conditions were abominable. Racial discrimination was rampant, medical services were meager, and no rehabilitation program was underway.

Confronted by such conditions, Judge J. Smith Henley might have issued a comprehensive decree with detailed requirements for new facilities, specific staff-inmate ratios, rehabilitation programs, and so forth. However, Henley preferred a more hortatory approach that stressed persuasion rather than coercion. Instead of requiring the immediate abolition of the trustie system, he called for adequate supervision of trusties, should trusties be retained. Instead of mandating specific staff-inmate ratios, he called upon the state legislature to appropriate funds sufficient to end constitutional violations. Instead of establishing rigid deadlines, he exhorted state officials to make a "prompt and reasonable start." Instead of appointing a master to remind defendants of their obligations, he held informal conferences with litigants. As Spiller (1977: 96) has noted, Henley's orders were "general, restrained, and limited in scope." While insisting on significant, timely reform ("The handwriting is on the wall, and it ought not to require a Daniel to read it," *Holt v. Sarver*, 1970: 383), he left the specifics in the hands of other state officials.

Henley's restraint paid off. Instead of alienating state bureaucrats, Henley enlisted them in the cause of prison reform. While prison administrators in other states were busy defending themselves before skeptical and impatient judges, Arkansas corrections officials directed their energies toward securing the necessary appropriations from the state legislature. After some initial problems traceable to partisan rivalries (the governor and the corrections commissioner in 1970 were Republicans, while the legislature was Democratic), the state legislature came around. By the mid-1970s legislative appropriations to the state's prisons had climbed from zero to nine million dollars per year.[13] At the same time, the Department of Corrections complied with the letter and the spirit of the court's orders by launching a vigorous program of internal reform.

By 1975 the state's prisons had been transformed. Although some serious problems remained,[14] evidence of significant change

13. The base appropriation for prison operations in the mid-1970s was approximately $6 million; in addition, about $3 million per year was appropriated for capital improvements (Spiller, 1977: 111).

14. The Cummins facility was still seriously overcrowded in 1975, but a new facility was being built to alleviate the problem.

was widespread. The trustie system had been completely eliminated and inmate safety had been improved significantly. Incidents of brutality and reprisals against inmates declined dramatically. Notable progress was made in race relations. Medical services and sanitation improved considerably. Restrictions on inmate correspondence were lifted and educational and rehabilitation services were made available to inmates. As Spiller (1977: 113) notes: "The changes in the prison system were more than cosmetic; they were broad and profound. The system bore little, if any, resemblance in 1976 to the system that existed before 1969."

It might be argued that Judge Henley's approach works only when both bureaucrats and politicians are receptive to the idea of institutional reform. However, this implies that legislative and bureaucratic attitudes are relatively fixed. In fact, they are both malleable and fragile. Bureaucratic support for institutional reform can quickly degenerate into hostility when the integrity of bureaucrats is questioned and when their discretion is reduced to zero. Without valuable allies in the executive branch, a judge will have a difficult time securing legislative support. Likewise, legislators can become very defensive when they perceive a full-scale assault on their "power of the purse." Indeed, legislative opposition in Arkansas hardened only when a federal appeals court opted for a tougher, less flexible approach in 1974 (*Finney v. Arkansas Board of Corrections*). In these matters, there is a strong element of the self-fulfilling prophecy. If legislators and bureaucrats are assumed to be recalcitrant, it should not surprise us if they behave this way.

It is difficult to state with precision the difference between a court order that is too coercive and one that applies just the right amount of pressure. A court order that specifies detailed staffing ratios, which mandates the physical dimensions of new facilities, which prohibits new admissions, and which imposes fixed deadlines for difficult tasks is probably too coercive. A court order that requires adequate medical treatment, sanitary conditions, and some efforts at rehabilitation along with periodic progress reports is often sufficient. But conditions do vary from state to state. An order too coercive for one set of circumstances may be unavoidable in a state where circumstances are far worse. Also, a state where politicians and bureaucrats are implacably opposed to any reform may require stronger remedies than one in which politicians and bureaucrats are wary but sympathetic.

Writing a court order in an institutional reform case is a challenging task; it is difficult to strike the right balance between firmness and flexibility. For this reason the wise judge will try to get the parties to write the order themselves. The preconditions for successful court orders are not well understood, but one pattern is beginning to emerge: some of the most successful institutional reforms have resulted from consent decrees drafted and signed by both plaintiffs and defendants. In Minnesota, for example, a consent decree (*Welsch v. Dirkswager*, 1977) resulted in significant staffing gains at the state's mental hospitals and a sharp improvement in both the quantity and quality of patient treatment plans (Moss, 1984: 428–29). In Maine a consent decree in a mental institution case (*Wuori v. Zitnay*, 1978) yielded significant gains within three years, including the elimination of large wards, greater privacy, new furnishings and decorations, and a more homelike atmosphere (Moss, 1984: 427). In New York, the Willowbrook consent decree on the rights of the mentally retarded (*New York ARC v. Carey*, 1975) resulted in deinstitutionalization that was both rapid and effective. Within a few years after the decree was signed the overwhelming majority of Willowbrook residents had been placed in group homes and their quality of life had improved noticeably (Rothman and Rothman, 1984: 177–253).

Institutional reform orders require a judicious mixture of firmness and flexibility. Neither muscles nor prayers alone will do. If a judge tilts too far in the direction of firmness, defendants may lack the ability to comply; if a judge tilts too far in the direction of flexibility, defendants may lack incentives to comply. The situation is complicated by the fact that these cases are often characterized by invisible defendants. The failure of bureaucrats to provide adequate services is frequently traceable to the failure of politicians to provide adequate funds. Depending on what they discover, judges may find it necessary to rebuke either politicians or bureaucrats. However, they should be wary of alienating both. With powerful allies in the executive branch or the legislative branch, judges may be able to secure constitutional rights in a timely fashion. With powerful opponents in both branches, they are unlikely to succeed.

Conclusion

During the 1970s federal courts used the concept of due process as a means of controlling state and federal bureaucracies. In *Goldberg v. Kelly*, *Morrissey v. Brewer*, and *Goss v. Lopez*, the U.S. Supreme Court established a right to a hearing in adjudicatory proceedings threatening liberty or property. In *Mobil Oil Corp. v. FPC* and *In-*

ternational Harvester Corp. v. Ruckelshaus, U.S. Appeals Courts required cross-examination and other procedures in supposedly informal rulemaking proceedings. In *Wyatt v. Stickney, James v. Wallace, Morales v. Turman*, and *Halderman v. Pennhurst*, federal district courts established a right to treatment for inmates in state mental institutions and required a wide variety of reforms in other state-run institutions such as prisons.

The due process reforms of the 1970s differed from one another in their conception of what due process means. By requiring a hearing in certain adjudicatory proceedings and cross-examination in certain rulemaking proceedings, the courts were pursuing a vision of due process understood as procedural fairness. By formalizing the administrative process, judges hoped to preserve and extend rights guaranteed in the Fourteenth Amendment and the APA. In contrast, the institutional reform cases were rooted in a vision of due process as substantive justice. By shifting legislative priorities and reforming administrative operations, judges hoped to preserve rights guaranteed in the Fourteenth Amendment, the Eighth Amendment, and pertinent statutes.

The due process reforms of the 1970s also differed from one another in their effects. The courts' hybrid rulemaking requirements made life a little easier for certain intervenors (usually corporations) and made life a little harder for front-line administrators. In practice, such requirements provided procedural protections to the parties who needed them the least. The courts' requirements of hearings in administrative adjudication cases had a more profound impact on the bureaucracy because they affected thousands and thousands of highly individualized administrative decisions. In some instances, these court rulings may have benefited their intended beneficiaries—prisoners, students, welfare recipients. However, the cases as a whole resulted in an uneven, illogical system of justice in which hearing requirements bore little relationship to the magnitude of the interests at stake. In addition, hearing requirements often backfired, because they were poorly understood (*Goss v. Lopez*) or because they required more time and energy than beleaguered bureaucracies could provide (*Goldberg v. Kelly*).

The courts' decisions in institutional reform cases are easier to defend. Whatever else may be said about them, they did help their intended beneficiaries—prisoners, juvenile delinquents, the mentally retarded, and the mentally ill. They resulted in significant improvements of conditions that were inhumane, unsanitary, dan-

114

gerous, brutal, and unconstitutional. In the case of mental institutions, they also resulted in numerous experiments in deinstitutionalization, many of which were successful. Yet in many instances problems were merely displaced from one institution to another—from state prisons to county jails and from state homes for the mentally retarded to private nursing homes. Moreover, some court decisions were unrealistic and extreme. Mandating cell space requirements, detailed staffing ratios, and judicial meddling in daily operations undermined judicial credibility and discouraged good faith cooperation. In addition, unreasonable court orders virtually guaranteed protracted litigation, which in some instances proved unfavorable to both the original plaintiffs and the lower courts. All of this could have been avoided had judges been more patient and more modest.

In retrospect, the courts were more successful in establishing rights than in designing remedies. Many observers would agree that prisoners have liberty rights under the Constitution, that corporations have procedural rights under the APA, and that the mentally ill have a right to treatment if they are placed in a state institution. Time after time however the courts went overboard in fashioning remedies to secure such rights. Instead of simply requiring a hearing before depriving a person of liberty or property, the courts often wrote a script for the way the hearing should proceed. Instead of simply remanding a case when an evidentiary record was too thin, the courts often required hybrid rulemaking procedures of questionable utility. Instead of working hard to secure a consent decree in institutional reform cases, many judges issued sweeping, unrealistic orders drafted by a single hand. In case after case, unreasonable judicial remedies made it difficult for conscientious administrators to collaborate with the courts in a joint effort to help the disadvantaged. By formalizing the administrative process and by limiting administrative discretion, judges affirmed the power of the courts, but often at the expense of both procedural innovation and substantive justice.

Management

If judges are poorly suited for the tasks of management, chief executives have both a greater legitimacy and a greater capacity for such tasks. As elected public officials with broad electoral bases, chief executives may speak with some credibility for the public at large. Moreover, chief executives have a special managerial role to play under the law. The U.S. Constitution says that the president shall "take care that the laws are faithfully executed." Many state constitutions carve out similar roles for governors. In addition, chief executives often have the advantage of appropriate training and experience. Many presidents have served as governors and many governors have managed a bureaucracy or a business firm.

Yet while a consensus exists that chief executives have an important role to play in managing the bureaucracy, it is not clear what that role should be. Jimmy Carter was roundly criticized for excessive meddling, for trying to do too much (surely, someone else could have decided who would have access to the White House tennis courts). In contrast, Ronald Reagan was condemned for the excessive delegation of responsibility, for allowing subordinates to run amok (surely, foreign policy should be made in the Oval Office and not in the basement of the White House). There is no doubt a happy medium between these two extremes. But specifying that middle path is not easy. Nor is sensible executive leadership a sufficient condition for a well-run government.

A well-managed bureaucracy is characterized not just by leadership but also by efficiency. Good management is a matter of both politics and economics. The bureaucracy should respond positively to the policy initiatives of the chief executive, provided that they are consistent with legislative intent. The bureaucracy should also pursue legitimate policy goals at the lowest possible cost and with a minimum of waste and duplication. Coordination and integration are usually consistent with both sets of objectives.

Over the years, chief executives have sought to promote leadership and efficiency in a variety of ways. Presidents and governors have appointed blue-ribbon commissions charged with streamlining the executive branch and making the bureaucracy more manageable. In keeping with recommendations by such commissions, chief executives have reorganized the executive branch, often with the implicit consent of the legislative branch. With less fanfare, chief executives have also changed the groundrules for appointments, promotions and dismissals; in addition, they have acted decisively to cope with crises and emergencies.

In many respects, the management reforms of the 1970s and 1980s provided more of the same—administrative reorganization, crusades against fraud and abuse, personnel reforms, and vigorous executive leadership to deal with urgent problems. There were, however, at least two new wrinkles. First, many chief executives opted for what might be called "strategic politicization," with a parallel emphasis on "supportive competence." The premise was that top appointees should have a commitment to the chief executive's values and the skills to pursue those values successfully. This constituted a departure from the old days when chief executives often perceived their choice to lie between loyalty and neutral competence, the spoils system and the merit system. In the 1970s and the 1980s, appointments were political, but seldom purely political. Instead of treating appointments as payoffs for past services, chief executives viewed them as strategic building blocks for the future. Second, many chief executives appreciated the virtues of both formal and informal reforms. Instead of viewing structural change as a panacea (too optimistic) or as a farce (too pessimistic), they recognized that new structures and new norms make for a formidable combination. Thus the creation of the Office of Management and Budget (OMB) and the Senior Executive Service (SES) provided strategic opportunities for a president who was willing and able to take advantage of them—Reagan. By piggybacking new informal norms (ideological screening and reductions in force) onto new structures (OMB, the Office of Personnel Management), Reagan was able to create the "administrative presidency" that had eluded Richard Nixon (Nathan, 1983). Less spectacularly, governors were able to combine formal and informal reforms to enhance their "power to persuade." By recognizing the importance of informal norms and by opting for strategic politicization, chief executives were able to pump new life into some old ideas for managerial reform.

Administrative Reorganization

One of the oldest management reforms in the chief executive's bag of tricks is administrative reorganization, described by March and Olson (1983: 281) as "a characteristic feature of twentieth century bureaucratic and political life." Actually, it is more accurate to describe administrative reorganization as a routine occurrence at the federal level and as an occasional occurrence at the state level. Most twentieth century presidents have merged, eliminated, or created a number of administrative agencies. In contrast, administrative reorganization was less common at the state level until a rash of reorganization efforts broke out in the mid-1960s.

Administrative reorganization became enormously popular in the 1970s at both the state and federal levels. In Maryland, Governor Marvin Mandel merged 247 agencies to yield twelve consolidated departments. In Washington, Governor Dan Evans created the first comprehensive Department of Ecology. In California, Governor Jerry Brown created an Energy Conservation and Development Commission and an Office of Appropriate Technology. During the 1970s alone, seventeen states underwent comprehensive reorganizations (Sabato, 1983: 61–62), and most states reorganized in some policy arenas.[1]

At the federal level, administrative reorganization was especially dear to the hearts of Presidents Nixon and Carter. Following a report by a presidential commission, the Ash Council, Nixon urged the creation of four "superdepartments" (human resources, natural resources, community development, and economic affairs) and took informal steps to institutionalize such an arrangement by designating four cabinet officials as having lead responsibility in these areas. Nixon's formal reform proposals were subsequently rejected by Congress, whereupon Nixon resorted to other attempts to bring the bureaucracy under control. Carter, who had reorganized state government as the governor of Georgia, was more successful than Nixon on this front. After much lobbying, he persuaded Congress to create a Department of Energy and a Department of Education. Like Nixon, he initiated other management reforms as well.

Although administrative reorganization is often justified on many grounds (responsiveness, effectiveness, efficiency, economy), the bedrock of administrative reorganization efforts has usually been the promise of cost containment. At the federal level the Congress has authorized presidents to reorganize if this will "reduce expenditures and promote economy" (March and Olson, 1983: 287). The same impulse is evident at the state level. For example, Hult (1987: 47) reports that Minnesota merged its Depart-

1. In environmental protection, for example, thirty-two states reorganized during a recent fifteen-year period (Lester et al., 1983: 300).

ment of Economic Development, state planning agency, state energy agency, and crime control planning board in the hope of "saving money and promoting efficiency in state government."

According to a careful study of reorganizations at the state level (Meier, 1980), administrative reorganization seldom leads to significant cost savings. Neither state expenditures nor public employment levels have declined in the long run as a result of recent state reorganizations. Salamon (1981: 64) reaches similar conclusions at the federal level. As he puts it, "The most often expected, though least often delivered, objective of reorganization is economy and efficiency."

Administrative reorganization has become the cod liver oil of government—an all-purpose cure for whatever ails the body politic. Yet there is much more to administrative reorganization than meets the eye. The problem with administrative reorganization is not that it is inconsequential but that its actual consequences differ substantially from its purported consequences. Illusory promises of greater economy and efficiency obscure the real impact that administrative reorganization can have on both public management and public policy. If viewed as a cost-saving device, administrative reorganization is a dud. If viewed as a catalyst for change (Hult, 1987), administrative reorganization is much more significant.

Administrative reorganization is a catalyst for change in several important respects. First, it throws people and organizations together who would otherwise operate in separate spheres. Second, it forces them to adapt to one another and to account to their overseers. Third, it introduces a healthy fluidity into the policymaking process, an antidote to incrementalism and inertia. Fourth, it presents a "window of opportunity" for talented policy entrepreneurs. Fifth, it creates expectations for policy innovation, expectations that must be taken seriously. Sixth, it generates media interest and heightens agency and issue salience, at least for a time.

Both case studies and aggregate studies confirm the potential utility of administrative reorganization. For example, the creation of the federal Department of Housing and Urban Development (HUD) in the late 1960s resulted in both process and policy changes: first, the agency became more hierarchical, with stronger leadership at the top; second, the network of actors with which the agency interacted became more diverse; third, the agency became less of a "bricks-and-mortar" organization, more of a social welfare organization; and fourth, the agency made significant progress toward established goals and it became more innovative too (Hult, 1987).

Administrative reorganization has succeeded at the local level as well. The creation of the Minneapolis Community Development Agency in 1981 had several tangible consequences: first, it resulted in a moderate increase in top-down influence within the agency; second, it resulted in closer ties between the agency and elected officials; third, it permitted important changes in outcomes, including less turnover in public housing units and higher sales of industrial revenue bonds (Hult, 1987).

A comprehensive study of environmental policymaking at the state level reveals equally important consequences of state-level reorganization (Lester et al., 1983). Specifically, states with more consolidated environmental bureaucracies (e.g., departments of natural resources) have more stringent hazardous waste regulations. The relationship is especially strong in low-waste states, where these issues are presumably less salient. Perhaps administrative reorganization matters more in those issue areas and those states where administrative discretion is relatively high and legislative involvement is relatively low. If legislators perceive a crisis, as in high-waste states, organizational form may matter less and legislative policy preferences may matter more.

Although administrative reorganization was not a hallmark of the Reagan administration, some Reagan executives did use administrative reorganization effectively to promote Reagan's policy goals. Ford B. Ford, head of the Mine Health and Safety Administration (MHSA), used reorganization to transfer power from mine inspectors to district supervisors. Ford anticipated (correctly) that this would shift the agency's orientation away from an adversarial approach and toward a partnership between government and the private sector. In addition, he expected that reorganization and related changes would permit the agency to focus less on outputs (the number of inspections and citations) and more on outcomes (reductions in injuries and illnesses). Whatever one may think of the Reagan administration's policies on mine safety, the reorganization was clearly a managerial success (Lynn, 1984: 349–51).

Administrative reorganizations do not always succeed. No matter how auspicious the circumstances, a "garbage-can" merger that brings together organizational units with largely unrelated functions is unlikely to work. For example, the creation of the Minnesota Department of Energy, Planning, and Development was conceptually flawed and ill-advised. Interdependent and coordinative mergers that combine organizational units engaged in identical or related enterprises are much more likely to work (Hult, 1987).

Even interdependent mergers may fail to live up to their potential, if they are hastily conceived and poorly executed. The creation of the federal Department of Energy (DOE) in 1977 offers sobering lessons in this respect. Despite reorganization, the government's energy agencies remain fragmented and decentralized. For example, the DOE includes a director of administration, a controller, an inspector general, and still another official responsible for procurement and contracting (Dean, 1981: 146); this proliferation of managers obscures responsibility for these functions. The Federal Energy Regulatory Commission (FERC), nominally a part of DOE, is in fact a quasi-autonomous unit independent of the secretary. Physically, the department's offices are scattered throughout the country, which is both inevitable and desirable, and throughout the Washington, D.C., metropolitan area, which is neither inevitable nor desirable. All of these factors limit coordination and undermine the potential for integrated policymaking.

Despite its weaknesses, we are probably better off with DOE than we were with the loosely connected assortment of energy fiefdoms that preceded it. As Rosenbaum (1987: 60) has argued, "the Department of Energy has improved energy management in important if limited ways." All energy research and development is now coordinated through a single agency. The creation of an Energy Information Administration within DOE enables the government to develop its own energy data base without relying on energy producers for such information. Fragmentation continues to be a problem, but the situation was even worse under the old regime.

Actually, DOE's fragmentation is symptomatic of a deeper problem—the absence of a national energy policy. Administrative reorganization is no substitute for a coherent government policy. However, if there is such a policy, administrative reorganization can make it work. By galvanizing career executives and by providing political executives with momentum, administrative reorganization can be a catalyst for change. It may not reduce the costs of government, but it does facilitate strong leadership. It may not make government more efficient, but it does make government more responsive. It may not provide easy solutions to urgent policy problems, but it does enable the government to pursue such solutions when they are found.

Inspectors General

For all its virtues, administrative reorganization does little to curb bureaucratic waste and inefficiency. Yet as government spending rose sharply during the 1970s, Congress became increasingly concerned about waste, fraud, and abuse. In 1976 Congress established an Office of Inspector General within the Department of Health, Education, and Welfare (now Health and Human Services). Two years later Congress made inspectors general mandatory in twelve major agencies. There are now statutory inspectors general in nineteen major agencies, including virtually all of the cabinet-level departments.[2]

Each inspector general's office consists of auditors and investigators who report to their agency's inspector general. The auditors and investigators are civil servants, most of whom have previously worked elsewhere within the agency. The inspector general is a presidential appointee who cannot be dismissed by the department or agency head. The inspector general may be dismissed by the president, but only after the president has given prior notice to Congress. The hope is that these arrangements will give inspectors general the courage to criticize their own agency or department without fear of reprisals.

Inspectors general have considerable staff resources at their disposal—more than twenty-three thousand auditors and investigators. This is nearly five times the number of staffers who work for the General Accounting Office (GAO). Inspectors general also have greater control over their budgets than most agencies. Unlike other executive branch officials, inspectors general have the right to ask Congress for more money if they disagree with OMB's budget request.

Despite these formidable resources and special protections, inspectors general have produced a mixed record of performance. According to widely publicized reports, inspectors general have ferreted out more than $55 billion in waste and corruption. However, that figure has been challenged by both the GAO and OMB. For example, David Stockman raised questions about billions supposedly recovered through improved debt collection. In fact, the

2. The Department of Justice and the Department of the Treasury do not have inspectors general.

money had accrued from crop loans that farmers simply repaid when market conditions improved (Campbell, 1986: 193).

The temper of inspectors general has also aroused concern. When White House Spokesman James Brady described President Reagan's criteria for inspectors general in 1981, he said the president would pick people "meaner than junkyard dogs" (Lanouette, 1982). Yet according to some critics, inspectors general have been more like lap dogs in practice (Eisendrath, 1986).

Some reports by inspectors general have whitewashed wrongdoing by agency officials. For example, the Interior Department's biggest coal sale in history was bungled by agency officials, who leaked sensitive data to coal companies, driving down the price of the coal and costing the government an estimated $46 million (Eisendrath, 1986: 17). Instead of leading the charge against the leakers, the Inspector General, Richard Mulberry, denied any wrongdoing. The Environmental Protection Agency's inspector general was equally lax during the scandalous Gorsuch years. Despite serious allegations by public officials and journalists, the EPA's inspector general failed to investigate alleged "sweetheart deals" with regulated industries, the political manipulation of funds, and gutted regulatory procedures. Indeed, only 3 percent of the inspector general's audits during that period focused on internal management problems.[3] In other instances, inspectors general have done their job, but slowly. For example, the Defense Department's inspector general eventually uncovered a corrupt competitive bidding system but only after dozens of lucrative contracts had been tainted (Cushman, 1988).

Some inspectors general have been vigorous and effective. The inspector general in Health and Human Services (HHS) has discovered surprisingly high profitmaking by hospitals that treat Medicare patients, inadequate discipline by state medical licensing boards, and an organ transplant system so loosely controlled "you could drive a Mack truck through it" (Schneider and Flaherty, 1986). These revelations, which received considerable publicity, appear to have triggered tougher discipline by state licensing boards, a better-integrated organ transplant system, and serious efforts to reform Medicare reimbursement procedures. Less dramatically, the inspector general in the Department of Labor (DOL)

3. The overwhelming majority of audits, 92 percent, focused on grants and contracts (Eisendrath, 1986: 20).

has been successful in documenting food stamp abuses, thus paving the way for reform (Lanouette, 1982).

How does one explain this mixture of successes and failures? To some extent, they may reflect the personal styles of the inspector generals themselves. Take, for example, Richard Kusserow, inspector general of HHS. An ex-marine with years of experience as a CIA operative and an FBI agent, Kusserow has been hailed as a tough, blunt, aggressive watchdog (Rich, 1987). He is the very model of a modern inspector general. In contrast, Richard Mulberry of Interior has been more of a Caspar Milquetoast. Under pressure, he has been timid and pliable (Eisendrath, 1986).

There is, however, more than personal style at work here. On balance, inspectors general have been much more vigorous and effective in pursuing waste and abuse outside their own agencies than inside their agencies. When focusing on outside contractors, state agencies, and ineligible benefits claimants, inspectors general have often been relentless. When focusing on fellow agency officials and their transgressions, inspectors general have often been cautious. In intermediate cases, such as bribery and fraud in military contracting where outsiders and insiders were at fault, the picture is mixed. Overall, inspectors general have played a useful hortatory role in their dealings with outsiders, but they have been far less successful in keeping their own houses in order.

In retrospect, this is entirely understandable. The idea of using bureaucrats to control other bureaucrats is a good one. It has worked well in other contexts, as illustrated by the victories of ombudsmen and proxy advocates. However it is unrealistic to expect bureaucrats to control their own peers on a sustained basis. Bonds of collegiality discourage public sniping and fault-finding aimed at fellow workers. When inefficiency is the fault of outside contractors or greedy claimants, inspectors general have a constructive role to play. When inefficiency is the fault of agency officials, inspectors general are apt to be paper tigers.

Central Coordination

Although the quest for economy in government has fueled many management reforms, other goals have also been prominent, including coordination, integration, leadership, and responsiveness. In pursuit of these goals chief executives have often opted for central coordination, hoping to overcome centrifugal tendencies within the executive branch by means of a central office or a combination of councils, task forces, and advisory groups. Central co-ordination is often a follow-up to administrative reorganization (Schick, 1981).

The coordination impulse was especially popular during the 1970s and 1980s at both the federal and state levels. At the federal level, it resulted in the establishment of a White House counter-bureaucracy and the creation of OMB under Nixon; the creation of a Regulatory Council, a Regulatory Analysis Review Group (RARG), and numerous interagency task forces under Carter; and the establishment of several cabinet councils under Reagan.[4] At the state level, coordination efforts were equally striking. Some governors have established a cabinet for the first time, while others have established a subcabinet system, with key agency officials assigned to broad issue groups such as natural resources and human resources. Governors have also expanded their personal staffs, created management and central planning offices and set up temporary interagency task forces to facilitate bureaucratic control. Some of these reforms have given coordination a bad name; others however have enabled chief executives to strengthen their control over the bureaucracy without eroding the integrity of the civil service or the cabinet.

The first major coordination effort of the 1970s was Richard Nixon's decision to establish a counterbureaucracy within the White House. Convinced that the federal bureaucracy was hostile to his policy goals,[5] Nixon set out to control the bureaucracy by enlarging the White House staff considerably and by expanding its authority over both policymaking and policy implementation. In doing so, he hoped to bypass disloyal subcabinet officials and to leave his personal imprint on numerous administrative decisions. To accomplish these goals, Nixon established a domestic council, headed by John Ehrlichman. Ehrlichman approached this assignment with his usual mixture of bluster and bravado.

Nixon's counterbureaucracy strategy backfired spectacularly—and not merely because Ehrlichman had a knack for rubbing people the wrong way. Cabinet members bitterly resented what they viewed as a transparent effort to usurp their authority. As the White House counterbureaucracy grew in importance, cabinet members found themselves excluded from important policy deci-

4. The Ford years were relatively quiet. Ford belatedly announced a President Management Initiatives program aimed at improving linkages between OMB's budget and management operations, but this did not get very far.
5. According to Aberbach and Rockman (1976), Nixon was right!

sions. This triggered a nasty public feud between the cabinet and the White House staff. Moreover, the White House staff, bogged down in operational details, began to lose sight of the broader picture. Ironically, as the White House staff intruded into the domain of administrative operations, fundamental policy decisions were being pushed deeper into the bowels of the bureaucracy (Nathan, 1983). The counterbureaucracy had become counterproductive.

Interestingly enough, many governors developed their own counterbureaucracies in the 1970s. In 1966, the average gubernatorial staff consisted of 6.6 people; by 1979, the average gubernatorial staff consisted of thirty-four people (Sabato, 1983: 85). Yet the dysfunctions of a counterbureaucracy have been less evident at the state level, perhaps because a staff of thirty-four is still more manageable than a staff of sixteen hundred (the size of the Executive Office of the president). Also, as gubernatorial staffs increased in size many governors simultaneously strengthened the role of cabinet and subcabinet officials, thus muting the resentment that surfaced at the federal level.

During the 1970s, approximately fourteen governors established a cabinet for the first time, and approximately twenty-five governors established subcabinets to advise and coordinate policy in selected areas. According to a 1982 survey of governors (Bodman and Garry, 1982), these reforms were very successful. Governor Pierre (Pete) DuPont of Delaware, who established a system of cabinet retreats, had these comments: "The collegiality developed at these cabinet retreats significantly contributes to interdepartmental cooperation as well as cooperation between the Executive Office and the various cabinet departments." Governor John Evans of Idaho had equally high praise for subcabinets, arguing that "small groups are able to focus better." Whether they opted for a cabinet system, a subcabinet, or both, governors found that regular meetings of top agency officials improved the atmosphere and facilitated policy integration.

Meanwhile, at the federal level, presidents were hard at work trying to devise viable alternatives to the discredited counterbureaucracy approach of the early Nixon years. Jimmy Carter's distinctive contribution was to establish a variety of temporary task forces and coordinating councils, including the Regulatory Council, the RARG, and interagency task forces on energy, productivity, consumer affairs, and so forth. According to a knowledgeable observer, Carter's Regulatory Council and RARG were somewhat successful in reducing inconsistencies and in sensitizing agencies to the concerns of other agencies (Schick, 1981). Carter's interagency coordinating councils were also reasonably effective, especially when the president took a personal interest in them.

Yet something seemed to be missing—a strong sense of purpose, vigorous participation by cabinet officials, or perhaps both. President Reagan improved upon the Carter experiments by establishing several cabinet councils, including a Cabinet Council on Economic Affairs and a Cabinet Council on Management and Administration. During Reagan's first year, the cabinet councils met 150 times, with the president presiding at some of the more important sessions. According to close observers, Reagan's cabinet councils were well-run and effective (Newland, 1984; Campbell, 1986). By giving cabinet officials a vital role in policymaking and policy implementation, the cabinet councils improved policy design and solidified cabinet support. By integrating cabinet officials and White House staff members from the very start, the cabinet councils reduced the friction associated with Nixon's counterbureaucracy strategy. In contrast to foreign affairs, where cabinet members were eventually eclipsed by a renegade national security staff, the Reagan administration's efforts at domestic policy coordination were both sensible and successful.

If Nixon's counterbureaucracy strategy was the most short-lived of the central coordination efforts, another Nixon initiative was easily the most important management reform of the decade. Following a recommendation by the Ash Council, Nixon converted the Bureau of the Budget (BOB) into OMB in 1970. The impetus for OMB was a widespread belief that management issues were being neglected by the White House. The hope was that a new high-profile office would integrate budget and management decisions and upgrade the importance of management within the executive branch.

Since its inception, OMB has been both powerful and controversial. It has been the driving force behind regulatory reform, management by objectives, procurement reform, zero-based budgeting, civil service reform, paperwork reduction, administrative reorganization, and other major initiatives. It has used budgetary threats to secure management concessions. It has extended its tentacles into long-forgotten nooks and crannies of the bureaucracy. It has used the executive clearance function to intimidate outspoken agency officials.[6] Always strong, it became even stronger un-

6. The practice of executive clearance requires executive branch officials to clear

der Ronald Reagan. In interviews with Reagan's White House staff, Kessel (1984) found that OMB was perceived as the most important organizational unit in the White House—even more important at the time (1981, 1982) than the powerful National Security Council (NSC).

OMB's critics—and there are many—make two principal points. First, they argue that OMB has become too politicized. Instead of developing a reputation for "neutral competence" or even purposive professionalism, OMB has become highly partisan and ideological (Mosher, 1984; Campbell, 1986: 153–98). Second, they argue that OMB continues to emphasize budgeting at the expense of management. That is due in part to the imperatives of the budget cycle and also to the low visibility of management issues (Mosher, 1984; Campbell, 1986: 153–98). The federal budget deficit crisis has probably exacerbated these tendencies.

There is another factor that OMB's critics often overlook. The OMB has neglected management questions not merely because of its understandable interest in the budget but also because it has strayed into the realm of policy analysis. In practice, OMB has become the Office of Management, Budget, and Policy Analysis. Instead of attempting to improve executive management, OMB has developed an elaborate process for reviewing administrative rules

TABLE 5.1

Relative Importance of Organizational Units
in the Reagan White House

Unit	Mean Rating	Mean Rating by Other Units
President	79.0	79.0
Office of Management & Budget	57.2	55.3
National Security Council	54.4	54.9
Legislative Liaison Staff	47.2	47.1
Office of Policy Development	45.1	36.6
Council of Economic Advisers	31.4	26.1
Office of the Press Secretary	31.4	25.8
Office of Public Liaison	14.1	14.3

SOURCE: John Kessel, "The Structures of the Reagan White House," *American Journal of Political Science*, Vol. 28, No. 2 (May 1984), p. 247. By permission of the University of Texas Press.

NOTE: A mean rating of 79.0 indicates that respondents regard the organizational unit as "extremely important." A mean rating of 14.1 indicates that respondents regard the organizational unit as "of minor importance."

their congressional testimony with OMB. This permits OMB to alter the remarks of officials who disagree with administration policies.

before they are issued. This trend, documented in the next chapter, has distracted the agency from very real management problems and opportunities. For example, OMB has allowed the Intergovernmental Personnel Act to languish, while relations between the federal government and other levels of government deteriorate (Gormley, 1987).

In broader terms, OMB has become quite heavy-handed in its dealings with administrative agencies. Indeed, an agency as big and powerful as OMB may be incapable of prodding agencies with catalytic recommendations. When OMB speaks, its utterances are likely to be perceived by administrative officials as coercive. An agency that defies OMB is uncommonly courageous or uncommonly foolish. A smaller, less powerful office of management might be both more commited to good management and more supportive of agency experiments to promote that goal.

Would a separate office of management be visible enough and powerful enough to have an impact on the bureaucracy? The National Academy of Public Administration thinks so, and many members of Congress agree (Gilmour and Sperry, 1986). Moreover, there is some evidence at the state level to suggest that a separate management office need not be a "toothless tiger." Indeed, in California an office with an even narrower mission has produced tangible results in a short period of time.

In 1979 the California State Legislature established an Office of Administrative Law (OAL) headed by a gubernatorial appointee to review administrative rules for clarity, consistency, authority, and necessity. One of OAL's missions was to curb the proliferation of emergency rules, which some agencies were using in order to bypass the "notice and comment" requirements of the state Administrative Procedure Act. Before OAL's creation, California agencies were issuing 232 emergency rules per year. Within two years after the OAL's creation, this number had plummeted to 105 emergency rules per year (Cohen, 1983). Moreover, the OAL seemed to do a sensible job of distinguishing between problems that warranted emergency rulemaking (expanding quarantine areas to prevent the spread of infestations) and problems that did not (expanding the authorized size of cauliflower containers). Even the OAL has strayed into the realm of policy analysis, substituting its judgment for that of administrative agencies in several questionable instances (Cohen, 1983). The California state legislature seems to have invited this by allowing the OAL to reverse a rule if it is "unnecessary." By striking that language, the state legislature could help to ensure that the OAL plays an effective management role without attempting to make or remake public policy.

California's experience may not be transferable to states with small populations or states where skilled professionals are scarce. To be successful, a separate office of management or administrative law must be rich in talent and large enough to coordinate numerous agencies with diverse goals and practices. Such an office might not work in Wyoming or Mississippi. California may also have benefited from personnel reforms that make it easier for political executives to control the bureaucracy. Specifically, the creation of a senior executive corps of civil servants who may be transferred from one job to another by the governor—California Executive Assignees—facilitates central control (Hamilton and Biggart, 1984). This reform, initiated in 1963 and fine-tuned in later years, set the stage for a similar reform at the federal level.

Personnel Reform

Jimmy Carter, who deserves credit or blame for the Civil Service Reform Act of 1978, described it as "the most sweeping reform of the Civil Service System since it was created nearly 100 years ago" (Thayer, 1984: 29). Both supporters and detractors would probably agree. The Civil Service Reform Act of 1978 split the old Civil Service Commission into two agencies: the Office of Personnel Management (OPM) and the Merit Systems Protection Board (MSPB). The Office of Personnel Management, headed by a presidential appointee, would set personnel policy and oversee the processes of hiring, training, promoting, and terminating personnel. The MSPB, a three-member commission insulated from the White House through relatively long terms of office, would oversee OPM, enforce merit principles, and protect civil servants from arbitrary treatment. The Civil Service Reform Act also established a merit pay system for middle-level managers (GS 13–15) and provided for performance evaluations of senior managers (GS 16–18). Most importantly, it created a Senior Executive Service (SES).

The SES, vigorously promoted by Alan Campbell and other public administration scholars, was the centerpiece of the Civil Service Reform Act. The SES is an elite corps of senior managers (approximately eight thousand persons above the GS–15 level), whose employment in the civil service is secure (except for political appointees, who constitute no more than 10 percent of the SES) but whose employment in a particular job is insecure. If their performance is judged favorably by their superiors, SES members are eligible for substantial cash bonuses; if judged unfavorably, they can be demoted or transferred to another job within their agency or another agency.

According to critics, the SES is a blatant attempt to politicize the upper echelons of the bureaucracy by rewarding loyalty and punishing disloyalty (Thayer, 1984). Yet one person's politicization is another person's leadership. Moreover, the SES idea differs significantly from other political strategies of bureaucratic management, such as the bureaucratic bypass (Nixon's early years) and bureau-bashing (by OMB and OPM). By giving the president an opportunity to redeploy senior managers to suit his strategic purposes, this reform gives the president some reason to trust senior managers in key positions. In addition, it might well discourage other more destructive efforts to politicize the bureaucracy.

The initial response to SES was highly favorable within the bureaucracy itself. Of several thousand senior managers eligible to join, approximately 98 percent did so. The overwhelming majority of senior managers had enough confidence in their ability that they were willing to risk demotion or transfer in the hope of greater financial rewards. Within two to three years, however, SES officials had been disillusioned. The number of SES members eligible for cash bonuses was slashed by Congress and slashed further by OMB (Ingraham and Colby, 1982). Stories circulated that bonuses were being awarded to persons with good political connections (Thayer, 1981). Also, liberal Democrats found themselves gagging at the prospect of serving a conservative president. For all these reasons, the SES experienced a "brain drain." Between July 1979 and March 1983, 40 percent of SES officials left government service (Levine, 1986: 200).

High turnover at the top was but one manifestation of a much deeper problem that had little to do with the SES—plummeting bureaucratic morale. A 1982 survey of federal executives and managers (mostly GS–15 and above) found that two-thirds would recommend private employment to others. Less than 25 percent would recommend a career in the federal government (Schmidt and Posner, 1986: 449). More recently, a Twentieth Century Fund commission headed by Charles Robb found that bureaucratic morale is alarmingly low and that the recruitment and retention of "independent and imaginative" professionals is increasingly difficult (Lawrence, 1987).

Clearly, the federal bureaucracy has a serious morale problem.

131

However, it is doubtful that the SES caused or even exacerbated this problem. Rather, low bureaucratic morale seems to be a result of other factors: 1) stingy appropriations by Congress and OMB; 2) the politicization of OPM under Reagan; 3) other Reagan policies and practices (especially reductions in force and budget cutbacks); and 4) the cumulative toll of a decade or more of bureau-bashing.

Confronted by a staggering budget deficit, the Congress in 1980 reduced from 50 percent to 25 percent the number of SES members eligible for bonuses. Shortly thereafter, OMB further reduced this to 20 percent. Thus, while one out of every two SES members expected to be eligible for a bonus, only one out of every five SES members was eligible in practice. Many SES members felt betrayed (Ingraham and Colby, 1982). Middle-level bureaucrats, anticipating an SES appointment in the future, probably shared the frustration of shattered expectations.

The Reagan administration's budget cutbacks and RIFs (reductions in force) had an even more devastating impact on bureaucratic morale. Within his first year in office, Reagan laid off eleven thousand employees (Meier, 1987: 157). Reductions in force were especially common at DOL, HHS, and other domestic agencies unpopular with the Reagan administration. According to Rubin (1985), who examined "cutback management" at five federal agencies, RIFs lowered both bureaucratic morale and productivity. "Mental health days" became more common,[7] and people grew afraid of making decisions. One bureaucrat directly affected by the RIFs described the atmosphere this way: "We were zero. Now we are minus ten. Morale was bad; now it's terrible. People who were friends aren't talking. It's so depressing" (Rubin, 1985: 150).

The politicization of OPM also contributed to fear, paralysis, and sagging morale. Donald Devine, an archconservative appointed to head OPM, declared war on the bureaucracy and vowed to "bring the tanks up to the border" (Levine, 1986: 203). He routinely observed that federal employees were overpaid, despite studies showing that pay was higher in the private sector (Peters, 1985: 24–25). Openly contemptuous of the career civil service, he slashed the number of civil servants at OPM and substantially increased the number of political appointees. At the same time, he presided over an increase in Schedule C positions, used by the White House for

7. The mental health day is a widely used but little-studied American institution. When an employee becomes so frustrated at work that he or she is ready to scream, the employee simply stays at home for a day or two, scrubbing floors or watching game shows to calm down.

patronage purposes.[8] He set a disturbing precedent by attending the 1984 Republican Convention as a delegate and by campaigning for thirteen Republican congressional candidates. When the Professional and Career Examination (PACE) test was declared discriminatory by a federal court,[9] he failed to develop a viable alternative. Instead he authorized agencies to make Schedule B appointments for two years without a written test.[10] Later, Devine converted these appointments to career positions. Congress was sufficiently outraged by these and other actions that it refused President Reagan's nomination of Devine to a second term. But the damage had been done. For many bureaucrats, it was the *coup de grace*. To be bashed by politicians and judges was upseting but in some sense tolerable. To be bashed by the head of the civil service was the last straw.

In assessing the personnel reforms of recent years, it is important to distinguish between the politicization of the SES and the politicization of the OPM. As a vital link between the president and the career civil service, the SES was of necessity politicized. That President Reagan appointed conservatives to key SES positions was not merely his prerogative; that was precisely what the Civil Service Reform Act was supposed to permit (a conservative appointing conservatives, a liberal appointing liberals). Indeed, as Goldenberg (1985: 73) puts it, "Increasing assignment flexibility was one of the central goals of establishing the Senior Executive Service and has been one of its clearest accomplishments." Democrats may not like the people Reagan appointed but they will undoubtedly sing a different tune when they have their chance.

The politicization of OPM on the other hand is another matter. It is difficult for the head of OPM to talk about merit principles with

8. Schedule C, first established by President Eisenhower, enables the White House to bypass examination requirements in appointing approximately sixteen hundred people to lower-level civil service positions.

9. For years, the PACE exam was the major recruiting device for administrative and professional people at entry levels in the federal civil service. In 1982, a federal court ruled that the PACE exam, as worded, discriminated against minorities. In an out-of-court settlement, the Reagan administration agreed to draw up a new set of exams. The Office of Personnel Management subsequently dragged its feet in order to permit political appointments. An alternative to the PACE exam did not emerge until June of 1988.

10. Schedule B appointments, which do not involve policymaking, normally require a competitive civil service exam. Previously, Schedule B appointments had been relatively few in number, reserved for bank examiners, Air Force intelligence officers, and other persons with highly specialized skills (Meier, 1987: 37).

a straight face when he simultaneously subverts them at every opportunity. And it is difficult to motivate career civil servants when the person in charge of appointments, promotions, salaries, and pensions openly demeans them. Civil servants are seldom shocked by subcabinet officials who pursue a partisan political agenda. But they are understandably shocked when the head of the civil service declares war on the bureaucracy and uses the appointments process to reward friends and punish enemies.

The politicization of the SES and OPM was made possible by the Civil Service Act of 1978. Both reforms made it easier for President Reagan to control the bureaucracy. In Peters's apt description (1985: 32), the Civil Service Reform Act was "Carter's gift to Reagan." Yet if Reagan was successful in creating an administrative presidency, much of the credit should go to Reagan himself, who not only took advantage of the formal reforms but who also changed informal practices in important ways. The president of the United States possesses formidable latent powers. In contrast to other recent presidents, Reagan instantly appreciated these powers and took advantage of them. More than his predecessors, Reagan took an active, personal interest in subcabinet appointments. More than his predecessors, Reagan used ideology as a litmus test in the appointments process. More than his predecessors, Reagan delayed appointments until he found the right people for the job.

Why did other presidents not take such steps to augment their managerial powers? Because they didn't think of the idea soon enough (Nixon). Because they wanted to reward constituencies for electoral support (Carter). Because they lacked a clear vision (Ford and Eisenhower). Because they valued continuity for symbolic purposes (Johnson and Ford). Because they thought the bureaucracy could be bypassed (Nixon). And because they viewed appointments as part of the transition process—a prelude to governance rather than the core of governance itself (all of the presidents). Reagan, whose gifts as a manager have been grossly underrated, was able to combine formal and informal powers to create the administrative presidency that had eluded his predecessors.

There is much to be said for the politicization of the federal bureaucracy's upper echelons, whether through formal or informal means. It eliminates the need for coercion by putting supportive individuals in key positions. It promotes policy coherence and integration—long thought to be missing in American politics. It strengthens the chief executive's power to persuade. It jolts the bureaucracy and facilitates change, experimentation, and innovation. All of this assumes, of course, that appointees are not merely loyal but competent as well.

Similar points might be made with respect to the politicization of state bureaucracies. During the 1970s, a number of states shortened their ballots, reducing the number of elected state officials and thereby strengthening the governor's appointment powers. In Oklahoma, for example, the state switched in 1975 from thirteen to eight elected officials within the executive branch. Between 1962 and 1978, the number of elected state executives declined by 10 percent nationwide (Sabato, 1983: 63) as states allowed governors to appoint insurance commissioners, agriculture commissioners, public utility commissioners, and so forth. Studies show that governors with more formidable powers of appointment are more successful in promoting a legislative program (Sharkansky, 1971) and in managing the bureaucracy (Dometrius, 1979a). Another study by Dometrius (1979b) demonstrates quite clearly that appointed executives regard the governor very differently than elected executives (see Table 5.2). Specifically, appointed officials are more likely to respect the governor's wishes.

The politicization of the bureaucracy does not necessarily mean a return to "spoils system" politics. Indeed, at the same time that states were shortening their ballots, they were also reducing the number of patronage positions (Sabato, 1983: 66–69). The trend at the state level seems to have been toward greater gubernatorial control over top state officials, reduced gubernatorial control over other appointments. In contrast, the politicization of the OPM at the federal level has resulted in an expansion of patronage posi-

TABLE 5.2

Governors' Appointment Authority and
Administrators' Perception of Gubernatorial
Control (N = 3,501)

Selection Method of State Administrators	Percentage of Administrators Stating Governor's Authority is High
Popular Election	9.1
Board	20.4
Department Head	39.9
Governor	57.5

SOURCE: Nelson Dometrius, "The Efficacy of a Governor's Formal Powers," *State Government*, Vol. 52, No. 3 (Summer 1979), p. 123. Reprinted with permission from *State Government*, © by the Council of State Governments. The data, derived from Deil Wright's survey of state administrators, encompass responses from 1964, 1968, and 1974.

tions, with Schedule B and Schedule C appointments increasing.[11] For all of these reasons, bureaucratic morale is probably higher at the state level than at the federal level. At the state level, personnel reforms have strengthened gubernatorial control without undermining merit principles. At the federal level, personnel reforms have strengthened presidential control while eroding the confidence of civil servants in their superiors and in themselves.

Executive Orders

Even with supportive personnel in place, a chief executive may find it tempting to resort to stronger bureaucratic control measures, such as executive orders. Executive orders are directives to administrative agencies that have the full force of law but that lack explicit legislative approval. Executive orders enable a chief executive to have a swift impact on public policy or government operations without the usual encumbrances of checks and balances. Not surprisingly, executive orders have been very popular with chief executives at both the federal and state levels. Since the days of Abraham Lincoln, presidents have issued more than twelve thousand executive orders (Cooper, 1986). Governors have also issued numerous executive orders to reorganize the executive branch, establish special commissions, and deal with natural disasters and other emergencies.

In recent years the number of executive orders has increased sharply at the state level. Thus, in Wisconsin, Governor Lee Dreyfus issued more executive orders in 1979 than his predecessors had issued during an earlier eighteen-year period (King, 1980: 333). Dreyfus's successor, Anthony Earl, issued even more executive orders (Kopca, 1987). Similar increases have been reported in Massachusetts, where the number of executive orders issued between 1965 and 1980 rose 206 percent over the preceding fifteen years (Bernick, 1984: 97).

At the federal level, no such upward trend is apparent. As Table 5.3 indicates, President Carter issued more executive orders than most modern presidents, while President Reagan issued fewer executive orders. If there is a pattern in these raw numbers, it is that presidents whose relations with Congress are poor (Carter, Ken-

11. The initial expansion of Schedule C appointments began under Carter, continuing under Reagan. The expansion of Schedule B positions occurred under Reagan.

TABLE 5.3

Executive Orders by President

President	Number of Executive Orders	Number of Months Served	Executive Orders/ Month
Kennedy	213	34	6.26
Johnson	323	62	5.21
Nixon	345	66.5	5.19
Ford	168	29.5	5.69
Carter	319	48	6.65
Reagan (through 1986)	291	71	4.10

SOURCE: Compiled by the author from *Public Papers of the Presidents*, 1961–83 and the *Code of Federal Regulations*, 1984–86.

nedy) issue more executive orders, perhaps to compensate for that weakness. Indeed, this is an important point, because it suggests that one of the underlying purposes of executive orders may be to bypass an unsympathetic legislative branch.

Although executive orders are no more numerous today at the federal level than before, they do seem to be more intrusive and more significant. Certainly, that is true of executive orders institutionalizing cost-benefit analysis in administrative rulemaking, to be discussed in the following chapter. That is also true of President Carter's unusually comprehensive executive orders relating to Iranian assets and energy policy. Finally, it is difficult to imagine executive orders bolder than two issued by President Reagan in 1986—one on drug testing for federal employees and one on the sale of arms to Iran. If presidents who get little respect from Congress are more inclined to issue executive orders, presidents who have little respect for the bureaucracy may be more inclined to issue strong executive orders. As contempt for the bureaucracy has become more widespread, executive orders have become both more forceful and more formidable.

Executive orders are both appropriate and necessary in emergency situations when other political institutions are unable to act in a timely manner or when it is important that the government speak with one voice. President Carter was able to secure the release of the American hostages in Iran by issuing an extraordinary series of executive orders that emerged from delicate negotiations with Iranian representatives. These executive orders, subsequently upheld by the U.S. Supreme Court as consistent with pertinent statutes (*Dames & Moore v. Regan*, 1981), ended a long and bitter ordeal for the hostages and the American people. Similarly, Presidents Nixon and Carter were able to cope with the energy crisis of the 1970s by issuing a number of executive orders—ones creating a federal energy office, mandating energy savings in federal buildings, establishing a ride-sharing program for federal employees, and so forth. While Congress would probably have adopted these measures if asked, Presidents Nixon and Carter were able to bring them into being quickly and decisively, saving both precious time and precious fuel.

At the state level, governors have also issued executive orders to cope with genuine emergencies. Thus, many governors promulgated odd-even gasoline purchase plans in the mid-1970s to end the queues that clogged service stations and city streets. As a result of these executive orders the purchase of gasoline became more orderly and more restrained. In a similar fashion, governors routinely issue executive orders to cope with natural disasters. For example, Wisconsin Governor Martin Schreiber responded to a devastating storm by issuing an executive order suspending time-consuming navigable stream crossing permit procedures. This expedited the removal of downed timber, which presented a major fire hazard (King, 1980).

Unfortunately, chief executives have also used executive orders to cope with controversies—as opposed to genuine emergencies—without securing legislative consent. In addition, they have used executive orders to bypass legal requirements for "notice and comment" opportunities as part of the administrative rulemaking process. Frustrated by political opposition, chief executives have used the executive order as a fig leaf for illegal or unconstitutional acts. At the same time, they have deprived themselves of the constructive criticism that lawmaking and administrative rulemaking afford.

Executive orders are sometimes coercive, illegitimate, overly intrusive, overly extensive, or based on questionable premises. President Reagan's drug testing order, issued in September 1986, illustrates many of these problems. Concerned about drug abuse, the president issued a sweeping executive order requiring all federal agencies to establish drug testing for civilian employees "in sensitive positions." According to OPM estimates, employees in sensitive positions include over half of the nation's two million federal civilian employees! Under OPM rules implementing the executive order, federal employees who test positively for drugs may be dismissed after the first offense and must be dismissed after the second offense. There is no need for supervisors to demonstrate a connection between drug use and work performance (Williams, 1986).

This executive order is flawed in several crucial respects and has been challenged in the federal courts. First, drug tests are notoriously unreliable and may result in either false positives or false negatives. Is it fair to fire or otherwise punish an employee who has never used drugs? Second, federal law states that there must be a connection between a disciplinary act and an employee's performance. Has this law suddenly become irrelevant? Third, if drug abuse is a problem, surely random testing is not the solution. Rather, a more selective approach in cases where persons exhibit the symptoms of drug abuse would seem to be less costly and less intrusive. Fourth, the executive order may well be unconstitutional, because it provides for a "search and seizure" without a warrant. Indeed, a federal judge reached just such a conclusion in a case involving a drug-testing program run by the U.S. Customs Service.

A narrowly focused, clearly circumscribed drug testing program may well be justified, especially where public safety is at stake (e.g., at the Federal Aviation Administration). However, such a program should be carefully designed by Congress, after public hearings, or by an administrative agency, after expert testimony. Instead the Reagan administration institutionalized an unreliable test to solve a problem of unspecified dimensions without legislative consent and without allowing any meaningful input from affected persons. The Reagan drug testing program is a slapdash, panicky effort that runs roughshod over civil liberties and that is almost certain to demoralize civil servants. Surely, the solution to drug abuse is not the abuse of presidential power.

If President Reagan's executive order on drug testing sent shockwaves throughout the federal bureaucracy, his executive order on the sale of arms to Iran sent shockwaves throughout the entire world when it was disclosed in November 1986. The classified executive order issued on 17 January 1986 authorized the shipment of arms to Iran in the hope that this good will gesture would secure the release of American hostages. It also instructed Central Intelligence Agency (CIA) Director William Casey to say nothing about the shipment to Congress because of its "extreme sensitivity" (Engelberg, 1986). During 1986, the United States shipped approximately 250 tons of military equipment worth an estimated $50 million to Iran. The Congress like the American people did not learn about this extraordinary transaction until November 1986.

The Iranian arms sale has been widely condemned as one of the most foolhardy foreign policy gambits in U.S. history. With the president's authorization, the U.S. government shipped arms to a sworn enemy of the United States in return for worthless assurances that some hostages might be released by their terrorist captors. The United States did this while publicly forswearing any negotiations with terrorists and while berating allies who traded with Iran. Moreover, the president and his aides conducted this transaction without notifying key members of the congressional intelligence committees, as required by law. The National Security Act did allow the president to forgo "prior notice" in an emergency if he subsequently informed the key committee members in a "timely fashion." However, a delay of eleven months does not constitute timely notice by anyone's reckoning.

The Iranian arms caper was flawed both substantively and procedurally. It has caused enormous and irreparable harm. It has eroded U.S. credibility abroad and exposed a huge gap between democratic theory and democratic practice. Had they been notified of this initiative, key members of Congress would almost certainly have opposed it and stopped it. Unwilling to take this risk, the president and his aides unilaterally suspended the laws of the United States, lying to Congress, our allies, and the American people in the process.

Some governors have also demonstrated a disturbing disregard for the rule of law in their use of executive orders. Governor Richard Thornburgh of Pennsylvania, unable to "privatize" Pennsylvania's state-run liquor stores due to determined legislative opposition, issued an executive order during the last days of his governorship privatizing state stores by fiat. Whatever the merits of privatization in this context, the executive order clearly violated legislative intent, since the Pennsylvania State Legislature had just considered and rejected the governor's privatization proposal. Thornburgh's executive order was subsequently overturned by a state court, which concluded that the governor had acted "without authority" (Warner, 1986).

It is tempting to dismiss these executive orders as aberrations—isolated instances of bad judgment. Yet such executive orders, deliberately drafted to evade legal or constitutional requirements, undermine respect for the rule of law and reflect contempt for democratic processes. They not only coerce bureaucrats but they do so contrary to legislative intent. They illustrate what can happen when bureau-bashing becomes so accepted that it eclipses other values.

If used properly, the executive order can be an effective and legitimate management device. It is especially useful in emergencies. But it has been widely abused in recent years. Chief executives have viewed the executive order as a license to bludgeon bureaucrats, bypass legislators, or both. They have ignored the legal rights of civil servants and the constitutional partnership that is supposed to exist between chief executives and legislators. Instead of viewing the executive order as an extraordinary tool to be used under extraordinary circumstances, chief executives have begun to treat the executive order as their personal ace in the hole. In doing so, they have lost sight of their place in the constitutional order.

Conclusion

Management reforms are both more and less exciting than other efforts to control the bureaucracy. They are more exciting in that they have the potential to integrate public policymaking. Because of the historical and cultural tendencies toward fragmentation that persist in American politics, coherence has long been elusive except in times of war. By strengthening the chief executive's leverage over the bureaucracy, management reforms do not usher in the millennium, but they do turn back the clock to an era when we had three branches of government, not four. In this respect, they promote integration by augmenting the chief executive's "power to persuade."

On the other hand, the management reforms of recent years have offered for the most part old wine in new bottles. Indeed, in many instances, even the bottles are old. Executive orders have been issued since George Washington and have been codified since Abraham Lincoln. Administrative reorganization has been a standard cure for bureaucratic malfunctions and disappointments throughout the twentieth century. Personnel reforms aimed at augmenting the chief executive's appointment power date back to Andrew Jackson, if not earlier.

To say that reforms are old is not to say that they are useless. The recurring popularity of administrative reorganization, for example, does not necessarily mean that previous reorganizations have failed but may confirm that reorganization is needed periodically to revitalize and energize the bureaucracy. In politics, as in music, new variations on old themes may be both pleasing and innovative in their own way. Of these new variations on old management reforms, the most interesting were the SES and the OMB.

The SES sought to harness the talents of top civil servants to better serve the policy goals of the president. Instead of writing off the bureaucracy or trying to bypass it, this reform viewed the bureaucracy as an enormous reservoir of talent. It relied on voluntary inducements to lure senior managers into service and a combination of incentives and disincentives to those who chose to join. It was a quintessential hortatory control, with its emphasis on pressure as opposed to coercion. If the SES was initially disappointing to senior managers, the fault would seem to lie with stingy congressional appropriations committees and not with the underlying concept. In the long run, the SES has the potential to convert what Heclo (1977) called a "government of strangers" into a government of colleagues.

The OMB, in contrast, was based on very different premises—namely, that the bureaucracy could not be trusted and required constant supervision. Conceived as a counterweight to the bureaucracy (and to Congress), OMB has become the single most important unit in the White House and, quite possibly, in the federal government itself. The Office of Management and Budget's powers are so awesome that it is difficult for bureaucrats to defy the agency when it demonstrates questionable judgment. Thus, when an OMB official states that anyone who opposes cost-benefit analysis opposes thinking, this is greeted by respectful silence rather than howls of derision. At times, it seems that bureaucrats are more willing to criticize the president himself than to take on OMB. That is because OMB takes an active interest in important operational questions that presidents typically ignore. If the president's power is the power to persuade, OMB's power is the power to intimidate. Such power is easily abused.

In addition to creating new organizational units, chief executives have taken advantage of their informal managerial powers in recent years. Governors have convened cabinet meetings and organized weekend retreats, reportedly with good results. President Reagan more than his predecessors has put latent presidential powers to good use. By combining formal and informal reforms, Reagan managed to create the "administrative presidency" that so obsessed—but eluded—Richard Nixon. Now that Reagan has shown the way, other presidents may follow suit. If the SES was

Carter's gift to Reagan, the administrative presidency may be Reagan's gift to his successor.

But there is a darker side to the Reagan legacy as well. In recent years, the morale of the federal civil service has plummeted to dangerously low levels. While this phenomenon did not originate with Ronald Reagan, he contributed to this trend by ordering massive layoffs (RIFs), by politicizing the OPM (through the appointment of Donald Devine), and by berating the federal bureaucracy at every opportunity. None of this has been good for bureaucratic morale and bureaucratic turnover has been high, especially in the upper reaches of government. Thus, the legacy of the Reagan years may be stronger presidential control over a bureaucracy so weakened that it is no longer threatening but also so demoralized that it is no longer creative. Reagan has shown how to control the bureaucracy but he has not shown how to energize it.

Policy Analysis

The Search for Rationality

Policy analysis was not invented in the 1960s, but it was popularized at that time. As the size and scope of government grew—the hallmark of the Great Society—interest in evaluating programs and enhancing program effectiveness increased. The War in Vietnam, which raised the specter of a painful choice between "guns" and "butter," provided an additional rationale for choosing programs with greater care in order to maximize effectiveness while minimizing costs.

During the 1960s a number of steps were taken to institutionalize policy analysis in the federal government and at other levels of government as well. The centerpiece of these efforts was Planning, Programming, and Budgeting Systems (PPBS), a budgeting format aimed at promoting effectiveness and efficiency. Planning, Programming and Budgeting Systems is the systematic comparison of input-output packages in the form of program alternatives. In Wildavsky's (1966) words, PPBS is a form of systems analysis that utilizes cost-benefit analysis. It differs from traditional budgeting techniques in that it focuses on outputs rather than inputs, results rather than resources. Also, it facilitates comparisons of programs, including programs that cut across agency lines.

Planning, Programming and Budgeting Systems, introduced by Secretary of Defense Robert McNamara at the Defense Department in 1961, was extended to all federal departments and agencies by President Johnson in 1965. Shortly after its adoption at the federal level, PPBS was institutionalized at the state and local levels. By the end of the decade, PPBS had been adopted by most state governments and by many local governments as well. In contrast to the federal government, most states tailored PPBS to fit existing organizational boundaries. With the exception of Pennsylvania, states did not attempt to create "crosswalks" that would permit policymakers to compare programs in different departments. Even at the state level, however, PPBS proved to be overly ambitious and unrealistic.

Planning, Programming and Budgeting Systems has been widely criticized for several reasons. First of all, it is extremely difficult to assign costs to a single program. Take, for example, a National Aeronautics and Space Administration (NASA) rocket developed for one mission but useful for others.[1] Should one assign the costs of the rocket exclusively to the program for which it was originally developed? If not, how does one allocate costs across programs? These problems, difficult enough for a single piece of equipment, are even more difficult for buildings and personnel assigned to multiple programs.

Second, PPBS assumes that all costs and benefits can be quantified so that comparisons across programs can be made. Yet the future costs of projects begun today are not easily predicted. Although economists use discount rates to take inflation into account, these discount rates are hotly disputed. Benefits are even more difficult to quantify. How does one quantify the benefits of national parks or clean air or national security?

Third, PPBS threatens many agencies and consequently discourages programmatic change. Under traditional budgeting, one could change objectives without threatening organizational survival, since funding was not explicitly tied to programs. Under PPBS, in contrast, a threat to a program is a threat to the agency as well. As Wildavsky (1984: 200–01) explains: "Budgeting by programs, precisely because money flows to objectives, makes it difficult to abandon objectives without abandoning the organization that gets its money for them." From the agency's point of view, PPBS facilitates the identification of error but increases the organizational risks of correcting error. Yet PPBS cannot succeed without the active cooperation and support of agency officials.

As these and other problems with PPBS became apparent, PPBS was dropped by the federal government as a formal requirement. In 1971 the Office of Management and Budget informed agencies that they were no longer required to submit multiyear program and financing plans, program memoranda, and special analytical studies along with their budget requests. Without actually saying so, OMB had abandoned PPBS (Schick, 1973). Disenchanted state and local governments also jettisoned the formal trappings of PPBS, although the ideals it sought to promote—efficiency, effectiveness, and rationality—remained as goals of the executive branch.

1. Wildavsky (1966) cites this example in his excellent discussion of the failings of PPBS.

The demise of PPBS did not put an end to efforts to institutionalize policy analysis. Rather, it seems to have convinced policymakers that policy analysis was too multifaceted to be limited to a single technique and too important to be left to the bureaucracy. As a result, policymakers took a fresh look at policy analysis, seizing upon it as an additional opportunity to achieve bureaucratic control. The chief executive, the legislature, and the courts all got in on the act. At the end of the 1960s, governmental policy analysis consisted of a tattered PPBS system, some legislative requirements for agencies to conduct program evaluations, and policy analysis shops created by and for the agencies. By the end of the 1970s, government policy analysis included environmental impact statements, regulatory impact analyses and provisions for regulatory review, zero-based budgeting (a successor of sorts to PPBS), a more aggressive General Accounting Office (with similar developments at the state level), and a new judicial vigor epitomized by the "hard look" doctrine.

In several respects, the policy analysis reforms of the 1970s were more significant, more realistic, and more effective than PPBS. While PPBS sought comprehensive rationality, the reforms of the 1970s sought rationality and other objectives as well. While PPBS assumed that a common measure could be found for all programs and policies, the reforms of the 1970s recognized for the most part that diverse goals cannot always be adapted to the same interval scale. While PPBS was rooted in economics, the reforms of the 1970s relied on the wisdom of various disciplines, including the natural sciences, economics, accounting, and law. The policy analysis reforms of the 1970s were more eclectic, more flexible, less orthodox, and less grandiose than PPBS.

There were, however, some troublesome trends—most notably, the judicialization, politicization, formalization, and proliferation of policy analysis. The judicialization of policy analysis threatened to transform policy analysis from a search for truth into a quest for perfection. The politicization of policy analysis threatened to undermine the integrity of policy analysis by blurring the distinction between public and private benefits. The formalization of policy analysis threatened to transform policy analysis from creative problem-solving into a ritualisitc exercise. The proliferation of policy analysis threatened to spread analytic resources too thin, diverting attention from really important problems and burying analysts underneath mounds of paperwork.

TABLE 6.1

Alternative Approaches to Policy Analysis

	1960s	1970s
The purpose of policy analysis	Search for comprehensive rationality	Search for rationality
Underlying values	Efficiency, effectiveness	Efficiency, effectiveness, safety, health, environmental protection, accountability, responsiveness
Methods	Quantification of costs and benefits	Quantification of costs and benefits where possible
Assumptions	Belief in a common metric	Recognition of diverse goals
Requisite professional skills	Economics	Variable (natural science, economics, accounting, law)
Locus of policy analysis	Concentration of analytic resources	Diffusion of analytic resources
Conception of policy analysis	A specialized enterprise	A shared activity
The timing of policy analysis	Prospective	Prospective, retrospective
Focus	Spending	Spending, regulation, rulemaking, enforcement
Relationship between policy analysis and politics	Antithetical	Complementary
Examples	PPBS, Systems analysis	Environmental impact statements, regulatory impact analyses and regulatory review, zero-based budgeting, the "new" General Accounting Office, the "hard look" doctrine

There are a number of questions to ask in assessing the policy analysis reforms of the 1970s. Did they promote the utilization of good, sound research? Did they encourage agencies to consider alternatives that would otherwise have escaped their attention? Did they convince agencies to take a "hard look" at the evidence? Did they encourage caution where caution was warranted? Did they permit innovation where innovation was needed? Did they broaden the perspectives of single-mission agencies? These are some of the questions that need to be answered.

Environmental Impact Statements

The first federal statute signed into law in 1970 was the National Environmental Policy Act (NEPA). The National Environmental Policy Act established a new federal commitment to environmental protection (e.g., the pursuit of productive harmony between man and nature) and created a new agency within the Executive Office of the President, the Council on Environmental Quality. In addition, it required federal agencies to prepare an environmental impact statement for all major actions "significantly affecting the quality of the human environment." It also required federal agencies to consider the merits of various alternatives and to utilize a systematic, interdisciplinary approach in planning and decision making.

The National Environmental Policy Act's environmental impact statement requirement has been heralded as the most innovative and most controversial feature of the act (Caldwell, 1975: 79). That is because the environmental impact statement requirement marked a new approach to bureaucratic policy analysis. That approach has sometimes been described as "action-forcing" or as an effort to promote "comprehensive rationality." Yet NEPA is not so much action-forcing as it is thought-forcing (the bureaucracy need not act, but when it does act, it must think about certain questions). Nor does NEPA seek to promote synoptic decision making. Unlike PPBS, it does not ask agencies to quantify intangible values and convert them into a common metric.

The National Environmental Policy Act's environmental impact statement requirement is perhaps best described as a catalytic control. It forces federal agencies to take environmental protection seriously without precluding or mandating specific substantive action. It does not require agencies to choose the alternative least harmful to the environment; however, it does require agencies to think carefully—and in writing—about alternatives. It prods the bureaucracy without narrowing bureaucratic options. Indeed, it broadens the perspective of single-mission agencies and expands the options available to such agencies.

The timing of the environmental impact statement is also important. All too often, policy analysis comes too late—after the cow has already fled the barn. Under such circumstances, bureaucratic policy analysis tends toward rationalization, defensiveness and self-justification. If self-evaluation has failed in the past, that is because agencies have been asked to evaluate decisions already made—decisions involving considerable "sunk costs," investments in established practices. In contrast, the environmental impact statement precedes final agency action. Although there is no guarantee that it will shape agency decisions, provisions for public scrutiny and judicial review encourage agencies to incorporate its insights into their plans. In this respect, NEPA recognizes that policy analysis is both a technocratic and a political exercise. While encouraging bureaucratic rationality, it also enables citizens and judges to challenge the bureaucracy's conception of rational decision making.

If it is ignored, an environmental impact statement may trigger a series of lawsuits and judicial reversals. Catalytic controls may give way to hortatory controls or even to coercive controls. Indeed, this spiraling effect has been observed in some instances. However, the EIS itself is fundamentally a prayer—an entreaty that is both respectful and earnest. If the agency responds by thinking soberly about environmental impacts, it has little to fear. Moreover, the agency has considerable discretion in its formulation of a response.

Following the passage of NEPA, many states adopted similar statutes, known as state environmental policy acts or SEPAS (Pearlman, 1977). Most state environmental policy acts parallel the federal statute in crucial respects (e.g., they provide for the issuance of environmental impact statements). However, some SEPAS are stronger than their federal counterpart. For example, Connecticut's statute expressly requires attention not only to primary environmental impacts but to secondary impacts as well. Also, a number of SEPAS extend the environmental impact statement requirement to the activities of local governments. Thus, in California environmental impact statements must be prepared for subdivision permits, local rezoning, and the proposed annexation of land by a city.

Environmental impact statements at both the federal and state levels have been disappointing in some respects. During the early 1970s, many environmental impact statements were skimpy and superficial; agencies, it seemed, did not take them seriously enough (Andrews, 1976). Later, many environmental impact statements were bulky and ponderous; to avoid judicial reversal, some agencies threw in everything but the kitchen sink. In the process, agencies blurred the distinction between critical and noncritical problems (Bardach and Pugliaresi, 1977). In other respects, the quality of environmental impact statements has often left a great deal to be desired. Some critics have noted weaknesses in the quality of their scientific analyses (Fairfax, 1978); others have noted insufficient attention being paid to social impacts, e.g., the effects of policies on cultural or ethnic subgroups or on the human community as a system (Friesema and Culhane, 1976). Perhaps the most serious criticism of environmental impact statements is that they have been ignored by certain agencies. For example, Andrews (1976) found that the number of watershed projects authorized by the Soil Conservation Service (scs) actually increased following the passage of NEPA. Although this was not flatly inconsistent with NEPA, it did suggest a certain hastiness inconsistent with the spirit of the statute.

Clearly, NEPA did not usher in the millennium. Environmental impact statements are often weak and their effects are often minimal. Perhaps the latter reflects the former. On the other hand, a considerable body of evidence confirms that NEPA has altered administrative decisions both directly and indirectly. Hill and Ortolano (1978), though critical of environmental impact statements, nevertheless found that approximately one-half of all Army Corps of Engineers respondents and one-third of scs respondents could point to new alternatives or project modifications that stemmed from environmental impact statements. Typical modifications included the limitation of some channel work, fish and wildlife mitigation and enhancement measures, the purchase of additional land for wildlife habitation, and different levels of flood protection. Similarly, Friesema and Culhane (1976) estimated that environmental impact statements altered Forest Service decisions about one-half of the time. In particular, impact statements helped the Forest Service to impose more stringent controls on development in national forests.

The effects of environmental impact statement requirements on the Corps of Engineers are especially impressive. Long regarded as an agency that built first and asked questions later, the corps was the bête noire of environmentalists. Consequently, many observers expected that the corps would drag its feet when NEPA was passed. In some corps districts, that appears to have been the case. However, the corps' central office strongly supported NEPA and many district offices followed its lead. As early as October 1971, the corps had canceled, postponed or significantly changed 20 percent of the projects for which detailed statements had been prepared (Andrews, 1976: 80). By 1973 the corps was beginning to give serious consideration to nonstructural alternatives for flooding problems. This constituted a major aboutface for an agency long accused of suffering from an "edifice complex."

The indirect effects of NEPA, although these are more difficult to document, are probably of equal or greater importance than the direct effects. In order to prepare environmental impact statements, the corps and other agencies hired significant numbers of biologists, botanists, chemists, hydrologists, and other scientists. To varying degrees these scientists working alongside engineers began to play an important role in the administrative decision-making process. For example, scientists in seven of eleven corps districts felt that they were involved in multidisciplinary planning (Mazmanian and Nienaber, 1979: 54). In nine out of eleven districts scientists recommended necessary project changes.

In addition, the environmental impact statement gave citizens' groups leverage to use in court. In this instance, policy analysis promoted not only rationality but interest representation as well. Approximately one out of every ten environmental impact statements has been challenged in court, many by citizens' groups.[2] Although environmental groups did not always win NEPA-related cases, they scored some significant victories (Liroff, 1976: 142–88; Wenner, 1982: 82–84). In addition, it should be noted that litigation often resulted in project modifications in districts where lawsuits were filed, though not necessarily in the projects against which the suits were filed (Andrews, 1976: 74). Thus even when agency personnel reacted defensively to judicial review, they modified other plans to avoid provoking similar challenges.

Environmental impact statements have not put an end to costly environmentally damaging dams, harbors, highways, power plants, and watershed projects. However, they have forced agencies to consider environmental impacts, to reduce them where possible, and to consider alternatives. This has not yielded comprehensive rationality but it has produced a more rational administrative decision-making process. Moreover, it has encouraged making project modifications and cancellations early in the decision-making process, before "sunk costs" become so huge that changes of direction are difficult to make.

According to Wildavsky (1979: 393–95), successful policy analysis requires both error identification and error correction. Envi-

2. During the early 1970s most plaintiffs in NEPA lawsuits were environmental groups. By the late 1970s industrial plaintiffs were as numerous as environmental plaintiffs (Liroff, 1981).

ronmental impact statements encourage error identification by forcing agencies to specify the premises behind their construction decisions and by giving citizens and judges a chance to rebut those presumptions; they also encourage error correction by providing policy analysis, citizen input, and judicial review at an early stage.[3] Finally, they encourage both error identification and error correction by encouraging agencies to hire professionals with diverse perspectives. The policy analysis that flows from this interdisciplinary dialogue is often illuminating and worthwhile.

Regulatory Impact Analyses

During the 1970s the White House required federal agencies to assess the costs and benefits of proposed rules and regulations before adopting them. These assessments in the form of inflation impact statements or regulatory impact analyses were to be submitted to the White House for review. Regulatory impact analyses, like environmental impact statements, were aimed at broadening the perspective of single-mission agencies. If some agencies were thought to be insensitive to environmental impacts, others were thought to be insensitive to economic impacts. By requiring agencies to take the costs of proposed rules into account, the White House hoped to promote such goals as economic efficiency and cost effectiveness.

The initial step in this direction was taken by President Nixon in 1971 when he instructed environmental, health, and safety agencies to submit drafts of proposed rules and regulations to the Office of Management and Budget (OMB), which in turn would invite other agencies to conduct "quality of life reviews." In practice, this requirement focused almost exclusively on the Environmental Protection Agency (EPA), which found its proposals attacked by the Department of Commerce and other agencies with close ties to the business community.

In 1974 President Ford further institutionalized the regulatory review process by requiring federal agencies[4] to prepare inflation

3. Wildavsky, a critic of the environmental movement, would probably dispute this application of his terminology. He might argue that environmentalists obstruct our view of certain errors by exaggerating the risks to public health and by ignoring the opportunity costs of environmental protection.

4. Independent regulatory commissions considered themselves exempt from Ford's executive order and from subsequent executive orders mandating White House review of regulatory rules. Presidents have accepted this exemption in practice, though they have not conceded the point in theory.

TABLE 6.2

White House Regulatory Review Strategies

Executive Action	Coverage	Documents Required	Reviewing Agency	Power to Reject	Nature of Control
Quality of Life Reviews–Nixon (1971–1976)	Regulations affecting health, safety, environmental quality (primarily EPA decisions)	Draft proposals	Interagency review, co-ordinated by OMB (budget staff)	None	advisory
Inflation Impact Statements, Council on Wage and Price Stability (COWPS)—Ford (1974–1977)	Major proposals (determined by agencies)	Quantified costs and benefits, to the extent possible	COWPS, OMB (management staff)	None	hortatory
Regulatory Analysis Review Group (RARG)—Carter (1978–1980)	Major regulations (determined by agencies, with guidelines from OMB)	Quantified costs and benefits, to the extent possible	OMB (delegated to COWPS, CEA), RARG, also Regulatory Council	None	hortatory
Executive Order 12,291, Task Force on Regulatory Relief—Reagan (1981–1988)	Major rules (determined by OMB), with exemptions granted for deregulatory proposals	Quantified costs and benefits	OMB (Office of Information & Regulatory Affairs), also Regulatory Relief Task Force (supported by OMB staff)	Yes (OMB may delay publication of proposed rule indefinitely)	coercive

impact statements when drafting "major" rules, regulations, or legislative proposals.[5] In these inflation impact statements, agencies were to quantify benefits and costs to the extent possible and to consider alternatives to the proposed course of action. The inflation impact statements were then submitted to the Council on

5. During the Ford years, it was up to each agency to decide what constituted a "major" rule.

Wage and Price Stability (COWPS) and OMB for review and comment.

In 1978 President Carter further refined the regulatory review process by specifying that major regulations were those with a $100 million impact or those that were likely to trigger a major price increase. Under Carter's executive order, regulatory analysis statements were to be submitted to OMB, which delegated review authority to COWPS and to the Council of Economic Advisers (CEA). Carter also created a Regulatory Analysis Review Group (RARG), chaired by the head of the CEA, which was to select approximately twenty major proposals per year for intensive scrutiny and analysis.

The regulatory review process under Presidents Ford and Carter was relatively informal and flexible. Costs and benefits were to be quantified to the extent feasible, but there was no requirement for a formal cost-benefit analysis. Alternatives were to be examined, but there was no requirement that the least costly alternative be adopted. The process was best described as an exercise in hortatory control. Through the regulatory review process, the White House exerted pressure on administrative agencies but did not stipulate a single overriding goal for the federal bureaucracy. In effect, the White House recognized that cost control, however important, was not the sole criterion for good public policy.

Agency responses to these requirements varied considerably. According to one account, the EPA's inflation impact assessments were of high quality; statements prepared by the Federal Energy Administration (FEA), the Department of Transportation (DOT) and the Occupational Safety and Health Administration (OSHA) were poorer (Vernon, 1977). A common tendency was to focus on direct compliance costs for particular industries and firms, ignoring indirect and opportunity costs (DeMuth, 1980). Other common problems that persist to this day include: the relative neglect of benefits, the failure to distinguish between transfer payments and efficiency losses, paying too little attention to distributional issues, too little attention to alternatives, making too little use of sensitivity analysis or other techniques to cope with uncertainty, and the use of a questionable discount rate (Grubb et al., 1984).

In contrast to assessments prepared by agencies, evaluations by RARG during the Carter years were consistently of high quality. However, RARG evaluations, which were expected to be selective (twenty proposals per year), proved to be even more selective than was originally envisioned. After two years, RARG had reviewed only nine agency regulations (DeMuth, 1980).

Despite their limitations, regulatory impact analyses and occasional RARG reviews appear to have done some good. In response to criticism from COWPS, the EPA revised its motorcycle emissions standards, OSHA conducted a more detailed economic assessment of its occupational safety noise standards, and DOT further studied the costs and benefits of its occupant crash protection program (Vernon, 1977). In broader terms, COWPS reviews resulted in some improvement between the proposed and the final form of a rule in seventeen of twenty-four cases (Portney, 1984). Regulatory Analysis Review Group reviews, though infrequent, also appear to have been modestly successful. According to one study (Litan and Nordhaus, 1983: 69–76), RARG reviews resulted in rule modifications in four out of six instances.

Admittedly, RARG interventions were unsuccessful in at least two highly celebrated cases. Charles Schultze, chairman of the CEA and of RARG, was unable to persuade EPA Administrator Douglas Costle to relax his agency's ozone standard. Schultze was also unable to convince OSHA to relax a controversial cotton dust standard. However, in both of these instances, the agencies were operating under a strong mandate from Congress. Thus, in resisting pressure from RARG, the agencies at least arguably were pursuing their statutory mission.

During the 1970s regulatory review by the White House sensitized health and safety agencies to economic considerations, enlarged the menu of alternatives, and contributed to a more rational decision-making process. This changed abruptly, however, when President Reagan took office. In 1981 President Reagan issued an executive order (number 12,291) transforming regulatory review in several key respects. Under the Reagan administration, federal agencies were required to conduct a formal cost-benefit analysis when drafting any major rule or regulation. Having done so, they were to choose the alternative involving the least net cost to society, unless expressly prohibited from doing so by law. If it was dissatisfied with the agency's regulatory impact analysis, OMB could delay publication of the proposed rule indefinitely, unless overruled by the President's Task Force on Regulatory Relief. The very title of that task force confirmed a blurring of the distinction between economic efficiency and regulatory relief.

With Executive Order number 12,291 President Reagan effectively instituted a new form of MBO—Management by Objections.

By objecting to a proposed rule, OMB could in practice quash the rule. The Office of Management and Budget's role was not hortatory but coercive. In addition, OMB's administration of Executive Order 12,291 was highly capricious, though not, one supposes, contrary to the president's desires. While objecting regularly to new rules and regulations, OMB simultaneously exempted deregulatory rules from the regulatory impact analysis requirement. In doing so, it redefined rationality as the singleminded pursuit of market solutions. Instead of broadening agency perspectives, OMB narrowed agency perspectives, forcing agencies to place regulatory relief ahead of other goals. It also elevated cost-benefit analysis from a useful tool to the litmus test of good public policy, deregulation excepted.

In a sense, cost-benefit analysis has always been a double-edged sword. As Andrews (1982) has observed, cost-benefit analysis may be viewed as an idealistic search for greater rationality (better policy analysis) or as the use of analytical requirements to support particular purposes and constituencies (political control). Under the Reagan administration, cost-benefit analysis became so politicized that its original rationale was obscured. But it is not just the politicization of cost-benefit analysis that is troublesome. The formalization of cost-benefit analysis attributes too much accuracy to an analytic technique that is at best a rough and imprecise guide to future consequences.[6]

An additional problem, often noted, is that cost-benefit analysis tells us nothing about the distributive consequences of alternative projects. Recognizing this, some states have wisely opted not for cost-benefit analysis but for economic assessments as guides to policymakers. In Illinois, for example, the Institute of Natural Resources must carry out economic impact assessments for all proposals presented to the Illinois Pollution Control Board. These economic impact assessments must take the distributional effects of policies into account. The impacts on agriculture, local governments, commerce, and industry must be examined separately (Croke and Herlevsen, 1982). In comparison to federal cost-benefit studies, these economic impact assessments provide valuable information on sectoral impacts. Here as in other areas state

6. The problems with discount rates have already been noted. In addition, cost-benefit analysis routinely overestimates compliance costs because it assumes static technology. In environmental policy, this ignores the realities of "technology-forcing," which expedites the pace of technological change and reduces the costs of compliance.

reformers have improved upon the practices of their federal counterparts.

Budget Reform

In 1974 Congress dramatically overhauled its budget-making machinery through passage of the Congressional Budget and Impoundment and Control Act. In addition to creating House and Senate budget committees and a Congressional Budget Office, Congress established a series of self-imposed deadlines to help keep pace with the executive branch. Congress also took steps to curb impoundment, a practice that had grown out of hand during the Nixon years.[7]

The congressional budget reforms of 1974, though important, were not really intended to control the bureaucracy. Rather, they were aimed at strengthening congressional control over the president and his budget staff. In some instances, a stronger congressional role in budgeting might be disadvantageous to the bureaucracy, to the extent that the bureaucracy shares the president's objectives. In other instances, however, a stronger congressional presence might be advantageous to the bureaucracy, e.g., when the bureaucracy favors the expenditure of funds appropriated by Congress but impounded by the president.

Thus, it is unclear whether the creation of the Congressional Budget Office (CBO) has reduced the power of the federal bureaucracy. Certainly, the CBO has given Congress a valuable analytical tool in its dealings with the president and OMB. Moreover, it appears that CBO outlay estimates and economic forecasts have been more accurate than those of the White House (Schick, 1980: 164–65). However, the love-hate relationship between the White House and the federal bureaucracy makes it difficult to assess the overall consequences of this development for the bureaucracy.

In one instance, budget reform has been explicitly aimed at administrative agencies, as opposed to the chief executive. Zero-based budgeting (ZBB)—the heir apparent to PPBS—was indeed an effort to promote efficiency and effectiveness by changing the budgeting procedures of administrative agencies. In discussing ZBB, it is important to distinguish between pure ZBB (which has

7. Under the 1974 law, the president may delay spending funds appropriated by Congress (impoundment). However, the president must eventually spend these funds unless Congress explicitly authorizes a funding cutback.

never been tried) and modified ZBB (as adopted by the federal government, at least twenty-five states, and a number of local governments). Jimmy Carter, who popularized ZBB, preached in favor of pure ZBB but settled for modified ZBB in practice—in Georgia and later at the federal level. As described by Carter, (pure) ZBB is a revolutionary budgeting technique that abandons incrementalism in favor of "total rejustification of everything from scratch—from zero" (Lauth, 1980: 115). If taken literally, this would require a wholesale reevaluation of every spending decision the government has ever made over the years. There is of course not enough time for such an exercise in synoptic decision making; moreover, there is very little enthusiasm for such an approach within the bureaucracy, where threats to dismantle well-established programs are viewed with alarm. Pure ZBB is a fiction, and politicians do little good by pretending otherwise in their speeches.

In contrast, modified ZBB does not mean starting from scratch but does mean that the previous year's budget base is not taken for granted. Thus in Georgia agencies were required to prepare alternative budgets for each program, based on different levels of effort in comparison with the previous year, e.g., 85 percent of the previous budget, 100 percent, 110 percent. Agency officials were then required to present programs in the form of decision packages that were ranked from the most to the least desirable. Modified ZBB is an exercise in generating alternatives and setting priorities. Although it is demanding, time-consuming, and somewhat threatening, it is more realistic than PPBS, which assumed that all programs could be evaluated on the same interval scale. In contrast to PPBS, modified ZBB merely assumes that managers are capable of ranking their programs on an ordinal scale. On the other hand, it does ask a lot of agency officials, because it is not easy to rank a wide variety of programs and because no program manager likes to provide superiors with a blueprint for sharp program cutbacks.

If Georgia's experience is any indication, modified ZBB appears to have been less successful than expected but more successful than PPBS. Despite ZBB, agency officials continued to start from their current budget, working backward and forward to generate alternatives for reduced and increased funding levels. Whether one looks at the budget-making process or at budget outputs over time, ZBB has not put an end to incremental budgeting in Georgia. There is no evidence of substantial spending reductions or significant funding reallocations across departments (Lauth, 1980).

On the other hand, modified ZBB has had some beneficial results not only in Georgia but in other states (LaFever, 1974), at the local level (Wholey, 1978), and at the federal level (Lynn, 1981: 81–84). It does seem to have provided useful information to managers, and it has encouraged managers to do a better job of justifying requests for funding increases. It has gotten program managers more involved in a process that might otherwise be dominated by accountants. In contrast to PPBS, it has tried to improve the budget-making process from the "bottom up" rather than the "top down." Finally, it has generated interest in program evaluation as a technique for promoting efficiency and effectiveness.

In the formal sense, ZBB is no longer utilized by the federal government or by Georgia, where it began. Indeed, in the formal sense, it can be found today only in Iowa and a handful of other jurisdictions. One might infer from this that ZBB has failed. Yet as Rose (1980) has suggested, some procedural innovations "evaporate" over time. While they cease to exist as a formal part of government, they are nevertheless absorbed into the managerial culture. This appears to have happened to ZBB. Despite the formal demise of ZBB, its kind of emphasis on the generation of alternatives, of program comparisons, and on the connection between program evaluation and budgeting endures.

In a way, the legacy of both ZBB and PPBS is a budget process that approximates Etzioni's (1967, 1986) conception of "mixed scanning." Agencies are encouraged to use both a wide-angle lens and a zoom lens in preparing their budget requests. In effect, agency officials scan the environment for a range of options, then narrow their focus to one or two of these, which they then analyze in detail. Fundamental strategic choices based on more information than ever before are succeeded by narrow, routine decisions that recognize the limitations of the human mind. "Giant steps" are followed by "baby steps." If this approach differs from synoptic rationality, it also differs from incrementalism. Budgetmaking today is not entirely rational, but it is more rational than it used to be—no small achievement.

The New General Accounting Office

For the most part, the policy analysis reforms of the 1970s relied on the bureaucracy to conduct policy analysis, subject to a variety of external constraints (review by the courts, the White House, and so forth). An exception to this general rule was the revitalization of the General Accounting Office—an effort to control the bureaucracy through legislative policy analysis. The General Accounting Office, created in 1921, had long been responsible for conducting financial audits of federal agencies to ensure that federal funds were being properly spent. An arm of Congress, the GAO was nevertheless headed by a presidential appointee, the comptroller general, who served a fifteen-year term and could be fired only with the greatest difficulty. This arrangement helped to insulate the GAO from political pressures and contributed to its reputation as a nonpartisan, professional watchdog agency.

During the 1960s, as program evaluation blossomed, the GAO became increasingly restive and uncomfortable with its traditional role. The Comptroller General, Elmer Staats, and other top officials at the GAO concluded that the agency would become irrelevant unless it became actively involved in program evaluation and policy analysis. Toward that end, the GAO began to hire professionals other than accountants—policy analysts, systems analysts, operations researchers, planners, statisticians, social scientists, and other professionals capable of conducting program evaluation and policy analysis. The Congress, receptive to these developments, officially authorized the GAO to conduct various program evaluations, such as an evaluation of the War on Poverty.

In 1970 the Congress expressly endorsed the GAO's growing interest in program evaluation and policy analysis. The Legislative Reorganization Act of 1970 provided for the Comptroller General to "review and analyze the results of Government programs and activities carried on under existing law, including the making of cost benefit studies," when instructed by members of Congress or congressional committees or on his own initiative. In response to this and other congressional mandates, the GAO took concrete steps to upgrade and institutionalize its policy analysis efforts. In 1974 the GAO established an Office of Program Review and Evaluation, which later evolved into the Program Analysis Division. The GAO also endorsed congressional proposals to shift some of the GAO's auditing responsibilities to the agencies themselves. By the end of the 1970s the GAO had been able to shed some of its auditing responsibilities and to move aggressively into the fields of program evaluation and policy analysis. According to one scholar (Mosher, 1979: 178), 49 percent of the GAO's reports in 1977 focused on program results, as opposed to 30 percent five years earlier.

As the GAO's role changed, its importance grew. The number of GAO reports increased dramatically, from approximately four hundred per year during the late 1960s to approximately eight hundred per year during the late 1970s (U.S. GAO, 1981). A growing number of GAO reports received considerable publicity. According to one estimate (Mosher, 1979: 248), the number of GAO reports that received nationwide, in-depth media coverage grew from 31 in 1972 to 180 in 1976, approximately one every other day. General Accounting Office officials were also in great demand as expert witnesses. During the late 1960s GAO officials testified on Capitol Hill approximately thirty times per year; during the late 1970s GAO officials testified approximately 156 times per year (U.S. GAO, 1981). By the 1980s the GAO had become the single most important policy analysis shop in the federal government.

Commentary on the GAO in the scholarly literature and in the popular press has been almost uniformly favorable (Morse, 1978; Mosher, 1979; Mosher, 1984). The agency has been given high marks for its professionalism, its timeliness, and its relevance. The agency is credited with having reduced the costs of government, having made constructive recommendations to Congress, and having kept administrative agencies on their toes. Yet there is reason to wonder whether the impacts of GAO reports on administrative agencies are always so benign. The GAO's emphasis on efficiency, effectiveness, and accountability is difficult to criticize. If the GAO can promote these goals, it is performing a valuable function. But the GAO's commitment to speed, compliance, immediate results, and maximum embarrassment is more problematic, especially when carried to an extreme. Consider, for example, some of the most common themes of GAO reports and how these may be perceived by agency officials:

1. *Speed*. Signal Sent—Agencies should move promptly to enforce the law. Signal Received—It is more important to make quick decisions than to make good decisions.[8]

2. *Compliance*. Signal Sent—Agencies should comply with the law. Signal Received—It is more important to adhere to the letter of the law than it is to solve the policy problems that led to passage of the law in the first place.

3. *Results*. Signal Sent—Agencies should demonstrate progress in meeting congressional goals. Signal Received—If it's

8. A variation on the same theme is the following: Signal Sent—Agencies should move promptly to spend money allocated by Congress. Signal Received—It is more important to spend money quickly than to spend it wisely.

too early to demonstrate real progress, resources should be diverted from outcomes to outputs in order to create the illusion of progress.

4. *Embarrassment.* Signal Sent—Agencies that misbehave will be publicly embarrassed. Signal Received—It is better to avoid embarrassment today than to earn praise tomorrow.

In emphasizing speed, compliance, immediate results, and maximum embarrassment, the GAO no doubt is producing the kind of policy analysis Congress desires. But is this kind of policy analysis as constructive as is commonly supposed? If incrementalism is the problem, is the solution speed or innovation? If parochialism is the problem, is the solution to be found in new data or new attitudes? If legislative goals are contradictory and confusing, is compliance a meaningful concept? If program success depends on bureaucratic commitment and program credibility, does it really make sense to destroy both bureaucratic morale and public support?

Critical to the GAO's "successes" are its muckraking style, its tendency to focus on rotten apples in the barrel, and its willingness to extrapolate based on extreme cases. When the GAO goes after a target, it does so with a vengeance. Small wonder that muckraking journalists find the GAO so appealing. General Accounting Office reports confirm two of the muckrakers' favorite beliefs—that fraud and abuse in government are rampant; and that the bureaucracy is slow and recalcitrant. As a result, a GAO report is frequently the tip of a large iceberg. When an agency is attacked by the GAO, there is usually a triple whammy: a GAO report, a congressional hearing, and adverse media coverage. An agency that has been GAO-ed is unlikely to forget it!

Critical reviews by the GAO, though unpleasant, can improve the performance of sheltered agencies whose programs are stable, well-established, and not very visible. A GAO report is a good cure for bureaucratic smugness. Thus, GAO reports on the Social Security Administration's disability claims processing system led to significant reforms of the agency's quality assurance program (Mashaw, 1983: 153–57). The GAO's study of the Department of Labor's federal employee disability program brought important problems to light, such as the use of forced disability retirements to get problem workers off the payroll (Causey, 1979). A GAO study of the Smithsonian Institution helped to clear up conflicts of interest and questionable banking procedures (Editorial, *Washington Post* 1977). Occasional studies of state bureaucracies such as public utility commissions and state insurance commissions have helped to identify important problems and possible solutions.

However, GAO reports can do a great deal of damage to new, fragile programs that cannot be successfully implemented overnight. A highly visible but vulnerable program, fighting for survival, may be so badly discredited that it never recovers. This appears to have been the case with the Comprehensive Employment and Training Act (CETA) program, which the GAO (along with congressional committees and muckraking journalists) portrayed as a veritable sinkhole of fraud and abuse. Following critical reports by the GAO and much adverse publicity, Congress tightened the screws, placing administrative compliance with spending restrictions ahead of all other values, including job creation. Eventually, CETA's failure became inevitable, as local governments paid more attention to federal paperwork than to possibilities for new approaches to employment problems (Baumer and Van Horn, 1985: 125–56).

A highly visible but popular program may also be harmed by a GAO report, though in different ways. Here there is no serious danger that the program will be terminated. However, there is the very real possibility of goal displacement, as agencies scramble to escape the unwelcome glare of adverse publicity. This may have happened to state hazardous waste management offices, accused by the GAO of moving too slowly on the enforcement front. After the initial resentment fades away, agency officials are likely to respond with rigid enforcement, playing a "numbers game" that will satisfy the GAO and other overseers. In Bardach and Kagan's words (1982), they are apt to "go by the book." This is likely to spell an end to improvization, imagination, and innovation. It may also divert attention from hazardous waste operators with deplorable records. Whether that is intended or not, GAO reports often encourage agencies to place outputs ahead of outcomes, to blur the distinction between urgent and less urgent problems, and to substitute impressive statistics in the short run for impressive performance in the long run.

It is difficult to know for sure whether the GAO's behavior is due to its ties to Congress, its domination by accountants, or both. In a sense, both characteristics incline the GAO in the same direction. As an accounting agency, the GAO believes in ferreting out fraud and abuse and expects full and immediate compliance with the law. As a congressional support agency, the GAO has incentives to emphasize similar priorities. Odd as it may seem, GAO accountants are probably more "legalistic" in their orientation than bureaucratic lawyers. To an agency lawyer, law enforcement is an important option, used most effectively as a threat. To a GAO accountant, law enforcement is the ultimate good and the principal criterion for measuring agency performance. General Accounting Office accountants and other GAO officials routinely out-lawyer the lawyers.

There are two different ways to assess the transformation of the GAO from a low-profile auditing agency into a high-profile policy analysis agency. The conventional interpretation emphasizes that an agency once dominated by accountants and devoted to auditing has become multidisciplinary in its composition, multifaceted in its methodologies, and diversified in its activities (Mosher, 1979, 1984). All of this is true. Yet it is equally true that an agency historically commited to accounting has in recent years become the single most powerful policy analysis shop in the federal government. Had the GAO not changed with the times, program evaluation and policy analysis responsibilities might have been vested in the Congressional Research Service, a legislative office of policy analysis and program evaluation, or perhaps in the executive branch. Such an office, never dominated by accountants, might have taken a different approach to policy analysis than that pursued by the GAO. Instead of emphasizing compliance with the letter of the law, it might have emphasized problem-solving. Instead of emphasizing quantifiable indicators of progress, it might have utilized both quantitative and qualitative measures of performance. Instead of rewarding speed, it might have rewarded innovation and imagination. The more one considers the transformation of the GAO, the more one realizes that this was no setback for accountants but a remarkable *tour de force* for an agency that might otherwise have become obsolete. The salient fact is not that accountants have become less numerous at the GAO but rather that an accounting agency has acquired enormous influence within the federal government.

The Hard Look Doctrine

Unlike Congress, the federal courts do not have their own stable of policy analysts. However, this has not prevented the courts from restructuring bureaucratic policy analysis authoritatively and profoundly through something known as the "hard look" doctrine. The hard look doctrine provides for strong substantive judicial review of administrative agency actions, including close and careful scrutiny of technical decisions. In invoking the hard look doctrine, judges ask whether agencies have taken a "hard look" at all relevant factors and alternatives. In addition, they assure themselves that the agency's findings are supported by the record and that the agency's ultimate policy choice is reasonable. In the words of the late Judge Harold Leventhal, "The function of the court is to assure that the agency has given reasoned consideration to all the material facts and issues" (*Greater Boston TV Corp. v. FCC*, 1970).

The hard look doctrine originated in 1969 when Judge Leventhal of the prestigious D.C. Circuit Court of Appeals articulated it in a pair of cases involving the Federal Communications Commission (*Pikes Peak Broadcasting Co. v. FCC*, 1969; *WAIT Radio v. FCC*, 1969). The hard look doctrine also received a surprising boost from the U.S. Supreme Court when it struck down a Department of Transportation decision on the grounds that the secretary had failed to take all relevant factors into account and had made a clear error of judgment (*Citizens to Preserve Overton Park v. Volpe*, 1971). The *Overton Park* ruling was important and surprising because it involved an informal agency decision, supposedly free from the strict evidentiary requirements that the Administrative Procedure Act imposes for formal decision making on the record. In effect, *Overton Park* paved the way for stringent judicial scrutiny of administrative agency actions in informal proceedings.

Although the Supreme Court subsequently eschewed the *Overton Park* standard, other courts embraced it with alacrity (Shapiro, 1983). The same was true of the hard look doctrine, not easily distinguished from the *Overton Park* standard. During the 1970s the number of decisions in which federal appellate courts explicitly invoked the hard look doctrine steadily increased.[9] During this same period the use of the doctrine spread from the D.C. Circuit Court of Appeals to other circuits as well. One reason for the growing popularity of the hard look doctrine with its emphasis on strong substantive judicial review is that strong procedural review was running into trouble. In 1978 the Supreme Court sternly rebuked lower courts for imposing procedural requirements above and beyond those required by the Administrative Procedure Act (*Vermont Yankee Nuclear Power v. NRDC*, 1978). This decision left federal ap-

9. A LEXIS search of federal appeals court decisions using "hard look" language reveals a 50 percent increase in hard look decisions from the early 1970s (1970–1974) to the late 1970s (1975–1979).

peals courts few alternatives besides strong substantive review, at one extreme, and judicial deference, at the other.

The hard look doctrine has been characterized by some scholars as an attempt to ensure fidelity to legislative intent (Garland, 1985; Bruff, 1984). Yet while many hard look cases do involve extensive inquiries into legislative history, such inquiries are often ancillary to the heart of the case. In *International Harvester Co. v. Ruckelshaus*, 1973, Judge Leventhal conducted an extensive inquiry into the legislative history of the Clean Air Act Amendments but ultimately found little legislative guidance on what he regarded as the key issue of the case—the reasonableness and reliability of the EPA's methodology. In other cases where the courts have engaged in strong substantive review, legislative intent has been equally obscure (e.g., *Columbia Gas Transmission Corp. v. FERC*, 1979).

In assessing the hard look doctrine, other scholars have characterized it as a movement toward synoptic rationality or comprehensive problem-solving (Diver, 1981; Shapiro, 1983; Bruff, 1984). While this comes closer to the truth, it goes too far. The hard look doctrine does indeed promote rationality but not comprehensive rationality. The courts have expected a great deal of administrative agencies, but they have repeatedly declined to require formal cost-benefit analysis (*Portland Cement Assoc. v. Ruckelshaus*, 1973; *Industrial Union Dept. v. American Petroleum Institute*, 1980; *American Textile Manufacturers Institute v. Donovan*, 1981). Instead, they have insisted that agencies take economic feasibility, technological feasibility, and other pertinent factors into account. The courts have insisted on reasonableness but they have not asked for comprehensive rationality.

In several respects, the hard look doctrine resembles other attempts to promote administrative rationality. Like requirements for environmental impact statements and regulatory impact analyses, the hard look doctrine requires administrative agencies to take a serious look at alternatives. Like environmental impact statements and regulatory impact analyses, the hard look doctrine broadens the perspective of single-mission agencies and single-minded administrators (see, for example, *U.S. v. Nova Scotia Food Products Corp.*, 1977; *H&H Tire Co. v. Department of Transportation*, 1972). Like zero-based budgeting, the hard look doctrine requires administrators to clarify their thinking and to make their assumptions explicit. Like all of these reforms, the hard look doctrine encourages reasoned decision making.

However, the hard look doctrine also differs in several critical

TABLE 6.3

Policy Analysis as a Form of Bureaucratic Control

Mechanism	Analysis	Time Frame	Value Invoked	Focus	Discipline
Environmental Impact Statement Requirement (NEPA)	internal, subject to judicial review	mainly prospective	environmental protection	construction decisions, licensing decisions, stream channelization decisions	multi-disciplinary
Regulatory Impact Requirement (Ford, Carter)	internal, subject to review by OMB, COWPS or RARG	mainly prospective	efficiency, cost-effectiveness	major regulatory rules (e.g., with impacts exceeding $100 million)	Economics
Zero-Based Budgeting (modified version)	internal, subject to review by central budget office	prospective	efficiency, effectiveness	spending recommendations, program design	Business Administration, Public Administration
The New General Accounting Office (program evaluation, policy analysis)	external, with rebuttal opportunities	mainly retrospective	accountability, compliance, efficiency, effectiveness	practices, procedures, implementation	Accounting, Social Sciences
Hard Look Doctrine (Leventhal et al.)	internal, subject to judicial review	retrospective	rationality	rules and other decisions	Law

respects from other policy analysis reforms of this period. First of all, it is the only one of these reforms that is both retrospective and coercive. In this respect, the hard look doctrine has much in common with the legislative veto. The hard look doctrine is a particularly intimidating form of judicial review. In effect it says that even if an agency has been faithful to legislative intent and has followed all the procedural requirements imposed by the Administrative Procedure Act, it may still be reversed by the courts if a federal judge does not find the agency's reasoning persuasive or compelling. As a result of the hard look doctrine, judicial review is far less predictable than it used to be. Prior to the development of the hard look doctrine, an agency could predict the scope of judicial review with some precision, based on the degree of formality in the agency's decision-making process. That distinction has broken down as judges have applied the hard look doctrine to informal and formal decisions alike. Consequently, an agency can only guess when a hard look judge will send it back to the drawing boards.

A second problem with the hard look doctrine is that it often reinforces administrative tendencies toward incrementalism—tendencies that the reforms of the 1970s were supposed to cure. In *Columbia Gas Transmission Corp. v. FERC*, 1979, Judge Bazelon struck down a FERC rate-setting formula that differed from the formula previously used by the agency. In doing so, Baselon argued that the previous formula must be the "starting point" in determining the "overall reasonableness" of pipeline rates. Judge Leventhal was even more explicit in linking the hard look doctrine to incrementalism. As Leventhal put it in *Greater Boston TV Corp. v. FCC*, 1970, "An agency's view of what is in the public interest may change, either with or without a change in circumstances. But an agency changing its course must supply a reasoned analysis indicating that prior policies and standards are being deliberately changed, not casually ignored, and if an agency glosses over or swerves from prior precedents without discussion, it may cross the line from the tolerably terse to the intolerably mute." Other courts, including the Supreme Court, have demonstrated this same commitment to incrementalism in more recent cases (e.g., *Motor Vehicle Manufacturers Assn. of U.S. Inc. v. State Farm Mutual Automobile Insurance Co.*, 1983).

A final problem with the hard look doctrine is that it requires judges to understand technical and scientific arguments for which their professional training has not adequately prepared them. One finds federal judges asking whether the EPA's measurements of emissions from portland cement kilns were methodologically sound, whether the fixed costs of natural gas transmission may be recovered primarily from commodity charges rather than demand charges, whether the risks of botulism are great enough to warrant an FDA requirement that hot-process smoked whitefish be heated for thirty minutes at a temperature not less than 180 degrees Fahrenheit in water containing 3.5 percent salt. According to one scholar (Shapiro, 1983), the courts may be sowing the seeds of their own destruction when they plunge into the thicket of such technical disputes. If this trend continues, agencies will probably respond by producing records even thicker and even more impenetrable than they are now. As this occurs, judges may find it impossible to exercise meaningful judicial review not because the record is incomplete (the complaint of hard look judges) but rather because it is too full of technical minutiae. Eventually, judges may find themselves deferring to administrative agency officials because they cannot understand what the officials are saying.

The hard look doctrine originated in an issue area where it was unusually appropriate—broadcasting regulation. The Federal Communications Commission (FCC) has long been accused of being "captured" by the industries it is supposed to be regulating (Bernstein, 1955; Edelman, 1964; Gormley, 1979; Krasnow, Longley and Terry, 1982). As an independent regulatory commission, the FCC is subject to few controls by the Congress or the White House. Indeed, it is subject to fewer legislative controls than most independent regulatory commissions, partly because of the low visibility of communications policy, partly because of the sensitivity of the issues with which it deals (freedom of the press, freedom of speech), and partly because its statutory mandate is extraordinarily vague—"the public interest, convenience or necessity." Without strong judicial review, the FCC would be virtually unfettered.

Moreover, the kinds of issues addressed by the FCC are for the most part ones the courts can be expected to handle competently. With the exception of common carrier cases (e.g., telephone rate cases), these issues are not unduly technical or complex. The issues in a broadcast license renewal proceeding, for example, can be readily understood by a generalist judge. Also many of the issues handled by the FCC (obscenity, the fairness doctrine, political advertising) have a constitutional dimension. Judges are of course uniquely able to grapple with these questions credibly and authoritatively.

During the 1970s the hard look doctrine spread from the FCC to other regulatory agencies, including both independent regulatory commissions and single-headed agencies. These agencies differed from the FCC in two critical respects. First, most of them were already subject to scrutiny by the White House, the Congress, or both. The Nuclear Regulatory Commission and the Federal Energy Regulatory Commission must file environmental impact statements when licensing a new power plant; the Food and Drug Administration and the National Highway Traffic Safety Administration must file regulatory impact analyses with OMB; the Environmental Protection Agency and the Occupational Safety and

169

Health Administration are subject to stiff statutory controls and receive considerable attention from the White House as well. Second, most of these agencies deal with extremely complex issues— rate-setting for natural gas pipelines, the design of nuclear power plants, safety standards for consumer products, and so forth. When judges wade into the thicket of these controversies they soon find themselves out of their depth. If judicial intervention in these cases truly promoted fidelity to legislative intent, it might be justifiable. However, serious questions have been raised about the willingness and the ability of federal judges to discern legislative intent in highly complex issue areas (Melnick, 1983).

A case can be made for the hard look doctrine when regulatory agencies are captured by the industries they are supposed to be regulating. However, numerous studies confirm that regulatory agencies are far less vulnerable to capture than they were two or three decades ago (Wilson, 1980; Quirk, 1981; Gormley, 1982). Moreover, the hard look doctrine can serve as an antidote to capture only if the plaintiff challenging the agency action represents broad, diffuse interests such as consumer protection or environmental protection. In practice, this is seldom the case. In reality, the hard look doctrine provides an opportunity for a regulated industry that lost in an administrative forum to seek redress in the courts. Far from curbing tendencies toward capture, the hard look doctrine provides that if a regulated industry cannot capture the agency, it may be able to capture the court. Many regulatory agencies today have the backbone to stand up to regulated industries. The hard look doctrine penalizes agencies with backbone and increases the likelihood that tough, aggressive regulations will be reversed.

Conclusion

The policy analysis reforms of the 1970s, in contrast to PPBS, sought to promote rationality but not comprehensive rationality. With the possible exception of ZBB, all of these reforms recognized the limitations of the human mind. And even ZBB was more realistic than PPBS. Although reformers were probably unfamiliar with Etzioni's (1967) work on mixed-scanning, these reforms did in fact promote mixed-scanning in the form of generating greater attention to diverse options, a more thorough examination of a single option, or both.

According to Etzioni, mixed-scanning is an alternative to incrementalist decision making. At one level, the process level, that is true. However, incrementalism has two dimensions: a process dimension and an output dimension. While mixed-scanning guarantees a nonincremental decision-making process, it does not guarantee nonincremental choices. The hard look doctrine, which embodies many of the classic features of mixed-scanning (the consideration of alternatives, taking a hard look at relevant evidence), nevertheless inhibits change by requiring agencies to justify departures from the status quo. Similarly, GAO reports discourage innovation by punishing bureaucratic deviations from statutory requirements, narrowly interpreted.

If mixed-scanning does not guarantee innovation, neither does it guarantee better decisions. In issue areas where broad, diffuse interests remain unorganized, the hard look doctrine punishes regulatory agencies that resist "capture" by industry by increasing the probability that tough regulations will be overturned. In issue areas where highly visible, controversial programs are at stake, GAO reports encourage agencies to divert resources from outcomes to outputs. In issue areas where uncontrollables (or nondiscretionary spending commitments) constitute a relatively high percentage of the budget, zero-based budgeting has little impact whatsoever.

Some of the policy analysis reforms of the 1970s do appear to have promoted both balance and innovation—a rare combination and a noteworthy achievement. Environmental impact statements have required construction-minded agencies to take environmental values into account. Environmental impact statements have even persuaded the once-notorious Army Corps Engineers to take a serious look at nonstructural alternatives—an important and surprising development. The old adage that you can't teach an old dog new tricks finds little support in the behavior of the corps during the 1970s.

Similarly, regulatory impact analyses have promoted balance by forcing health and safety agencies to take costs into account unless otherwise prohibited by law. Whether the regulatory review process has in fact stimulated bureaucratic innovation is unclear. However, the EPA's "bubble" policy of 1979, which seeks to reduce the costs of air pollution control without lowering air quality, is at least consistent with the spirit of regulatory impact analysis. President Carter's commitment to cost control probably encouraged "bubbles" and other cost-saving innovations in the same sense that President Nixon's commitment to "dirty tricks" encouraged break-ins, enemies' lists, and schemes to remove the hair from Fidel Castro's cheeks. Atmospherics, though difficult to measure and control, are nonetheless important.

In a sense, the policy analysis reforms of the 1970s are more consistent with the thinking of the Progressive Era than are other reforms of the same period. They are based on the premises that there are correct answers to policy problems, that better information will yield better decisions, and that reasoned decision making is superior to partisan mutual adjustment. Yet there is no denying a political side to these reforms as well. Policy analysis is a continuation of politics by other means. It furnishes a lever for altering power relationships between political institutions. It promotes some interests at the expense of others. Thus, while the policy analysis reforms of the 1970s promoted competence, they did not promote neutral competence. Also, they departed significantly from the Progressive view that technical decisions should be made by bureaucratic experts and be as removed from politics as possible. The policy analysis reforms of the 1970s ensured that politicians and judges would play key roles in structuring policy analysis within government. In this respect, it is difficult to imagine a more fundamental departure from the premises of the Progressive Era.

Federalism

If intergovernmental conflicts have all the elegance of a barroom brawl, that is because they involve such a wide variety of disputes. The disputes pit one level of government against another, one branch of government against another, one ideology against another, one political party against another, and one issue network against another. This makes for a hopelessly tangled melange of friends and enemies. These disputes are fueled by high financial stakes. Money, the mother's milk of politics, is also the mother's milk of intergovernmental relations. Hard pressed by angry taxpayers, state and local officials have sought relief from the federal government. Beleaguered by a staggering budget deficit, federal officials can no longer afford the generosity of yesteryear. After a while, the disputants begin to act like Humphrey Bogart and Walter Huston in "The Treasure of the Sierra Madre." Their eyes bulging, half-crazed with greed and desire, they struggle passionately over a contested fortune.

Yet there is more than money at stake here. If one looks closely at the twists and turns of federalism since 1969, one sees ample evidence of bureau-bashing as a recurring theme. It was Richard Nixon's animus toward the federal bureaucracy that led to the New Federalism: general revenue-sharing and block grants as alternatives to categorical grants. Later, it was congressional dissatisfaction with state and local bureaucracies that led to various forms of regulatory federalism, such as mandates, quality control, and partial preemptions. Here as elsewhere politicians could agree on little else, but they could agree on the congenital weaknesses of bureaucrats and bureaucracies.

Table 7.1 summarizes some key features and examples of federalism initiatives popular in the 1970s and the 1980s. It is interesting to note that different patterns of intergovernmental relations have characterized different policy domains in recent years. Thus, revenue-sharing has focused on relatively popular economic development and community development programs, while quality control has focused on relatively unpopular public assistance programs. Civil rights programs, which involve constitutional

TABLE 7.1

Federalism's Many Faces

Intergovernmental Relationship	Modus Operandi	Target	Examples
Revenue-Sharing	catalytic controls, vague goals	federal bureaucracy	general revenue-sharing; block grants (CETA, CDBG)
Mandates	coercive controls, clear goals	state and local governments	direct orders and cross-cutting requirements (civil rights, environmental protection, handicapped accessibility)
Quality Control	hortatory controls, deceptive goals	state bureaucracies	quality assurance systems (AFDC, Medicaid, social security disability)
Partial Preemptions	hortatory controls, clear goals	state and local governments	state and local enforcement of federal standards (clean air, clean water, occupational health)

guarantees, have depended on congressional mandates for their enforcement. New social regulations concerning environmental protection, public health, and worker safety have encompassed a variety of approaches including cross-cutting requirements, cross-over sanctions, and partial preemptions.

It is difficult to develop a chronological story line out of this messy pattern. In part, that is because the president, the Congress, and the courts have often been out of sync. Thus during the early 1980s, as President Reagan was attempting to weaken the federal government's grip on the states, the U.S. Supreme Court was tightening that grip. In *United Transportation Union v. Long Island Railroad Company* (1982), the Supreme Court permitted railroad employees to strike under the federal Railway Labor Act, despite a state law to the contrary. In *Equal Employment Opportunity Commission v. Wyoming* (1983), the Supreme Court extended the federal government's ban on age discrimination to state and local governments. In *Garcia v. San Antonio Metropolitan Transit Authority* (1985), the Supreme Court required state and local governments to honor federal minimum wage and overtime pay provisions, effectively reversing an earlier decision in *National League of Cities v. Usery* (1976).

Another source of confusion is that the same actors have endorsed different controls in different policy arenas. For example, the Nixon administration supported highly coercive environmental mandates at the same time that it promoted general revenue-sharing and loosely structured block grants for employment and training and community development. With similar inconsistency, the Reagan administration supported a great deal of delegation to state environmental agencies while endorsing tighter restrictions on state welfare agencies. Presidents, it seems, have been policy-driven, not theory-driven. If there is a theory of federalism lurking here somewhere, it is well-hidden.

Despite these complexities and inconsistencies, there has been one discernible trend over the past two decades. During the early 1970s the president and the Congress opted for relatively weak intergovernmental controls in order to bypass the Department of Labor (DOL) and the Department of Housing and Urban Development (HUD) and chose relatively strong intergovernmental controls in order to prevent foot-dragging by state environmental and worker safety agencies. By the late 1980s, these catalytic and coercive controls had given way to hortatory controls—a mixture of incentives and disincentives that preserved some discretion for state and local governments while retaining some federal control. In short, there has been a regression toward the mean, with weak and strong controls evolving over time into more moderate controls that stress intergovernmental bargaining. Pure revenue-sharing and pure mandates have both lost their luster.

In fact, that is as it should be, given the special character of American federalism. Inevitably some state and local governments will lack the skill to achieve federal goals, while others will lack support for such goals. Under these circumstances, federal laissez-faire is a recipe for state and local inertia. On the other hand, state and local governments must be treated with respect for both political and constitutional reasons. They enjoy considerable political clout on Capitol Hill, and the Tenth Amendment to the Constitution does grant them a good deal of discretion. For these reasons, federal officials who reach for a stick of dynamite every time they detect a trace of recalcitrance in the provinces should think again.

In intergovernmental relations, selective, hortatory controls are usually best.

Revenue-Sharing

Federal grants-in-aid have long constituted an important source of federal leverage over state and local governments. By attaching conditions to such grants, the federal government has been able to promote a wide variety of goals—affirmative action, a head start for disadvantaged children, highway beautification, and so forth. Historically, the overwhelming majority of federal grants-in-aid have been categorical grants, earmarked for specific purposes. Many of these grants have been project grants awarded by the federal bureaucracy on a discretionary basis. The combination of categorical grants and project grants, popular during the 1960s, strengthened the leverage of the federal bureaucracy in its dealings with state and local governments. However, such grants also raised the hackles of state and local officials who objected to "heavy-handed" treatment by federal bureaucrats.

It was against this backdrop that Richard Nixon proposed revenue-sharing. The linchpin of Nixon's New Federalism program, revenue-sharing offered aid to state and local governments with fewer strings attached. General revenue-sharing, a radical departure from categorical grants, was almost completely open-ended. Block grants, such as the Comprehensive Employment and Training Act (CETA) and the Community Development Block Grant program (CDBG), were more restrictive than general revenue-sharing but less restrictive than the old categorical grants. Both forms of revenue-sharing were packaged as formula grants that allocated money through congressionally specified equations.[1] This served to strengthen congressional control and to weaken the leverage of the federal bureaucracy.

To a visitor from another planet or even another country, the voluntary transfer of power from the federal government to state and local governments might seem a bit puzzling. It is understandable, however, if one views the New Federalism not as an attack on the federal government but rather as an attack on the federal bureaucracy. This helps to explain President Nixon's mighty efforts

1. For example, one CDBG formula included the age of housing (50 percent), poverty (30 percent), and lag in population growth (20 percent) as determinants of federal aid (Kettl, 1980: 29–30).

on behalf of the New Federalism, which he characterized as "the New American Revolution." To Nixon, the New Federalism offered an opportunity to strike a blow against a bloated federal bureaucracy, which he was struggling to control. In his memoirs Nixon rejoices that revenue-sharing "threatened sections of the bureaucracy with obsolescence" (Nixon, 1978: 768). To Nixon and to members of Congress sympathetic to him, the New Federalism offered a golden opportunity to put federal bureaucrats in their place.

Revenue-sharing flourished during the early 1970s and remained relatively popular into the late 1970s. As Table 7.2 indicates, federal grants-in-aid increased sharply during the Nixon years as a percentage of federal outlays and as a percentage of state and local outlays. The Ford and Carter years were more troublesome, but revenue-sharing weathered several storms during this period. Under President Reagan, however, federal grants-in-aid declined sharply as a percentage of federal outlays and as a percentage of state and local outlays. Indeed, general revenue-sharing was abolished in 1986 and other revenue-sharing programs were trimmed. At the present time, federal aid is about as important to state and local governments as it was at the end of the Johnson administration.

The rise and fall of revenue-sharing illustrates the need for clear statutory goals and hortatory controls in intergovernmental relations. Without clear statutory goals, federal grants-in-aid are likely to be gobbled up by politically powerful constituencies, not by those communities or groups that most need federal assistance. And without hortatory controls, federal grants-in-aid will be subject to waste, fraud, and abuse. At the other extreme, coercive controls can backfire, especially if they are applied across-the-board and if they emphasize paperwork (beancounting) rather than results (performance). To be successful, revenue-sharing must combine just the right mixture of statutory clarity, monitoring by federal bureaucrats, and experimentation by state and local bureaucrats. Unfortunately, these conditions were seldom met in the 1970s.

General Revenue-Sharing

From its inception, general revenue-sharing (GRS) was a program in search of a mission. When the Congress enacted GRS in 1972, it stipulated no substantive goals. Rather, the hope was that state and local governments would adopt programs responsive to the

177

TABLE 7.2

Federal Grants-in-Aid

	As a Percentage of Federal Outlays	As a Percentage of State-Local Outlays
1964	8.6	15.4
1965	9.2	15.1
1966	9.6	16.1
1967	9.7	16.9
1968	10.4	18.3
1969	11.0	17.8
1970	12.3	19.0
1971	13.4	19.7
1972	14.9	21.7
1973	17.0	24.0
1974	16.1	22.3
1975	15.0	22.6
1976	15.9	24.1
1977	16.7	25.5
1978	17.0	26.5
1979	16.5	25.8
1980	15.5	25.8
1981	14.0	24.7
1982	11.8	21.6
1983	11.4	21.3
1984	11.5	21.0
1985	11.2	21.0
1986	11.4	20.6
1987	10.8	19.1
1988	10.4 (est.)	17.1 (est.)

SOURCE: Office of Management and Budget, *Historical Tables: Budget of the U.S. Government*, Fiscal Year 1988; Advisory Commission on Intergovernmental Relations, *Significant Features of Fiscal Federalism*, 1988 Edition, vol. 1.

needs of their constituents. Inevitably, such an open-ended program degenerated quickly into an exercise in pork barrel politics, with powerful constituencies demanding a fat slice of pork for themselves. The Congress aided and abetted this process by making virtually every local government eligible for GRS funding. Thus 97 percent of all U.S. cities wound up receiving GRS assistance (Kettl, 1983: 40). This "scattershot" approach diluted the impact of GRS, spreading financial resources far and wide. General Revenue Sharing funding was available to needy and nonneedy communities alike; prosperous communities received funding along with their hard-pressed counterparts.

Within states and communities, GRS money was allocated with short-run political considerations in mind. State and local governments stressed capital spending projects that were easily finished rather than social services projects that might take a longer period of time to bear fruit. In part, this reflected understandable anxiety that the GRS program might be terminated or cut back. If that could happen, it might be unwise to invest in projects that would require continued long-term financial support to succeed. However, another critical factor was the greater popularity of capital spending projects in the business community and in upper-class neighborhoods. Social services projects, in contrast, were more likely to benefit disadvantaged members of the community with less political clout.

Community Development Block Grants

Like GRS, CDBG was widely distributed throughout the nation. All cities with populations of fifty thousand or more were automatically eligible for CDBG funding. In addition, funding formulas favored counties and suburbs at the expense of cities. These congressional decisions diluted the impact of CDBG awards. Instead of targeting funds where they were most needed, Congress adopted a familiar "scattershot" approach.

Even more disturbing were the decisions being made within communities. Although the enabling legislation passed by Congress called for "maximum feasible priority" to low- and moderate-income families, state and local governments easily circumvented this vague injunction. According to one estimate, only 50 to 60 percent of CDBG funding benefited low- and moderate-income families (Van Horn, 1979: 128). Horror stories began to surface. Community Development Block Grant funds were used to build a tennis court in one affluent neighborhood and a marina elsewhere; in another community, CDBG money was used to upgrade a stretch of road used by people going to a country club (Kettl, 1980: 25). When HUD attempted to clamp down on such abuses in 1977, Congress intervened on the side of state and local governments, thus preventing an ostensibly redistributive program from having this effect.[2]

2. Housing and Urban Development Secretary Patricia Harris announced that 75

Comprehensive Employment and Training Act

The CETA program suffered from similar problems. The enabling legislation adopted in 1973 offered little concrete guidance on the relative importance of employment and training programs or long-term versus short-term employment. In Van Horn's words (1979: 80), "The statute was vague about the who, what, when, and how of program design and expenditure decisions." Relatively unconstrained by Congress and the federal Department of Labor (DOL), state and local governments proceeded to use CETA dollars to substitute for existing programs and services, e.g., by laying off local government employees and rehiring them with CETA funds. Estimates of such substitution effects range from 16 to 50 percent of Public Service Employment funds during CETA's early years (Van Horn, 1979: 86). Other local governments viewed CETA as an opportunity to provide tax relief.

As unemployment increased during the 1970s, CETA's focus began to shift from the problems of the hard-core unemployed (chronic unemployment) to those of the temporarily unemployed (structural unemployment). It became increasingly clear that some CETA programs were not benefiting those who needed help the most.[3] It also became clear that some CETA programs were benefiting persons who did not need help at all. Tales began to surface of lawyers and engineers whose salaries were augmented by CETA funds. Magazine articles describing a CETA-funded "nude sculpting workshop" in which naked men and women ran hands over one another's bodies further undermined CETA's credibility (Baumer and Van Horn, 1985: 130).

In 1978 Congress took two steps to address these problems. First, Congress explicitly targeted long-term unemployed and low-income people for special attention. Second, Congress imposed a plethora of procedural rules to prevent waste, fraud, and abuse. The first of these measures proved successful. For example, between 1978 and 1980 the enrollment of poor people rose 20 percent in CETA's training components and between 10 and 30 percent in CETA's public service employment programs (Baumer and Van Horn, 1985: 149). In contrast, the second measure proved coun-

---

percent of a community's CDBG grant should go to low- and moderate-income groups; the Congress overruled that decision in 1978.

3. For example, under Title I, which provided comprehensive manpower services, enrollment of nonwhites and the economically disadvantaged declined during CETA's early years in comparison to previous categorical grant programs (Van Horn, 1979: 88).

terproductive. Through massive paperwork requirements, audits, and investigations, DOL was able to ferret out waste, fraud, and abuse. The horror stories came to an end. However, by stressing process over substance the federal government redirected the attention of state and local officials from performance to paperwork, from results to regulations. Under intense pressure to "count beans," state and local officials stopped trying to design better, more innovative programs that would help people to get jobs and hold onto them. Unfortunately, the new reign of terror was not selective—it was applied to all CETA prime sponsors including those with excellent track records. Thus, while it succeeded in shaping up a few embarrassing programs, it also stifled the initiative of many local programs that were working rather well.

In broader terms, the CETA experience signaled a significant shift in sentiment regarding intergovernmental relations. In particular, it marked the demise of the New Federalism and the rise of regulatory federalism. What began as an effort to make the government more responsive to the people evolved into an effort to make state and local bureaucracies more responsive to the federal government. What began as a quest for breadth evolved into an insistence on uniformity. What began as an effort to institutionalize flexibility and innovation evolved into a fairly rigid system. If revenue-sharing epitomized the approach of the early 1970s, mandates epitomized the approach of the late 1970s.

Mandates

Intergovernmental mandates include direct orders and conditions of aid. Direct orders require state and local governments to adopt certain policies or to follow certain procedures. Civil rights laws prohibiting discrimination based on race, color, or national origin are good examples of direct orders. Conditions of aid in contrast exact certain concessions from state and local governments if they wish to receive federal funding for a particular program or project. The stipulation that state governments enforce the fifty-five mile-per-hour speed limit if they are to receive federal highway funds illustrates a condition of aid.

Theoretically, direct orders are coercive while conditions of aid are hortatory. However, the distinction blurs in practice, depending on how vigorous enforcement is. Weak enforcement of a direct order may be less coercive than strong enforcement of a condition of aid. That is especially true when the aid involves a large amount of money. Indeed, the very threat to withhold federal funding for a large grant-in-aid program (like those for higher education) may be intimidating enough to be viewed by recipient governments as coercive.

Intergovernmental mandates are not new. In recent years however there has been a proliferation of intergovernmental mandates. There has also been a diversification of methods of intergovernmental control. Increasingly, one finds crossover sanctions, which impose financial penalties on one program (e.g., transportation) if state and local governments fail to comply with requirements for another program (e.g., energy or environmental protection). In addition, one finds cross-cutting requirements that cut across all or several grant programs at once. For example, racial discrimination is prohibited in all state and local programs supported by federal funds.

The number of cross-cutting requirements enacted into law increased dramatically during the 1970s (see Table 7.4). Examples include the Age Discrimination Act of 1975, the Rehabilitation Act of 1973, the Endangered Species Act of 1973, the Fair Labor Standards Act Amendments of 1974, and the Archaeological and Historic Preservation Act of 1974. The Office of Management and Budget (OMB) also imposed a wide variety of across-the-board requirements on state and local governments during the 1970s. Most OMB requirements were procedural in nature. Most conditions of aid are also procedural (Lovell and Tobin, 1981: 320).

There is a strong case to be made for intergovernmental mandates in some policy domains. In education, for example, persistent violations of black Americans' civil rights would not have

TABLE 7.3

Intergovernmental Mandates

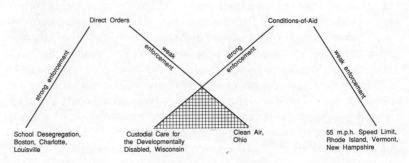

School Desegregation, Boston, Charlotte, Louisville — Direct Orders / strong enforcement

Custodial Care for the Developmentally Disabled, Wisconsin — weak enforcement

Clean Air, Ohio — strong enforcement

55 m.p.h. Speed Limit, Rhode Island, Vermont, New Hampshire — Conditions-of-Aid / weak enforcement

TABLE 7.4

Cross-cutting Regulations

Date Established	Social/Economic		Administrative/Fiscal		Total	
	N	%	N	%	N	%
Prior to 1960	4	11	2	9	6	10
1960s	9	25	9	39	18	31
1970s	23	64	12	52	35	59
	36	100	23	100	59	100

SOURCE: Office of Management and Budget, *Managing Federal Assistance in the 1980s* (Washington, D.C.: GPO, 1980).

ended without the strong intervention of Congress, the Justice Department, and the federal courts. Racist attitudes were too deeply entrenched, especially in the Deep South. According to one careful study of thirty-one Georgia school districts, coercion was indispensable in securing compliance with federal civil rights laws. Specifically, Rodgers and Bullock (1976: 40–45) found very high correlations between coercion and compliance with school desegregation orders in the early 1970s.

There is also much to be said for intergovernmental mandates in relation to environmental protection, because pollutants may be exported from one state to another. Here again the problem often lies with the attitudes of state bureaucrats. For example, bureaucrats at the Ohio EPA do not share the federal government's strong commitment to clean air. This is evident in their attitudes on a variety of specific policy questions (Gormley, 1987). Ohio's high unemployment rate and heavy dependence on high-sulfur coals, much of it mined in Ohio, help to explain the attitude of Ohio bureaucrats. Until federal acid rain legislation is passed, Ohio will continue to spew large amounts of sulfur dioxide into neighboring states.

In health and mental health areas the problem tends to be different. State bureaucrats are often committed to federal goals but may lack the staff to adequately address the needs of the elderly, the poor, the developmentally disabled, and the mentally ill. Under such circumstances, threats to cut off federal aid unless staff resources are augmented may be both necessary and effective. A case in point is the Southern Wisconsin Center for the Developmentally Disabled in Union Grove, Wisconsin, where beleaguered staff members frequently resorted to physical and chemical restraints in order to cope with an impossible situation. When the

U.S. Health Care Financing Administration (HCFA) threatened to cut off $17 million in Medicaid money to the Union Grove center, state officials immediately took notice. Within a few months, Wisconsin had committed itself to hire ninety additional staff members, and HCFA lifted its threatened decertification of the center (Kole, 1986; "U.S. Won't Cut Funds," 1987).

Unfortunately, intergovernmental mandates are seldom so selective. Pressed for time and afraid of being charged with unfairness, the federal government has imposed a wide variety of requirements on saints and sinners alike. In the interest of expediency the federal government has defined fairness as uniformity. Thus states with excellent nursing homes are obliged to conduct inspections as often as states with poor nursing homes; and nursing homes with excellent track records are scrutinized as closely as nursing homes with poor track records. The same basic pattern holds true for environmental protection, occupational safety, mine safety, and other areas. States with spotless reputations may lay up for themselves treasures in heaven, but they receive few rewards from the federal government here on earth.

Another problem is nitpicking. Instead of focusing on the spirit of the law, federal officials often focus on the letter of the law narrowly defined. For example, the Urban Mass Transit Administration (UMTA) invalidated a local public hearing in Janesville, Wisconsin, because the city advertised the popular local name for the location instead of its street address (Kettl, 1983: 11). Had UMTA been in charge, Ingrid Bergman would have been obliged to ask for Humphrey Bogart's street address rather than just "Rick's." It is of course true that one person's nit is another person's principle. Nevertheless, the federal government has undermined its credibility and wasted a lot of time by failing to distinguish between important and unimportant rules, serious infractions and harmless errors.

A third problem with intergovernmental mandates is their enormous inefficiency. Worthwhile objectives are often pursued with little or no attention to the costs they impose. In Section 504 of the Rehabilitation Act Congress required local governments to make mass transit fully accessible to the handicapped. According to the Congressional Budget Office (CBO), full accessibility would cost $6.8 billion over thirty years with few tangible benefits for the handicapped (Katzmann, 1986: 120). An alternative approach, stressing effective mobility (a combination of structural modifications, minivans, free taxi services, and so forth), would have been much less expensive. After a long and protracted battle, the federal government finally retreated from a full accessibility policy. In the meantime, however, many local governments had complied with regulations that offered few benefits but imposed considerable costs.

A final problem with intergovernmental mandates is their cumulative weight. When Mayor Ed Koch of New York refers to the "mandate millstone" (1980) he is alluding to an extraordinary number of burdensome regulations. If one examines the fifty-nine cross-cutting requirements identified by OMB in 1980, one finds many good ideas. But fifty-nine good ideas may be one very bad idea! When the total weight of intergovernmental mandates becomes so crushing that state and local governments lose their capacity to cope, some adjustments are needed.

Quality Control

During the 1970s Congress established comprehensive quality control systems for several major entitlement programs, including Aid to Families with Dependent Children (AFDC), Food Stamps, and Medicaid. In 1980 Congress streamlined a preexisting quality control system for social security disability payments. By the end of the decade, several major quality control systems were flourishing. Under a quality control system, state agencies review a sample of their awards and denials, calculating both case error rates (e.g., an award to an ineligible person) and payment error rates (e.g., an overpayment). The federal agency then reanalyzes a sub-sample of the state cases to determine compliance with federal statutes and regulations. From these figures, state error rates are computed. As stipulated by Congress, state error rates provide the basis for financial penalties imposed by the federal government. For example, in 1979 Congress specified that a state with an AFDC error rate higher than 4 percent in fiscal year 1983 should be penalized.

If properly designed, quality control systems are excellent examples of appropriate hortatory controls. By requiring state agencies to furnish case data to federal agencies they enable one bureaucracy to control another. By imposing financial penalties on states with high error rates, they provide incentives to reduce mistakes. At their best quality control systems promote what Mashaw (1983) calls a "bureaucratic rationality" model of justice. Through the use of financial incentives and disincentives they encourage state agencies to achieve accuracy and efficiency.

185

Unfortunately, real quality control systems do not live up to their advance billing. Their ostensible goals are accuracy and error reduction. Yet federal formulas for calculating error rates subject to financial penalties routinely ignore nonpayments to eligibles, focusing instead on payments to ineligibles. The real purpose of quality control, it seems, is not accuracy but cost containment. Under the guise of quality control, federal politicians have attempted to transform entitlement programs into discretionary benefit programs.

The AFDC quality control system provides a good illustration of this pattern. Although negative errors are counted, only positive errors trigger financial penalties. As a result, quality control biases state administrative performance, reducing "errors of liberality" but increasing "errors of stringency" (Brodkin and Lipsky, 1983). The same pattern is found in quality control systems for Medicaid and social security disability payments. Only the food stamps quality control system encourages states to reduce both positive and negative errors.

There is in short a gap between the stated and actual goals of quality control systems in place today. There is also a somewhat puzzling gap between congressional requirements and administrative practices. Despite clear congressional language concerning financial sanctions, the penalty system has broken down. For example, the U.S. Department of Agriculture (USDA) has levied sanctions on forty-two states for food stamp payment errors, but only one state (Connecticut) has paid up (U.S. GAO, "Food Stamp Program," 1986). The other states have received waivers or have challenged the sanctions in court. Thus at the enforcement stage neither the stated goal (accuracy) nor the hidden goal (cost containment) is being vigorously promoted.

There are three possible explanations for the gap between the tough congressional language and weak administrative enforcement. One possibility is that the Congress was interested in symbolism in the first place—that the real goal of Congress was not to reduce federal expenditures (cost containment) but to placate federal taxpayers (political containment). A second possibility is that the Congress meant what it said but that the USDA doesn't support congressional goals. A third possibility is that the threat to impose sanctions has already been effective. If so, the actual imposition of sanctions would be overkill.

In fact, there is some evidence to support the third hypothesis. Specifically, error rates have declined since quality control systems were established. The AFDC error rate declined from 16.5 percent in 1973 to 6.5 percent in 1983; the Medicaid error rate dropped from 6.6 percent in 1978 to 2.8 percent in 1983; and the Food Stamps error rate plunged from 16 percent in 1975 to 8.4 percent in 1983 (U.S. GAO, "Managing Welfare," 1986: 17). Clearly behavior modification in intergovernmental relations does not depend on the actual imposition of financial penalties.[4]

Yet there is less to these figures than meets the eye. One problem is that states can artificially reduce their error rates by omitting certain kinds of cases from their quality control figures. This is perfectly legal. In relation to food stamps, for example, states may (and do) exclude cases when a personal interview is difficult or impossible to arrange. According to the General Accounting Office (GAO), error rates would be substantially higher if such cases were included because they are more likely to involve ineligibles (U.S. GAO, "Food Stamp Program," 1986). It is also important to distinguish between "technical" errors (which do not affect payouts) and "substantive" errors (which do). By requiring all family members to produce social security numbers and by requiring all ablebodied persons to register for nonexistent jobs, state welfare agencies have been able to reduce "paper" errors without actually affecting welfare caseloads. Indeed, with federal dollars at stake, many state agencies have shifted their focus from real fraud and abuse (which are difficult to document) to paper errors (which are easy to spot), thus keeping their overall error rate as low as possible. Here as elsewhere procedure drives out substance and "beancounting" becomes more important than performance.

Another weakness of existing quality control systems is that they direct state agencies away from such goals as the quality of service, timely decision making, administrative cost reductions, and managerial effectiveness (Gardiner and Lyman, 1984: 134). Without incentives to improve their performance along these dimensions, state agencies focus instead on those indicators stressed by federal overseers. In Massachusetts, for example, social workers seem to have lost interest in clientele service, formerly an important administrative goal (Brodkin and Lipsky, 1983). Intentionally or not, federal overseers have weakened an important bond between

4. There are, however, other possible explanations for these declines. For example, the federal government picked up 75 percent of the administrative costs of state fraud control units to encourage cost containment in food stamps and Medicaid (Gardiner and Lyman, 1984: 132). This may have contributed to reduced error rates.

"street-level" bureaucrats and the persons they are supposed to be helping.

Partial Preemptions

Partial preemptions are control strategies whereby the federal government assumes jurisdiction over a policy domain but then relinquishes some of that authority to the states. Under partial preemptions, federal law establishes the basic policies but administrative responsibility is delegated to state governments that agree to uphold national standards. Partial preemptions combine delegation and control. A good example is the Surface Mining Control and Reclamation Act of 1977, which grants states the option of running their own strip-mining programs, provided that federal standards are accepted. If a state declines to accept these standards, the federal government opts for full preemption, running the program out of a regional office.

Partial preemptions exemplify hortatory controls. They combine pressure and restraint in an effort to ensure both progress and cooperation. By setting federal standards they recognize the need for some uniformity in matters that transcend state boundaries (e.g., pollution). By delegating administrative authority to responsible states, they afford some discretion in implementation and enforcement to those public officials who are most familiar with the idiosyncrasies of their state. Potentially, they institutionalize a mutually beneficial bargain between federal and state officials.

Partial preemptions have become standard adjuncts of the new social regulations aimed at securing clean air, clean water, and a safe workplace. They are especially appropriate for such policy domains. Without a relatively vigorous federal role in promoting environmental protection and public health, interstate competition for jobs could result in weak state regulations, weak state enforcement, or both. States willing to despoil their environment could become magnets for paper mills, steel mills, smelters and other heavy manufacturing industries. Moreover, many of the pertinent issues are sufficiently complex that federal officials are in a better position than state officials to identify appropriate thresholds for benzene, cotton dust, and other harmful substances. On the other hand, the federal government could not possibly manage all of these programs without the cooperation of the state governments. Furthermore, state administrators are less threatening to regulated industries than federal administrators. In short, there is a strong case to be made for hortatory controls that harness the energies of state bureaucracies in pursuit of national policy goals.

Like other hortatory controls, partial preemptions do lead to coercion in some situations. Indeed, if they did not, hortatory controls would lose their bite. Coercion is most likely to emerge, as it should, in situations where state bureaucracies are low in skill or low in support. The federal Office of Surface Mining (OSM) took over strip-mining programs in Tennessee and Oklahoma when it became apparent that state staff resources were woefully inadequate. In Tennessee, only nine inspectors were attempting to run a program that required twenty-five inspectors; in Oklahoma, state administration was characterized by poor training, lost or misplaced records, and erratic enforcement (Pasztor, 1984; Derthick, 1987: 70; Reagan, 1987: 190). The U.S. Environmental Protection Agency (EPA) has also found it necessary to take over state programs when confronted by clear evidence of state recalcitrance.

In fact, the U.S. EPA has threatened to take over state programs much more often than it has done so. When a large state like Ohio balks at implementing federal air pollution standards, the U.S. EPA must reach some sort of *modus vivendi*. A federal takeover is both expensive and unpopular. This gives state governments considerable leverage, as Ingram (1985: 200) has pointed out: "Instead of a federal master dangling a carrot in front of a state donkey, the more apt image reveals a rich merchant haggling on equal terms with a sly, bargain-hunting consumer." Partial preemptions trigger a bargaining process in which both sides have impressive resources. The threat of a federal takeover is indeed alarming, but so too is the threat of state defiance.

Occasionally, federal courts have deprived federal bureaucrats of flexibility in their dealings with the states. For example, the First Circuit Court of Appeals barred the U.S. EPA from granting any air pollution variances after 1975 (Melnick, 1983: 156). While conceding that the Congress had not explicitly disallowed such variances, the court argued that open-ended exemptions undermined the purpose of the Clean Air Act. In effect, the court insisted on a coercive strategy. This made little sense for a number of reasons. To cite but one, the OPEC oil embargo required the pragmatic modification of regulations for coal-burning power plants because the option of burning oil was no longer viable. Eventually, the Congress interceded to restore the EPA's authority to grant variances to states. In the meantime, however, federal coercion resulted in confusion, delays, and animosity.

Despite this episode, other federal courts have explicitly endorsed partial preemptions and the flexibility they bring to intergovernmental relations. In *Hodel v. Virginia Surface Mining and Reclamation Association* (1981) and a related case in Indiana, the U.S. Supreme Court concluded that the Surface Mining Control and Reclamation Act did not interfere with states' "traditional governmental function" of regulating land use. As the Court pointed out, the federal government would have been justified in totally preempting state strip-mining regulations, since interstate commerce is involved. Surely, the Court reasoned, the federal government's willingness to grant some role to the states is constitutional in a policy domain where full preemption would have been constitutional. The Supreme Court upheld another partial preemption statute—the Public Utility Regulatory Policies Act—the following year (*Federal Energy Regulatory Commission v. Mississippi*, 1982).

Although partial preemptions have caused state bureaucracies a good deal of frustration and anxiety, they do appear to have succeeded in most instances. Certainly we have made remarkable progress in reducing air pollution since the Clean Air Act Amendments of 1970 were passed. Moreover many states have proven to be as vigorous in enforcing social regulatory statutes as the federal government itself. In occupational safety and health, for example, Thompson and Scicchitano (1985) found that state enforcement is not noticeably weaker than federal enforcement. Although states impose less burdensome financial penalties, they conduct more inspections per employee and they issue more citations. Furthermore, state administration has proved to be a source of stability and consistency as presidents with different social regulatory agendas have come and gone. Thus when President Reagan opted to cut back on federal enforcement of strip-mining and occupational safety statutes, the impact was softened because strong state programs were already in place.

In general, delegation to the states is most likely to succeed when both bureaucratic skill and bureaucratic support are high. More specifically, successful delegation seems to depend not just on bureaucratic characteristics but on interest group characteristics as well. Thompson and Scicchitano (1985) found stronger enforcement of occupational safety laws in states with strong unions. In fact, there may be a close link between bureaucratic support and interest group support, especially in policy domains marked by high visibility and high levels of controversy. For example, in Wisconsin, where environmental groups are relatively strong, bureaucratic support for clean air is greater than in Ohio where environmental groups are relatively weak (Gormley, 1987). By strengthening and broadening interest representation at the state level, it might be possible to increase state bureaucratic support for important national goals.

Bureaucratic skill is another important contextual variable and a manipulable variable as well. Indeed, one of the more significant consequences of partial preemptions has been to professionalize state bureaucracies. The Office of Surface Mining has insisted on sufficient numbers of administrative and technical personnel in state strip-mining offices (Reagan, 1987: 190). Similarly, the Occupational Safety and Health Administration (OSHA) has insisted on having qualified personnel in state occupational safety offices (Thompson and Scicchitano, 1985: 688). Partial preemptions like conditions of aid have given the federal government leverage to professionalize state bureaucracies. As this happens, the level of bureaucratic support may change as well (Derthick, 1970: 158–89; Peterson et al., 1986: 160–90). Thus the very conditions that prompt the threat of a federal takeover may change significantly over time as states adapt to the federal threat.

This, of course, is a far cry from "cooperative federalism." On the other hand, it also differs from a hierarchical view in which state bureaucracies are mere "vassals" of the federal government. The prevailing norm in intergovernmental relations today is what Reagan and Sanzone (1981: 157–79) call "permissive federalism." State bureaucracies are permitted by the federal government to run important programs, provided that they take federal standards seriously. Permissive federalism is bound to involve a degree of intergovernmental conflict. It will involve occasional excesses and occasional lapses. At times federal overseers may turn state bureaucrats into beancounters; at other times federal overseers may tolerate lethargic behavior. In the long run, however, there is no substitute for hortatory controls in intergovernmental relations, especially in regard to social regulation, where the states cannot be left to their own devices but where the federal government cannot go it alone.

Conclusion

Federalism is more than a power struggle between the federal government and the states; it is also a struggle between bureaucrats and politicians. The New Federalism originated in an atmosphere of deep suspicion toward the federal bureaucracy. Regulatory federalism emerged later as a response to the perceived weaknesses of state and local bureaucracies. Bureau-bashing has been a recurring theme in intergovernmental relations since 1970.

Neither the New Federalism with its emphasis on federal deference to the states nor regulatory federalism with its emphasis on federal control has proven satisfactory. Gradually, weak and strong controls have regressed toward the mean with hortatory controls emerging as the instruments of choice. It is difficult to know whether this trend reflects disenchantment with bureaus or disenchantment with bureau-bashing. In any case, hortatory controls now permit federal and state officials to strike a balance between change and stability, uniformity and flexibility. That balance may not be optimal, but it constitutes an improvement over the extremes of laissez-faire and nitpicking.

Hortatory controls in intergovernmental relations have helped to promote clean air, clean water, and occupational safety at prices most Americans can accept. They have helped to professionalize state bureaucracies and to legitimize federal standards. They have accelerated the tempo of change without mandating unrealistic commitments. In addition, they have survived a variety of challenges in the federal courts.

Where hortatory controls have been disappointing, the problem seems to lie not with intergovernmental bargaining per se but rather with the goals federal officials claim to promote. In particular, members of Congress have been disingenuous in specifying their goals. Thus, the CETA and CDBG block-grant programs, supposedly aimed at the neediest citizens and communities, were in fact designed as "pork barrel" programs with high electoral payoffs. Congress's refusal to adopt truly redistributive legislation may have facilitated political coalition-building initially but ultimately it undermined the credibility of both programs. Similarly, Congress has disguised its real intent in institutionalizing quality control systems for intergovernmental entitlement programs. Wrapped in language that stresses accuracy and error-reduction, these programs are in fact aimed at cost containment. Congressional dissembling has made it difficult for both federal and state bureaucrats to know whether they should pursue the ostensible or the hidden goals.

The Reagan administration's approach to intergovernmental relations was less consistent than those of previous administrations. While loosening civil rights mandates, the Reagan administration tightened welfare eligibility requirements. While substituting block grants for categorical grants, the Reagan administration also reduced the overall level of federal aid in real terms. In the short run, this caused a good deal of consternation in state capitols and city halls. In the long run, however, it could protect state and local governments from misguided federal requirements. Now that federal aid has declined, state and local governments are less vulnerable to federal bullying than they were in the 1970s. If this persists, federal officials may select hortatory controls rather than coercive controls, not because they prefer them but because determined state and local governments leave them no other choice.

Oversight

Legislative Freelancing

During the 1970s legislative bodies in the United States strength-ened their capacity to control the bureaucracy, to curb abuses by the chief executive, and to adjust the balance of power between the legislative and executive branches. The Congress, stung by the ac-cusation that it had become an accessory to crimes committed by imperial presidents, adopted a number of measures aimed at checking the president (the War Powers Act, restrictions on im-poundment, limitations on claims to executive privilege). In addi-tion, Congress took steps to control the bureaucracy. Legislative oversight, previously erratic and ineffective, became a powerful tool of congressional control. The legislative veto, which had been used from time to time since the 1930s, was revived and used with great frequency. The power of the purse was strengthened by the creation of budget committees and a Congressional Budget Office (CBO) and by provisions for annual legislative authorizations. Stat-utes, once derided as irresponsible delegations of authority (Lowi, 1969), were made tougher and more precise.

Similar changes were underway at the state level. Legislative oversight, unfamiliar to many state legislators in the 1960s, became a staple of legislative activity in the 1970s. At least three-fourths of the state legislatures provided for some formal legislative review of administrative rules and regulations. Nearly three-fourths of the state legislatures adopted sunset laws providing for the automatic review of designated administrative agencies at regular intervals and for the possible termination of such agencies if the legislature considered that desirable. In addition, some state legislatures adopted tough, clear legislation in certain issue areas, such as coastal zone management (Rosenbaum, 1980).

By the end of the 1970s, legislators had become the most impor-tant (and the most feared) actors in the bureaucracy's external en-vironment. A distinguished scholar analyzed the world of six bu-reau chiefs at the federal level and found the Congress to be "preeminent" (Kaufman, 1981: 168). Although bureau chiefs were mindful of department heads, presidential advisers, judges, interest groups, and journalists, they were most attentive to members of Congress and their staffs. As Kaufman put it (1981: 47), "At the center of the pattern of relationships for all the chiefs was Congress—its members, collectively and individually, its committees, its staffs, its evaluative arms (the General Accounting Office in particular). This set of congressional and congressionally related workers in the machinery of government seemed rarely to be out of the administrators' consciousness."

The situation at the state level was remarkably similar. In a questionnaire survey of top agency officials in ten states, Elling (1985) asked respondents to assess the impact of a wide variety of actors (the governor, the state legislature, the state courts, federal agencies and Congress, the federal courts, the state budget office, clientele groups, and interest groups) regarding a variety of important decisions, including the determination of overall budget levels, budget levels for specific programs, major policy or program changes, the content of rules and regulations, day-to-day operations, and the establishment of administrative procedures. In five out of six instances, the state legislature was perceived as the most important actor in the agency's external environment.

Despite the perceptions of bureaucrats and despite all the reforms, many legislators continued to complain that the bureaucracy was out of control (Kaufman, 1981: 169). Bureaucrats, quivering at every thunderbolt hurled by legislators from their Olympian heights, must have marveled at such lamentations. Yet, this difference of perspective is easy enough to explain. As Fiorina (1981) has argued, the 1970s witnessed an increase in "uncoordinated control" but not in coordinated control. Another way to put this is that while individual legislators increased their leverage over the bureaucracy, the legislature as a whole was seldom in charge. Instead, the kind of control that emerged in the 1970s was for the most part legislative freelancing. Individual legislators, responding to constituency pressures or to their own personal agendas, proceeded to tell bureaucrats what to do, what not to do, and what would happen if they did or didn't do as they were told.

From a bureaucrat's perspective, the freelancing legislator is a menacing figure who inspires fear, though not necessarily respect. Although bureaucrats realize that individual legislators do not speak for the legislature as a whole, that merely adds outrage to obligation. In fact, commands from individual legislators (or from legislative subcommittees) are more difficult to ignore than com-

195

mands from the legislature as a whole. Individual legislators know what they want; their commands tend to be sharp, explicit, unambiguous. In contrast, the legislature as a whole seldom knows what it wants (although it does expect bureaucrats to know what it wants). Thus, as Lowi (1969) has noted, legislative language tends to be ambiguous. While this changed somewhat in the 1970s, the number of commands issued from the legislature as a whole grew far less rapidly than the number of commands issued from individual legislators. As one rough measure of this difference, consider that the number of statutes passed by Congress was no greater in the 1970s than in the 1950s and the number of pages per statute was not substantially greater either (Sundquist, 1981: 410). In contrast, the number of oversight hearings—occasions for legislative freelancing—doubled between 1969 and 1975 (Aberbach, 1979: 506–07).

Thus while legislative control of the bureaucracy increased during the 1970s, control usually reflected the views of legislative freelancers rather than the collective will of the legislature or of the majority party. The principal reason for this is that important legislative reforms were occurring simultaneously, involving both changes in external relations and changes in the internal distribution of power. As legislative bodies strengthened their capacity to control the bureaucracy, they also decentralized power within the legislature. The impetus for decentralization was a sharp rise in legislative individualism, attributable in part to the decline of political parties as recruiting agents, as sources of campaign funds, and as electoral cue-givers. As political parties diminished in importance, legislators became more self-reliant, more willing to challenge party leaders, and more desperate for media attention. The result was pressure for a more egalitarian distribution of power within the legislative branch.

Legislative decentralization took somewhat different forms at the federal and state levels—a reflection of different levels of dispersion, specialization, and institutionalization as the decade began. At the federal level, where power was concentrated in the hands of congressional committees (and committee chairs), decentralization involved an increase in the number of subcommittees and in the number of individuals chairing subcommittees. By the end of the 1970s, one of every three House members (and one of every two House Democrats) chaired a subcommittee (Sundquist, 1981: 382). At the state level, where power was concentrated in the hands of party leaders, decentralization involved the strengthening of legislative committees (and committee chairs). As a result, Rosenthal (1981: 191) could report that state legislative committee systems were stronger and more authoritative than ever. Internal legislative reforms proceeded along different paths at the state and federal levels. However, the more striking fact is that both sets of reforms weakened party leaders, diffused responsibility, and encouraged legislative freelancing. Although the power of party leaders was strengthened in certain respects within Congress and within many state legislatures, these centralizing tendencies were more than offset by reforms promoting decentralization. As a result, the legislative bodies that sought to control the bureaucracy in 1980 were far more fragmented than the legislative bodies of a decade earlier had been.

It is important, however, not to equate a fragmented legislature with a weak legislature. A fragmented legislature may not be responsible or cohesive, but that does not diminish its capacity to influence the bureaucracy. The distinction between clarity and consistency is also important. Signals sent by a fragmented legislature may not be consistent but they are likely to be very clear. Uncoordinated legislative control is not very pretty but it should not be lightly dismissed. Moreover, if one looks not just at coordinated control but at uncoordinated control as well, a key conclusion emerges: legislative control of the bureaucracy is far stronger as a result of the reforms of the 1970s. Legislative oversight, the legislative veto, and greater statutory specificity have indeed made the bureaucracy more responsive to legislators, as reformers hoped they would. Unfortunately however they have not solved the deeper problems they were supposed to cure—clientelism, incrementalism, and so forth. Instead, in many instances they have actually made matters worse. These tendencies have been most pronounced in areas where legislative freelancers have been free to perform "hit and run" attacks on the bureaucracy—attacks that typically secure responsiveness to individual legislators at the expense of collective responsibility. Such hit and run attacks have become common as legislative oversight has developed into a virtual cottage industry within the legislative branch.

Legislative Oversight

During the 1970s legislative oversight hearings increased dramatically at the federal level (Aberbach, 1979: 505–06) and at the state level (Rosenthal, 1981).[1] It is not just that oversight has increased but that it has been institutionalized in various ways. The U.S. House of Representatives in 1974 required each committee to create a special oversight subcommittee or to conduct oversight through regular subcommittees. State legislatures have also institutionalized oversight through sunset reviews and other forms of systematic oversight of state administration.

But what exactly is oversight and what are we to make of it? Many political scientists define oversight rather narrowly, as backward-looking legislative review of bureaucratic actions, programs, or policies (Schick, 1976; Aberbach, 1979; Rosenthal, 1983). In contrast, Ogul (1976) offers a much more expansive definition of oversight: "behavior by legislators or their staffs, individually or collectively, which results in an impact, intended or not, on bureaucratic behavior." The problem with narrow definitions of oversight is that a great deal of legislative behavior is simultaneously backward-looking and forward-looking (e.g., a legislative hearing where bureaucrats are scolded for not solving a problem and are then told what they should do about it). Legislators like the ancient god Janus often look backwards and forward at the same time. Ogul's definition sidesteps this problem by recognizing that legislative oversight can be both retrospective and prospective (either or both). However, Ogul's definition suffers from two principal drawbacks. First, by treating lawmaking and the legislative veto as forms of oversight, Ogul blurs the distinction between binding and nonbinding legislative control. Second, Ogul implies that only effective legislative intervention should be regarded as oversight. In effect, this definition prejudges the question of effectiveness.

There is much to be said for a different conception of oversight, one that excludes binding legislative behavior but does not exclude forward-looking legislative activity. Legislative oversight might be defined as legislative inquiries into bureaucratic performance that result in either formal or informal recommendations being made to the bureaucracy. This definition of oversight excludes lawmaking and the legislative veto because they are more than mere recommendations; it also excludes casework that is purely informa-

1. At the local level, there does not appear to have been a significant increase in legislative oversight. Perhaps, as Abney and Lauth (1982) suggest, this reflects the amateurish quality of most city councils. Or perhaps it reflects tensions between oversight and the Progressive ideals of neutral administration institutionalized in so many cities during the early twentieth century.

tional and nondirective in character. On the other hand, it includes casework accompanied by legislative advice; it also includes legislative hearings that result in either explicit or implicit recommendations to the bureaucracy. As Table 8.1 suggests, there are four common forms of legislative oversight: (1) Casework—intervention in bureaucratic decision making on behalf of an individual constituent who is confused, impatient, or aggrieved; (2) Pork barrel Politics—the pursuit of goods and services (especially public works projects) that benefit a particular district or state; (3) Entrepreneurial Politics—the pursuit of policies that promote widely distributed benefits; and (4) Sunset Review—the automatic termination of an agency on a fixed schedule unless the legislature acts affirmatively to continue it. Entrepreneurial politics and sunset review typify what Ogul (1976) calls "manifest" oversight (legislative activity explicitly aimed at overseeing the bureaucracy); casework and pork barrel politics exemplify "latent" oversight (legislative activity that contributes to oversight while another activity is ostensibly being performed). Of these forms of oversight, casework and pork barrel politics are relatively old, while entrepreneurial politics and sunset review are relatively new. However, all forms of oversight appear to have increased in the 1970s.

Casework. Casework has long been a high priority for legislators at various levels of government. Studies of congressional behavior reveal that members of Congress and their staffs devote approximately one-fourth of their time to constituency service (Saloma, 1979: 183–87). At the state level, legislators rank constituency ser-

TABLE 8.1

Common Forms of Legislative Oversight

Type of Oversight	Member Incentives	Style	Legislative Role	Issue Area
Casework	strong	informal	ombudsman	distributive, redistributive
Pork barrel politics	strong	informal	procurer	distributive
Entrepreneurial politics	moderate	fairly formal	watchdog	foreign affairs, intelligence-gathering, regulatory (social)
Sunset review	weak	formal	fine-tuner	regulatory (economic)

vice high on their list of priorities, second only to lawmaking itself (Elling, 1979). Legislators have ample incentives to play an "ombudsman" role on behalf of their constituents. It is an easy way to make friends without making enemies. Not surprisingly, casework has increased in recent years (Johannes, 1979) and it shows no signs of abating.

As noted earlier, much casework is merely a request for information with no real significance for legislative oversight. However, casework has the capacity to influence bureaucratic behavior in both positive and negative ways. On the positive side, casework may stimulate the introduction of new legislation or the revision of an administrative rule. Nearly two-thirds of all congressional respondents agree that there are occasional "attempts to generalize about problems discovered in constituency service operations so that some remedial action, such as introduction of legislation, might be taken" (Johannes, 1979). Similar percentages of state legislators and administrators agree that casework sometimes alerts them to broader problems, bottlenecks, and so forth (Elling, 1980). There are however reasons to doubt that this occurs very often. Caseworkers employed by individual legislators have few opportunities or incentives to compare notes in an effort to identify common problems. Moreover, caseworkers are often isolated from the committees where new legislation is proposed, formulated, and discussed. At both the federal and state levels, many caseworkers are located in district offices where they have frequent contacts with constituents and infrequent contacts with legislators or other legislative aides. For all these reasons, the capacity of casework to contribute to new public policy initiatives or across-the-board revisions in agency rules and practices is minimal at best.

But casework is more than an innocuous distraction. In many instances, casework constitutes a thinly veiled request for special treatment for a favored constituent, ranging from expedited review to the breaking of rules, at the expense of other citizens or the taxpayers as a whole. In Parsons' (1960) terms, casework encourages bureaucrats to apply "particularistic" rather than "universalistic" norms in their dealings with individual citizens. According to one study of casework in Kentucky and Minnesota, requests for special favors or exceptions are commonplace, especially in Kentucky where the norm of an independent civil service has yet to take root (Elling, 1980). Subjected to such pressures, bureaucrats often acquiesce, even though they believe that they acted correctly. Although they resent legislative interference, bureaucrats would rather accommodate an insistent legislator than face budget cutbacks or blistering criticism at a legislative hearing. Such favors please constituents and help to guarantee the legislator's reelection. Yet in the process they weaken legislative elections as potential referenda on legislators' voting behavior. In addition, they may undermine public confidence in government as a whole. One wonders whether the universalization of a "ticket-fixing" mentality really restores public confidence in government.

Pork Barrel Politics. The bureaucracy is a prime target for legislators who seek to procure special benefits for their district or their state. Moreover, this appears to be true at all levels of government. At the local level, 44 percent of all department heads report at least one legislative request a year for a project or service for a particular district (Abney and Lauth, 1982). At the federal level, members of Congress have long been interested in "bringing home the pork" for their constituents (Ferejohn, 1974). Much of this activity takes place behind the scenes where legislators apply informal pressure on the bureaucracy to allocate funds or to locate a government facility in their district. This informal pressure, hidden from journalistic scrutiny, is often intense and irresistible.

A careful study of water and sewer grants and military base closings at the federal level reveals that legislators on key committees and subcommittees secure a disproportionate share of benefits for their constituents (Arnold, 1979). Membership on the Banking and Currency Committee or the pertinent appropriations subcommittee resulted in favorable Housing and Urban Development (HUD) decisions on water and sewer grants, while membership on the Armed Services Committee helped to prevent the closing down of military facilities.[2] Another systematic study, based on Federal Trade Commission (FTC) actions against antitrust law violators, reached similar conclusions in a regulatory policy arena. Specifically, the FTC brought fewer formal actions against firms located in the congressional districts of members of the House who serve on committees with oversight or budgetary authority over the FTC. The authors refer to this favoritism, also evident in the Senate, as the "antitrust pork barrel" (Faith et al., 1982).

2. Although the Congress alone can appropriate funds, the Congress often delegates discretionary authority to the bureaucracy to fund or not fund particular projects. For example, before the Army Corps of Engineers can undertake a proposed water project, it must secure congressional approval. However, once that approval is granted, it is up to the corps to decide which projects are worthy enough to receive funds for further investigation (Ferejohn, 1974: 18).

Although comparable studies at other levels of government have yet to be made, there is reason to believe that pork barrel politics is both widespread and effective. One in every five local department heads reports that interventions by city council members resulted in favoritism in service delivery (Abney and Lauth, 1982). Nearly one out of every three public works department heads reports such results.

Like casework, pork barrel politics is not new. What is new is that more legislators are strategically situated to exercise the influence once exercised by a few. At the federal level, bureaucrats must be attentive not merely to key committee chairs but to key subcommittee chairs and subcommittee members as well. At the state level, bureaucrats must be attentive not merely to party leaders but also to key committee chairs and committee members. Legislative decentralization has multiplied the number of powerful legislators with whom favor must be curried. At the federal level, the trend toward annual authorizations and annual appropriations provides more frequent opportunities for strategically situated legislators to engage in pork barrel politics. Although a similar pattern is not yet apparent at the state level, the trend toward annual sessions[3] provides greater opportunities for pork barrel politics in state government as well.

The consequences of pork barrel politics are very similar to the consequences of casework, although the beneficiaries are whole districts rather than individual constituents. Like casework, pork barrel politics promotes particularism, because bureaucrats are encouraged to deviate from merit-based norms. In some sense it promotes a more responsive bureaucracy. Yet it promotes bureaucratic flexibility at the expense of bureaucratic justice, sensitivity at the expense of equity. It also promotes the protection of incumbents. Legislators who successfully play the pork barrel politics game are not easily defeated at the polls. As a result, voters have less control over legislative behavior on other issues. Moreover, there are losers in this game, although they don't always know who they are. When bureaucracies respond to pressure to save one military base rather than another, the district with the less influential congressperson loses out. If the less fortunate district also happens to be the one with the higher unemployment rate, the nation as a whole may lose out as well. In short, the skewing of bureaucratic

3. At the present time, four-fifths of all state legislatures meet every year (Rosenthal, 1981: 142).

decision making to accommodate powerful legislators promotes the reelection of individual legislators but does not promote the public interest.

Entrepreneurial Politics. A new style of politics emerged in the 1970s spawned by the consumer movement, the environmental movement, and the growing power of television to turn legislative hearing-rooms into dramatic scenes far more riveting than anything imagined in a Hollywood studio. Wilson (1980) refers to this new style as "entrepreneurial politics" or the pursuit of policies that promote distributed benefits and concentrated costs.[4] Many legislators view entrepreneurial politics with fear and suspicion, preferring to avoid highly conflictual issues such as illegal spying and toxic waste disposal. However, the high visibility of such issues entices other legislators who thrive on controversy, either because they enjoy the challenge of difficult policy problems or because they crave the publicity that such issues generate for the participants. These legislators enjoy playing a "watchdog" role calling errant bureaucrats to account for various sins of omission or commission. The setting for such confrontations is often a formal congressional investigation, though press conferences will do in a pinch.

A number of the congressional investigations conducted in recent years have contributed to the triumph of broad, diffuse interests over narrow, parochial interests, whether inside or outside of government. For example, the Senate Select Committee on Intelligence established in 1975 conducted a widely publicized investigation into illegal and unethical activities by the Federal Bureau of Investigation (FBI), the Central Intelligence Agency (CIA), and the National Security Agency (NSA). These investigations resulted in shocking disclosures of CIA assassination attempts and covert operations (including an ill-fated effort to remove Fidel Castro's facial hair), illegal bugging by the NSA, and a wide variety of infringements on the civil liberties of American citizens by the FBI. Following these disclosures, Congress adopted the Foreign Intelligence Act of 1978, which required a judicial warrant for bugging in most instances. Congress also adopted the Intelligence Oversight Act of 1980, which required the executive branch to notify key members of Congress prior to a CIA covert operation. These

4. Wilson further distinguishes between entrepreneurial politics (distributed benefits, concentrated costs) and majoritarian politics (distributed benefits, distributed costs). As used here, the phrase "entrepreneurial politics" encompasses both of these categories.

provisions have enabled Congress to modify or cancel covert operations in subsequent years (Johnson, 1985: 262).

More recently, congressional investigations into Anne Gorsuch Burford's stewardship at the U.S. Environmental Protection Agency (EPA) led to sharp reversals of several Burford efforts to weaken the federal government's environmental protection efforts. When the EPA announced its intention to suspend a ban on dumping toxic liquid wastes into unlined landfills, congressional pressure (and the threat of a lawsuit) prompted an abrupt about-face (Mosher, 1982; Rosenbaum, 1985: 211). The EPA also backed away from plans to relax or repeal restrictions on lead in gasoline after strong congressional opposition and critical reactions from health experts (Stein, 1982; Shabecoff, 1982; Kenski and Kenski, 1984: 101). Most dramatically, Burford's refusal to provide documents to congressional investigators resulted in her being cited for contempt by Congress. Her credibility destroyed, she had become a liability to the Reagan administration and was persuaded to resign in 1983. Clearly congressional investigators played a major role in reversing the Reagan administration's efforts to dilute environmental protection statutes through rules changes or weak enforcement.

Although entrepreneurial politics in legislative settings has done much to promote environmental protection, consumer protection, civil liberties, and other widely distributed benefits, it has not been without its costs. In particular, entrepreneurial politics often encourages goal displacement as bureaucrats defer to questionable legislative judgments on the measurement of success. By demanding instant results, congressional investigators often demonstrate a "beancounting" mentality that encourages bureaucrats to play a "statistical numbers game" in order to appease congressional watchdogs. For example, Wilson (1978) notes that congressional oversight of the FBI in the 1970s led to demands for statistics to confirm that progress was being made in fighting crime. As a response to congressional pressure, FBI field agents redirected their attention from real criminal informants (less numerous but extremely valuable) to potential criminal informants (more numerous but far less valuable) in order to impress Congress with their success in identifying informants. The results, according to Wilson (1978: 128), were unfortunate: "The pressure for statistical accomplishments in the FBI was clearly making things hard for the agents by forcing them to divert substantial resources from cases they and their supervisors regarded as important and toward matters that were significant only because somebody counted them." Similar experiences seem to have plagued the Drug Enforcement Administration (DEA), which redirected its priorities in order to satisfy congressional demands for better statistics (Wilson, 1978: 46). Ironically, this resulted in less emphasis on "big cases" and more emphasis on "small cases" than Congress would have preferred. If statistics must be generated, small cases offer richer, quicker rewards to bureaucrats under the gun.

In an analysis of budget incentives facing the Food and Drug Administration (FDA), Quirk (1981: 125) found similar forces at work. Jamie Whitten, chair of the House appropriations subcommittee in charge of the FDA's budget, pestered the agency for statistics on food plant inspections as proof that the FDA was doing its job. To satisfy Whitten, FDA officials conducted large numbers of inexpensive food plant inspections with poorly trained personnel (e.g., evaluations of sanitary conditions), while neglecting lengthier but more important investigations by highly trained personnel (e.g., inquiries into possible chemical contamination). These priorities enabled the FDA to protect its budget but were difficult to justify on other grounds.

The consequences of entrepreneurial politics as practiced by legislative overseers are often beneficial for society as a whole. Entrepreneurial politics helps to prevent illegal acts and helps to guard against foot-dragging by bureaucrats who are not really committed to carrying out the law. On the other hand, entrepreneurial politics also contributes to goal displacement. Impatient legislative investigators often place greater emphasis on outputs than on outcomes, greater emphasis on short-term results than on long-term results, greater emphasis on quantitative than on qualitative measures of success. Entrepreneurial politics protects us from the worst excesses of bureaucratic malfeasance, but it also prevents rapid progress toward important goals through methods that do not lend themselves to impressive statistical tables.

Sunset Laws. Of all the checks and balances reforms of the 1970s perhaps the most original was the sunset law, which provides for the automatic termination of an agency on a fixed schedule unless the legislature votes affirmatively to retain the agency. Proposed by Theodore Lowi in 1967, sunset legislation was subsequently endorsed by Common Cause, which championed its adoption at both the state and federal levels. On Capitol Hill, sunset legislation was approved by the Senate in 1978 but it was blocked by the House. At the state level, however, Common Cause was far more successful. At the present time, approximately thirty-five states have some form of sunset legislation.

At first glance, sunset review seems a particularly formidable form of legislative oversight, because the target agency goes out of business unless it can convince legislators that it is doing a vital and worthwhile job. Under sunset laws, the burden of proof is on the agency to demonstrate that it has not outlived its usefulness. If ever there was a "bureau-busting" reform, surely this was it! Yet sunset review is far more coercive in theory than in practice. The executioner's song is seldom heard at the conclusion of sunset review. Indeed, sunset review often looks more like a love feast than a last supper. In many cases, it provides an opportunity for agencies to submit a wish list of recommendations to sympathetic legislators who proceed to strengthen the agency's authority and augment its resources (Gormley, 1983: 87).

The principal reason for this is that sunset review requires legislators to pay attention to agencies they would rather ignore. The low visibility of most agencies targeted for sunset review means that legislators have few incentives to take sunset seriously.[5] There are few benefits to be derived in the home district and few headlines to be obtained outside the district. Consequently, the success or failure of sunset review depends heavily on the motivation, competence, and imagination of staff members within the agency and within the legislature itself. Timing is probably also very important. If an issue arrives on the legislative agenda simultaneously through sunset review and another route (e.g., a gubernatorial proposal to abolish or reorganize an agency), the issue may be salient enough to command serious legislative scrutiny.

Sunset review has not been a complete failure. Some agencies have been abolished in some states (Gregson, 1980). More commonly and more significantly, sunset review has led to certain changes in statutes and agency rules. In Colorado, for example, bans on advertising by health professionals were lifted and continuing education requirements for nurses and optometrists were abolished (Gregson, 1980). In other states, licensing exam guidelines have been strengthened or clarified, auxiliary health care providers have been granted broader discretion, and reciprocity

5. In some states, sunset laws apply to all or most agencies; in others, however, they apply to a subset of agencies, usually occupational licensing boards and other regulatory agencies. In states where large, important agencies are excluded from sunset review, legislative incentives to take sunset seriously are apt to be particularly weak.

between states has been encouraged (Roederer and Palmer, 1981). More broadly, sunset laws have focused some modest legislative attention on agencies that form the "soft underbelly" of state government (e.g., occupational licensing boards)—agencies that are all too often ignored.

On the other hand, sunset review should be viewed with some caution. In many, perhaps most instances, sunset review degenerates into an exercise in symbolic politics. Legislators who feel obliged to do something often recommend a procedural reform— like instituting lay membership on occupational licensing boards— that has no discernible consequences for public policy (Thain and Haydock, 1983; Schutz, 1983). Such cosmetic changes may undermine efforts to adopt more meaningful reforms. In Pennsylvania, a sunset review recommending some modest changes in the operation of the state's Liquor Control Board (e.g., expanded hours) weakened support for a gubernatorial proposal to abolish state stores altogether—a reform that could well have benefited the state's consumers. In several states, provisions for having lay members on occupational licensing boards may have saved such boards from extinction or from a more thorough overhaul. In short, sunset review may promote incrementalism at the expense of innovation.

In conclusion, sunset review has the advantages and disadvantages of legislative oversight by relatively disinterested legislators. In contrast to casework and pork barrel politics, it is less likely to encourage bureaucratic deviations from universalistic norms. In contrast to entrepreneurial politics, it is unlikely to generate the publicity needed for major reform. Sunset review is not merely a form of legislative oversight but a form of policy analysis as well. Like other forms of policy analysis, it seeks to promote efficiency as well as accountability; it is heavily dependent on the technical competence of staff; its primary audience is a professional community rather than journalists or citizens. Yet, in contrast to other forms of legislative policy analysis, it is conducted according to a fixed schedule that bears no relationship to the actual lifecycles of political issues. If sunset review were somehow to elevate obscure issues to a place of real prominence on the legislative agenda, this would be an extraordinary accomplishment with potentially far-reaching results. At the present time, however, sunset review appears to stimulate no more than a modest amount of legislative attention to less visible issues.

Legislative Oversight: An Overall Appraisal. A number of scholars, quite properly, have raised questions about the quality of legislative oversight (Ogul, 1976; Fiorina, 1981; Sundquist, 1981; Rockman, 1985). Unfortunately, other scholars have gone a significant step further, asserting that legislative oversight is largely ineffective (Dodd and Schott, 1979: 247; Schick, 1983: 166). The evidence reported here does not support that conclusion. On the contrary, legislative oversight has had a wide variety of consequences, some intended, some unintended, some procedural, some substantive, some short-term, some long-term, some desirable, some undesirable. Casework and pork barrel politics protect incumbent legislators and encourage bureaucrats to abandon universalistic norms in favor of particularistic norms. They sometimes alert legislators and bureaucrats to problems that transcend a particular individual or district, but this is relatively rare. Entrepreneurial politics promotes broad, diffuse interests in highly salient issue areas (e.g., environmental protection, consumer protection) but also contributes to goal displacement and "beancounting." Sunset review promotes broad, diffuse interests in less salient issue areas (e.g., competition among licensed professionals) but also contributes to incrementalism and symbolic politics. In addition, sunset review has produced its own form of goal displacement as cost-cutting goals have yielded to other objectives.

The cumulative burden of legislative oversight is considerable. For example, in the ninety-fifth Congress, Food and Drug Administration (FDA) representatives made a total of eighty-five appearances before thirty-two separate congressional bodies (Kaufman, 1981: 48). It is not merely that this is time-consuming but that this steady barrage of legislative pressure chips away at one of the most precious advantages of the bureaucratic perspective, namely, a capacity to think about and pursue long-term benefits. If there is a common denominator to the many diverse forms of legislative oversight, it is a quest for immediate gratification through instant results. Another common denominator is intense, often irresistible pressure by individual legislators (legislative freelancers), not the legislature as a whole or the majority party. Legislative oversight, according to Sundquist (1981: 317), is "the power to persuade." In fact, Sundquist does not go far enough. Legislative oversight is not merely the power to persuade but the power to intimidate as well. In some instances, the power of legislative freelancers to intimidate the bureaucracy has been used to undermine universalistic agency norms and to substitute an individual legislator's understanding of the law for the stated (albeit unclear) will of the legislature as a whole. In still other instances, the power to intimidate has encouraged bureaucrats to divert priorities to create the illusion of progress so that impatient legislators can claim a quick success. In short, legislative oversight does promote a certain kind of responsiveness but it also encourages bureaucrats to behave irresponsibly as a response to the irresponsible demands of powerful legislators.

The Legislative Veto

A legislative veto is a legislative act invalidating a rule or decision proposed by an administrative agency or the chief executive. A legislative veto is made possible by a legislative veto provision attached to enabling legislation. The Federal Trade Commission Improvements Act of 1980 permits Congress to veto any trade regulation rule proposed by the FTC. The first legislative veto provision, adopted in 1932, granted the president authority to reorganize the executive branch subject to a one-house veto. Over the next fifty years, legislative veto provisions were attached to other bills from time to time, including public works and foreign affairs statutes.

During the 1970s, as Congress struggled to control the presidency and the bureaucracy, legislative veto provisions multiplied dramatically. Approximately three-fourths of all congressional veto provisions on the books today were adopted during the 1970s (Cooper, 1985: 368). The legislative veto was also institutionalized by numerous state legislatures during the same decade. At the present time, approximately thirty state legislatures provide for the legislative suspension or disapproval of proposed agency rules (Jones, 1982). Another dozen or so state legislatures provide for advisory legislative review of administrative rules.

For years, legal scholars have raised questions about the constitutionality of the legislative veto, especially the one-house veto and the committee veto, because they depart from established constitutional procedures for lawmaking (passage by both chambers and submission to the chief executive for approval). In 1983 in *INS v. Chadha* the U.S. Supreme Court appeared to resolve this lingering controversy once and for all by invalidating a one-house veto not merely on the grounds that it violated the constitutional principle of bicameralism but also on the grounds that it violated the Presentment Clause of the Constitution and the principle of the separation of powers. The Supreme Court also affirmed without comment two appellate court decisions invalidating legislative vetoes, including one involving a two-house veto. In Sundquist's (1983) words, the legislative veto looked like a "bounced check."

However, rumors of the legislative veto's demise were greatly exaggerated. Refusing to take the Supreme Court literally, Congress continued to adopt legislative veto provisions remarkably similar to those that had been invalidated by the Supreme Court. As one congressional insider put it, "It's like the Queen Mary. You can't turn it around that quickly" (Tolchin, 1983). Even if constitutionally suspect legislative veto provisions are eventually stricken down by the federal courts, it is clear that "law forms of the veto" (e.g., joint resolutions of approval or disapproval submitted to the president) are perfectly constitutional (Cooper, 1985). Moreover, the *INS v. Chadha* ruling leaves state legislative vetoes undisturbed.

At first, one might imagine that the legislative veto would be applied most often to highly salient controversies in which large numbers of legislators have a keen interest. In reality, however, this is not the case. For a variety of reasons, committee members would rather not bring highly salient controversies to the floor for a veto vote, because the veto is a rather blunt control instrument, because passage of a veto resolution is difficult, and because it might become clear that committee members do not speak for the legislature as a whole. But that does not mean that the matter is simply dropped. On the contrary, it means that legislative freelancers badger frightened bureaucrats who have little choice but to accept their remonstrations and to heed their instructions.

A good illustration of this phenomenon is the implementation of the highly visible Basic Educational Opportunity Grants (BEOG) program during the 1970s (Bruff and Gellhorn, 1977; Craig, 1983). Through informal negotiations and bargaining, members of the House Subcommittee on Postsecondary Education and the Senate Subcommittee on Education (and their staffs) persuaded the Office of Education (OE) to relax eligibility criteria so that more middle-class families would qualify for grants. This was accomplished over a period of several years without ever bringing a legislative veto resolution to the floor.[6] In contrast, committee members took four minor issues to the House and Senate floors in 1980 when the newly created Department of Education proved less co-

6. As a result of legislation passed in 1972, OE's schedule of "expected family contributions" was subject to a one-house legislative veto; in 1974, the legislative veto was extended to all OE rules of general applicability.

operative than its predecessor agency.[7] In all four cases, the full Congress approved the veto resolutions (Craig, 1983: 96–106). At first, the Department of Education resisted. Eventually, however, a penitent department returned to the familiar pattern of negotiations accepted by its predecessor agency.

Ethridge's (1984) research suggests a similar phenomenon at work at the state level. In a study of legislative vetoes in three states, Ethridge found that a disproportionate number of disapproved agency rules came from small agencies and boards. A reasonable inference is that state legislators were most likely to exercise the veto in less salient issue areas. But that is not to say that the legislature exercised no control over more salient disputes. In another study of all fifty states, Ethridge (1981) found that legislative veto provisions were associated with the adoption of less aggressive air pollution standards by administrative agencies. This suggests that the threat of a legislative veto at the state level as at the federal level is sufficient to alter bureaucratic behavior in highly salient issue areas.

Who benefits from legislative vetoes and legislative veto threats? There is no simple answer to this question, but two patterns are especially common. One pattern, often seen in the actual exercise of a legislative veto, is the triumph of special interest groups (especially business groups), at the expense of broad, diffuse interests (such as consumer interests). For example, in 1982 Congress vetoed a used car rule proposed by the FTC. The FTC's rule was a relatively modest one. It did not require used car dealers to examine cars from bumper to bumper for defects; rather, it merely required them to reveal any defects with which they were familiar. Moreover, it protected them from future liability for defects beyond their knowledge. This was hardly a draconian measure. Nevertheless, Congress, pressured by lobbyists, vetoed the proposed rule. Congress also vetoed a Federal Energy Regulatory Commission (FERC) incremental-pricing rule that would have mitigated the impact of natural gas deregulation on residential consumers (and other high-priority users such as hospitals and schools) (Craig, 1983: 132). The winners in this instance were powerful industrial groups who would have paid somewhat more for natural gas under the proposed rule. Congress also bowed to spe-

7. The four minor issues involved arts-in-education requirements, an education appeals board, law-related education requirements, and federal funds for gym equipment (Craig, 1983: 96–106).

cial interests when it overturned a tough energy conservation policy adopted by the Department of Housing and Urban Development (HUD) after masons objected to thermal insulation standards that would have made masonry construction more expensive (Craig, 1983: 64–68).

Another pattern, often seen in relation to a threat of a legislative veto, is the triumph of the middle class or whites over the poor or minorities. The threat of a legislative veto appears to have been sufficient to convince the Office of Education (OE) to broaden the number of persons eligible for Basic Educational Opportunity Grants (BEOGs), thus diluting the redistributive impact of the program (Bruff and Gellhorn, 1977: 1383–85; Craig, 1983: 83–85). Whether intentionally or not, these actions harmed the poor. As one individual put it, "To the extent you provide money to the middle income students when there are limited amounts for BOG . . . you are taking it away from lower income kids" (Craig, 1983: 92). Similarly, HUD responded to a legislative veto threat by withdrawing a spatial deconcentration rule that would have guaranteed equal opportunity for minority applicants for housing constructed with federal funds.[8] In this instance, the beneficiaries were whites who were competing with blacks for scarce housing space (and whites who preferred not to live in close proximity to blacks).

There are to be sure examples where the legislative veto has been used to promote broad, diffuse interests, as in the House Interior Committee's veto of coal-leasing at "ridiculously low prices" by Interior Secretary James Watt.[9] By and large, however, the legislative veto has been used to dilute the impact of programs targeted at the poor and to promote the interests of powerful business groups. These conclusions emerge not only from case studies but also from more systematic studies. For example, Ethridge (1984) found that state legislatures were most likely to reject administrative rules that imposed tough restrictions on the business community.

8. The Department of Housing and Urban Development would have done this by requiring advance marketing in minority neighborhoods and by prohibiting residency requirements as a condition for occupancy.

9. Interestingly enough, the House Interior Committee exercised the veto after the INS v. Chadha decision. A federal district court judge upheld the coal-leasing veto despite INS v. Chadha on the grounds that the Constitution grants Congress "power to dispose of and make all needful rules and regulations respecting the territory or other property belonging to the U.S." (Shribman, 1983).

The procedural side effects of the legislative veto are equally disturbing. The legislative veto has been used to stifle administrative innovations (at the FTC) and to revise administration decisions based on considerable public input (at HUD). The legislative veto has enabled committee chairs and staffs to substitute their wills for that of the legislature as a whole and to unravel carefully crafted legislative compromises (OE). It may also have discouraged rulemaking, since agencies can escape the threat of a veto by opting instead for case-by-case decision making. If so, the legislative veto has encouraged precisely the sort of bargaining (at the case level) that proponents of a stronger legislative presence have sought to eradicate (Lowi, 1979: 92–126).

In some respects, the threat of a legislative veto is even more troublesome than the veto itself. That is because the veto is less likely to be applied to matters that really count. On the surface, the threat of a legislative veto is far less coercive than the actual exercise of a legislative veto. In practice, however, the threat of a veto is both more common and more significant. Following the congressional veto of its used car rule, the FTC simply abandoned that rule in favor of a weak informational disclosure requirement. Following a congressional decision to subject all of its trade regulation rules to a two-house veto, the FTC dropped its children's television inquiry, declined to propose rotating warnings on cigarette boxes, softened a proposed funeral rule, and declined to ask for congressional permission to resume its insurance studies (Pertschuk, 1982: 113). While the changing composition of the commission undoubtedly contributed to these decisions, FTC commissioners could hardly ignore the Sword of Damocles hanging over their heads.

Statutory Specificity

For years scholars have criticized Congress (and other legislative bodies) for adopting vague, ambiguous legislation devoid of substantive content. Statutory vagueness according to Lowi (1969) is the root cause of many of the worst features of interest group liberalism—endless bargaining and equivocation, incestuous relations between bureaucrats and their clients, incrementalism, and so forth. Stung by such criticism, Congress has pursued a strikingly different approach in tackling several of today's most controversial policy problems, including air pollution, water pollution, consumer product safety, occupational safety, mine safety, and toxic waste disposal. Instead of instructing new regulatory agencies to promote "the public interest, convenience, or necessity" in the pattern of earlier years, Congress has issued instructions to the bureaucracy in sharp specific terms.

The best examples of statutory specificity can be found in environmental legislation, especially the Clean Air Act Amendments of 1970 and the Federal Water Pollution Control Act Amendments of 1972. These statutes are exceptionally specific in three respects: they contain clear priorities, specific standards, and fixed deadlines.

1. *Clear Priorities.* The environmental statutes of the 1970s established the overriding importance of public health and safety goals as opposed to economic efficiency. In most instances, statutes relegated cost considerations to a position of secondary importance, permitting regulators to consider costs but requiring them to place primary emphasis on environmental protection. In other instances, Congress excluded cost considerations from regulatory calculations altogether, as in the requirement that national air quality standards be set without regard to economic feasibility.

2. *Specific Standards.* The environmental statutes of the 1970s ordained highly specific standards linked to the "best available" or the "best practicable" technology. In most instances, Congress left it up to the EPA administrator to determine exactly which technologies were practicable, available, and the best (scrubbers for stationary sources of air pollution, catalytic converters for automobiles, treatment systems for sewage). However, Congress usually insisted that such technological controls apply to all polluters or to an entire class of polluters (e.g., all new sources of air pollution or all new nonmunicipal sources of waste). Congress specified not only that the standards would be technology-based but also to whom the standards would apply.

3. *Fixed Deadlines.* The environmental statutes of the 1970s required the EPA to achieve certain goals by a fixed date. For example, the Clean Air Act Amendments of 1970 required a 90 percent reduction in auto emissions of hydrocarbons and carbon monoxide by 1975 and a 90 percent reduction in nitrogen oxide emissions by 1976. Similarly, the Federal Water Pollution Control Act Amendments of 1972 speci-

fied that all industrial plants must install the best practicable technology for pollution control by 1977 and the best available technology by 1983; the same statute required municipal treatment plants to install the best practicable technology by 1983.

Although the consequences of these statutes cannot be specified with precision, it is clear that the United States has made considerable progress in combating pollution during the 1970s. From 1970 to 1979, the amount of sulfur dioxide in the atmosphere declined by 40 percent, particulates declined by 17 percent, and carbon monoxide declined by 40 percent. The reduction in auto emissions was especially dramatic. By 1978 the emission of hydrocarbons by new automobiles had declined by more than two-thirds and that of carbon monoxide and nitrogen oxides by one-half and two-thirds respectively (Schwarz, 1983: 65–66). Significant reductions in lead emissions were also achieved.

Progress in eradicating water pollution was slower, partly because legislators virtually ignored water pollution from nonpoint sources, which accounts for approximately one-half of all water pollution. In contrast to point-source pollution, which can be traced to a municipal sewage treatment plant or some other facility, nonpoint pollution emanates from diffuse sources. Examples include urban storm water runoff, mine runoff, and runoff from agricultural activities. Nevertheless, overall water quality remained stable at a time when population growth and industrial growth might have been expected to yield greater quantities of water wastes and greater amounts of water pollution. Moreover, certain changes were both positive and dramatic. The quality of water in the Great Lakes improved significantly as evidenced by the renewed popularity of fishing and swimming in Lake Erie. In addition, a number of major rivers including the Mississippi, the Cuyahoga, the Willamette, and the Hudson reported reductions in various organic and chemical pollutants.

These are significant achievements and there are reasons to believe that they would not have been possible without the strong, specific statutes of the 1970s. Yet, before extolling the virtues of statutory specificity, it is important to consider three counterarguments: First, that significant progress in environmental protection could have been achieved without clear statutory priorities; second, that significant environmental progress could have been achieved through less costly means or methods; and third, that statutory specificity guarantees disappointment and cynicism by creating unrealistic expectations and positing unattainable goals.

At first glance, the critics make a strong case that statutory specificity was not a prerequisite to significant progress in environmental protection. Sweden, which abjured fixed deadlines, a health-effects-only approach, and a technology-forcing strategy, nevertheless appears to have achieved air pollution reductions comparable to those in the United States during the same period (Lundqvist, 1980). Britain, which adopted a strategy similar to Sweden's, also has achieved air pollution gains roughly comparable to those of the United States (Vogel, 1983). The authors of these studies conclude that the United States has much to learn from Sweden and Great Britain, which accomplished as much as we did without resorting to draconian measures and a confrontational style.

There is however another way to interpret these cross-national comparisons. In contrast to both Britain and Sweden, the United States is characterized by a federal structure and a tradition of weak, decentralized parties (which are getting weaker all the time). Such systemic elements make dramatic changes extremely difficult because they frustrate coalition building and magnify problems at the policy implementation stage. Given the American political system's bias against rapid progress on any front, especially domestic policy where states' rights and decentralized political parties are particularly pertinent, it is remarkable that the United States accomplished as much as it did in environmental protection so quickly. Lundqvist (1980) may be correct when he suggests that the Swedish tortoise advanced as far as the American hare. But an American tortoise might have been much slower than either. Without specific statutory standards, it is unlikely that the United States could have moved so far so rapidly.

A second criticism of statutory specificity is more difficult to rebut. Some economists acknowledge that the United States has made remarkable progress in cleaning up the air and the nation's streams, but they contend that technology-forcing inflates costs unnecessarily. Consider, for example, the Clean Air Act Amendments of 1977. Among other things these amendments required emissions reductions for new sources of air pollution. This statutory provision encouraged the EPA to require all new coal-burning power plants to use "scrubbers" when a more cost-effective strategy would have been to permit the use of low-sulfur coal without scrubbers as an alternative (Crandall, 1983). The more general criticism is that Congress has relied too much on "command and control" (regulatory) strategies, too little on incentive-based (market) strategies for protecting the environment, such as bubbles, offsets, and banks.[10]

There is much to be said in favor of greater administrative discretion in these matters and in favor of greater emphasis on incentives as an alternative to command-and-control regulation. However, it is important to distinguish between problems caused by overly specific statutes and problems caused by overly directive committee reports. The key reason for the EPA's universal scrubbing rule was not the Clean Air Act Amendments of 1977,[11] but rather a conference report that tied the hands of the EPA administrator by requiring some percentage reduction in emissions, even for plants using low-sulfur coal (Ackerman and Hassler, 1981: 48–54). Similarly, one can argue that the worst side effects of the Clean Air Act Amendments of 1977 (e.g., the reluctance of utility companies to abandon old, dilapidated power plants) are attributable not to technology-forcing as such but rather to the gap between requirements for new and old facilities. A statute requiring existing facilities to install the best available technology by a fixed date would have effectively eliminated the escape hatch that has discouraged the construction of new, cleaner facilities. In broader terms, highly specific environmental statutes do not preclude the incentive-based approach that many economists endorse. For example, the EPA has been granting "bubble" requests with varying degrees of enthusiasm and apprehension since 1979. The fact that more bubbles have not been issued is due more to problems with bubbles themselves (and the opposition of environmental groups)

10. Bubbles are imaginary enclosures placed over several emissions sources within the same plant. A firm may exceed emissions ceilings at one source, provided that it reduces emissions by a greater amount elsewhere within the "bubble." Offsets enable a firm to open a new plant in an air quality region that does not meet national standards. The new plant may open if its emissions are "offset" by a comparable reduction in emissions from other plants within the region. Banks promote pollution-reducing exchanges between plants by giving firms credit for emissions reductions that exceed requirements. Firms may "bank" these credits for future use themselves or sell them to other firms as offsets.

11. The statute itself required the EPA to establish emissions reduction standards for all new sources but did not require universal scrubbing. Rather, the statute prescribed emissions standards that reflect "the degree of emission limitation achievable through the application of the best system of emission reduction which (taking into account the cost of achieving such reduction) the administrator determines has been adequately demonstrated." In addition, the statute clearly allowed for variable emissions reductions among different categories of polluters.

than to statutory constraints. While the Congress has not gone far enough to encourage incentive-based approaches like bubbles, statutory vagueness seems less likely to encourage bubbles than statutory specificity aimed at promoting bubbles and other devices that take costs into account.

A third and final criticism of statutory specificity has been that it creates unrealistic goals and expectations, fostering public cynicism and distrust. As Melnick (1983: 383) puts it, "It is poor regulatory policy to set goals that greatly exceed the resources the political community is willing to expend." A related argument made by Rosenbaum (1980) is that highly specific statutes are often unenforceable. Based on a careful content analysis of coastal zoning statutes in fourteen states, Rosenbaum (1980) found no relationship between statutory specificity and enforcement powers. If as Rosenbaum (1980: 576) suggests, "the more stringent the mandate for change, the more stringent the enforcement process must be," then the absence of a relationship between specificity and enforcement powers means that highly specific statutes will often be difficult to enforce. Rosenbaum cites Maine and Rhode Island as good examples of states with very specific coastal zoning statutes that are extremely difficult to enforce. Melnick (1983) argues that federal air pollution statutes have proven to be equally difficult to enforce.

These are serious and troublesome criticisms. However, there are two possible remedies: statutes that are more enforceable because they try to accomplish less; or statutes that are more enforceable because they provide the tools to accomplish more. There are, in short, two very different ways to bridge the gap between ambitious goals and the grim realities of regulatory practice. Nor is it clear that unrealistic goals are as disastrous as critics contend. In retrospect, it is obvious that auto emissions deadlines set by Congress in 1970 were unrealistic. However, these "unrealistic" goals sent a powerful message to the EPA, to citizens' groups, to judges, and to Detroit. Other "unrealistic" goals put water polluters and toxic waste manufacturers on notice that environmental damage would no longer be tolerated.

In comparison to other forms of legislative control, there is much to be said for lawmaking generally and for statutory specificity in particular. A key advantage of lawmaking is that it constitutes collective action as opposed to legislative freelancing. Because collective action is more visible and more enduring than other forms of legislative intervention, legislators have the incentive to appeal

TABLE 8.2

An Overview of Alternative Forms of Legislative Control

	Legislative Oversight		Legislative Veto		Law
	Latent	*Manifest*	*Threat*	*Exercise*	*Statutory Specificity*
Form of legislative action	freelancing	freelancing	freelancing	collective action	collective action
Issue visibility	low	low to high	moderate to high	low to moderate	high
Apparent coercion	threatening	threatening	threatening	binding	binding
Actual coercion	moderate to high	moderate to high	high	high	moderate
Consequences	error correction, compassion; particularism, favoritism, discrimination	environmental protection, consumer protection, competition; goal displacement, beancounting, symbolic politics	middle-class politics, distributive politics, something for everyone, incrementalism	special interest politics, clientelism, capture, incrementalism	public health and safety, technological innovation; inefficiency, rigidity

to broad, diffuse constituencies, provided that the issues at stake are high in salience. Indeed, in some instances legislators find themselves taking a long-term perspective, something that does not come naturally to politicians. In contrast, other forms of legislative control exhibit many of the worst features of legislative freelancing. More often than not, they promote particularism at the expense of universalism; they substitute short-run political gains for long-run policy benefits; they subvert the will of the legislature as a whole; they strengthen iron triangles; and they reduce the bureaucracy's capacity for innovation. Legislative freelancing is usually a poor alternative to lawmaking.

Nor is statutory specificity as coercive as it seems to be. Although statutes with clear priorities, specific standards, and fixed deadlines are binding on bureaucracies, they almost always leave bureaucrats some discretion. Even specific statutes contain loopholes, as well they should. Such loopholes, if properly fashioned, preserve a degree of bureaucratic flexibility and permit the formulation of innovative rules that are consistent with overall policy objectives. In contrast, other forms of legislative control are openly coercive or they are more coercive than they seem to be. The legislative veto flatly prohibits certain forms of bureaucratic behavior, thus discouraging important bureaucratic initiatives. More insidiously, legislative veto threats induce bureaucratic capitulation to a handful of legislative freelancers who dominate a particular policy arena. Paradoxically, "binding" forms of legislative control such as specific statutes are less coercive in practice than "nonbinding" forms of legislative control such as legislative oversight and the threat of a legislative veto.

An important exception to these general patterns involves entrepreneurial politics, which has more in common with statutory specificity than with other forms of legislative oversight. In fact, it may be that entrepreneurial politics and statutory specificity constitute different stages of the same phenomenon—a commitment to a common good that is more than the mere sum of special interests. Neither statutory specificity nor entrepreneurial politics is a perfect remedy for all bureaucratic maladies. Like statutory specificity, entrepreneurial politics may contribute to inefficiency and rigidity in some instances. It may even discourage "optimal" innovations by locking in "sub-optimal" innovations, as when the pressure for catalytic converters diverted Detroit from the search for alternatives to the internal combustion engine (Jacoby and Steinbruner, 1973; Wilson, 1974: 149; Marcus, 1980: 16). Nevertheless, entrepreneurial politics like statutory specificity does promote broad, diffuse interests such as environmental protection and consumer protection. It promotes some vision, however flawed, of the common good. It helps curb bureaucratic tendencies toward clientelism. It also overcomes systemic tendencies toward incrementalism. For all these reasons, entrepreneurial politics and statutory specificity are superior to other forms of legislative control.

Conclusion

There is much more legislative control of the bureaucracy today than there was in 1970 when bureau-bashing began in earnest. Legislative oversight has increased sharply at both the state and federal levels as a result both of official reforms (the creation of oversight subcommittees, sunset review, and so forth) and of unofficial trends (decentralization, professionalization). The legislative veto, used intermittently over the years, became extremely popular in the 1970s. Despite *INS v. Chadha*, the legislative veto continues to prosper in Washington, D.C., and in many states (Levinson, 1987). Finally, legislative bodies in several instances have adopted clear, specific statutes, as recommended by various scholars years ago (Jaffe, 1955; Lowi, 1969). Statutory specificity is most striking in the areas of environmental protection, occupational safety, and consumer protection.

Despite these reforms, there has been no concomitant decline in bureaucratic incrementalism, clientelism, or parochialism—the problems these reforms were supposed to curb or cure. Indeed in many instances legislative control has actually made matters worse. In part, this is because legislative control is coercive in form or substance or both. Far more than the power to persuade, it is the power to intimidate. Bureaucrats fear legislators and for good reasons. Legislators have been impatient, abusive, insistent, and vindictive. As a result legislative pressure makes bureaucrats uncommonly cautious. Although legislative pressure encourages a certain kind of responsiveness (to legislative freelancers in particular), it seldom encourages innovation. On the contrary, certain legislative control mechanisms such as the legislative veto have served the express purpose of quashing bureaucratic innovations that are unpopular with legislators who sit on key committees or subcommittees.

The deeper tragedy is that legislative pressure serves so often to narrow rather than to broaden the bureaucracy's perspective. This is because legislative control of the bureaucracy almost always suffers from a visibility problem of some sort. At first, this assertion seems implausible because legislative efforts to control the bureaucracy are in some respects more visible than ever before. Yet as Table 8.3 suggests, there are in fact two important kinds of visibility that need to be considered simultaneously: issue visibility and process visibility.[12] Issue visibility refers to the salience of the substantive controversy (e.g., federal funding for abortion), while process visibility refers to the salience of the decision-making procedure (e.g., a congressional subcommittee vote). Unless both issues and processes are visible, journalists and public interest groups lack both awareness and interest. Without their attentiveness, broad, diffuse interests are unlikely to triumph. As Schattschnei-

12. In general, scholars have been far more attentive to issue visibility (Cobb and Elder, 1972; Price, 1978; Ripley and Franklin, 1984) than to process visibility. There has been little recognition of interaction between the two.

TABLE 8.3

Issue Visibility, Process Visibility, and Legislative Control

	Issue Visibility	
	Low	*High*
Process Visibility	Sunset review (public hearings, committee reports)	Statutory specificity (public hearings, committee reports, lengthy floor debates)
High	Legislative veto, exercise (public hearings, committee votes, floor debate)	Entrepreneurial politics (press conferences, public hearings, committee reports)
	Casework (telephone calls, letters)	Legislative veto, threat (informal negotiations, bargaining)
Low	Pork barrel politics (telephone calls, letters)	

der (1960) has argued, the "scope of conflict" must be expanded if special interests are to be overcome. Aware of this, special interest groups and public officials often conspire to limit process visibility when issue visibility is high. Because issue visibility and process visibility are seldom high at the same time, most legislative control mechanisms do little to promote the common good.

When issue visibility and process visibility are both low (as they are in casework and pork barrel politics), legislators are free to function as ombudsmen and procurers on behalf of their constituents (individual or collective). Bureaucrats respond by abandoning universalistic norms in order to accommodate powerful legislators. When issue visibility is low but process visibility is high (e.g., as in sunset review and the exercise of the legislative veto), neither journalists nor public interest groups care enough to pay much attention. Indeed, legislators themselves are often uninterested, so that legislative staffs play a critical role in structuring alternatives and brokering solutions. When issue visibility is high but process visibility is low (e.g., as in the threat of a legislative veto), the attention span of journalists and the persistence of public interest groups are put to a severe test. Having covered this story before, journalists would rather move on to something else (stale news is not the stuff of which Pulitzers are made). Having intervened already in the administrative process, citizens' groups lack the stamina for an eleventh hour defense of gains achieved in other forums. Special interest groups, in contrast, are willing and able to fight. Not surprisingly, policy outcomes reflect the greater resources and efforts of these latter groups.

When issue visibility and process visibility are both high (as they are in entrepreneurial politics and statutory specificity), legislative control that promotes the common good is indeed a possibility. With journalists and public interest groups looking over their shoulders, legislators have ample incentive to function as policy entrepreneurs or trustees. Yet entrepreneurial politics has its dysfunctional aspects, as noted. In particular, the glare of publicity encourages quick solutions to problems that do not lend themselves to quick solutions. Short-term results become more important than long-term results, the appearance of short-term results becomes more important than the reality of short-term results, and outputs become more important than outcomes. Goal displacement is an ever-present danger. Specific statutes also create expectations for quick results. Yet, such expectations are less damaging than the demands of legislative freelancers. The expectations of the legislature as a whole can be satisfied in a variety of ways; the demands of individual legislators are much more confining. Paradoxically, specific statutes are less coercive than other forms of legislative control, including legislative oversight through entrepreneurial politics. Statutory specificity and entrepreneurial politics are alike in their pursuit of widely distributed benefits. However, that pursuit is more likely to succeed when undertaken by the legislature as a whole than when undertaken by legislative freelancers. Statutory specificity and entrepreneurial politics have the common advantage of high issue visibility and process visibility, but they differ in this crucial respect: specific statutes, though nominally more restrictive, are in fact more likely to preserve the bureaucracy's capacity for innovation and flexibility.

Conclusion

Muscles

Following the Iran-Contra hearings, Ben Wattenberg was asked to comment on the meaning of this experience for American politics. In his view, the hearings were neither surprising nor extraordinary: "This is a muscular, sweaty democracy we live in where people beat up on each other's head" (1987). This is an apt description not just of the Iran-Contra hearings but of the past two decades in American politics. Legislators, chief executives, and judges have beaten up on one another. Even more frequently, they have beaten up on bureaucrats. Not to be outdone, federal bureaucrats have beaten up on state bureaucrats, who in turn have beaten up on local bureaucrats. And the beating goes on. If bureau-bashing peaked during the 1970s, it continues to flourish during the 1980s.

Like Wattenberg, I have stressed the muscles and the sweat of checks and balances. There are however three hidden premises behind the Wattenberg statement that I would like to challenge. The first is that the muscular quality of American democracy is deeply rooted in our culture, that it is a persistent trait dating back to Teddy Roosevelt, Davy Crockett, George Washington, and the Minutemen. It is true that we have celebrated our warriors, especially when they have participated in a patriotic cause. But so too have other societies. It is also true that Americans are known for being blunt, outspoken, direct, boorish, and impatient. Our political system accentuates these traits by emphasizing checks and balances, which institutionalize tension and conflict. There is, however, an important distinction between checks and balances and a running brawl.

The recent rash of bureau-bashing reforms, though in keeping with the spirit of checks and balances, has in fact unbalanced our system of government by placing an extraordinary emphasis on one kind of check (muscles) aimed at one kind of institution (the bureaucracy) and by developing few if any counterchecks to permit self-defense. More subtly, we have shifted our expectations of the bureaucracy from problem-solving to compliance. Ironically, this has happened at the same time that the bureaucracy's capacity for creative problem-solving has increased substantially, especially at the state level. In a sense, we seem to have decided that the bureaucracy should have twentieth-century responsibilities but eighteenth-century powers. In the short run, this contributes to bean-counting, proceduralism, avoidance, particularism, defeatism and other pathologies identified in this book. In the long run, it means that the bureaucracy will spend more time making excuses than making policy.

A second premise behind Wattenberg's statement is the notion that beating up on someone draws attention to a problem. In a society where a public brawl is an unusual event, that is no doubt true. But if bureau-bashing becomes routine, and it has, we may become so jaded that the only people who really notice are those who are being bashed. By relying frequently on the most formidable weapons in their arsenal, politicians and judges may have dulled our sensitivity to those weapons and what they imply. As a result, ordinary citizens are unable to distinguish between bureaucratic felonies and misdemeanors. When bureau-bashing becomes commonplace, it loses its capacity to rivet our attention.

A third premise behind Wattenberg's statement is the proposition that muscles and democracy somehow go hand in hand. Yet we normally associate muscles with totalitarian societies, not democratic societies. To be sure the muscular feature of tolalitarian societies that frightens us the most is government coercion of citizens, not government officials coercing other government officials. But coercion, once unleashed, may not be easily channeled. If government officials lack respect for one another, why should they respect citizens and why should citizens respect one another?

From the vantage point of the bureaucracy's overseers, one form of coercion may be a cure for another more disturbing form of coercion. Judge William Justice coerced Texas prison officials and state legislators into providing humane treatment to prisoners when it became apparent that the constitutional rights of prisoners were being violated. Conditions in Texas prisons have improved somewhat, and Judge Justice has been the prime mover behind that progress. However, the costs have been high. The Texas prison system was a powder keg waiting to explode and Judge Justice seems to have lit the match. According to close observers, the court orders triggered a breakdown in the state penitentiary's informal norms, engendered a growing restiveness among inmates, and encouraged a breakdown in authority resulting in frequent personnel turnover, riots and deaths (Alpert et al., 1984; Press, 1986; DiIulio, 1987). Judge Justice did not create the unconstitutional conditions in Texas prisons and he had no choice but to intervene. However, there is a critical distinction to be maintained between judicial intervention and judicial coercion. Had Judge Justice worked harder to secure the cooperation of state authorities, progress in the state prison system might have been achieved without these tragic upheavals. Beating up on each other's head is seldom a solution to virulent social problems.

Prayers

It is often remarked that business occupies a "privileged position" in our society and that this poses problems for democratic theory (Lindblom, 1977). This is accurate and worrisome. Thanks to some recent reforms, however, consumers, environmentalists, the poor, and the elderly also occupy a privileged position in the sense that they are guaranteed a voice in the administrative process. They have been designated by elected officials as groups that deserve a chance to be heard—in public utility commission (PUC) ratemaking proceedings, at Environmental Protection Agency (EPA) rulemaking proceedings, in welfare benefit decisions, in nursing home inspections. The privileges of these broad, diffuse groups are perhaps not as great as those of organized business or even of organized labor. Their prayers are not as eloquent; their chants are not as vigorous. As Schattschneider (1960: 35) would put it, "the heavenly chorus (still) sings with a strong upper-class accent." Nevertheless, these reforms have been both durable and important.

There is in fact a significant gap between the theoretical and the empirical literature on interest representation in the administrative process. The theoretical literature tells us that broad, diffuse groups will not organize (Olson, 1965), that they will be pacified by symbolic concessions (Edelman, 1964), and that they will be stymied by bureaucratic inertia and imperialism (Niskanen, 1971). Yet the empirical literature tells a very different story. Ombudsmen have secured important victories for citizens at the state and local levels, including nursing home residents who have difficulty speaking for themselves. Proxy advocates have successfully promoted consumer protection and energy conservation in public utility regulation. Public hearings have enabled environmental groups to promote clean air, clean water, and land preservation. Freedom of information acts and open meetings have provided valuable opportunities to expand the scope of conflict and to sharpen the submissions of resource-poor groups.

It is worth noting that much of the theoretical literature antedates the reforms of recent years. Whatever may have been true twenty years ago, prayers on behalf of large constituencies are no longer figments of the imagination or exercises in futility. In the 1980s, prayers have several components that account for their success:

1. *The Blessing.* The Congress and other legislative bodies have established new organizations and have designated them as having special missions to perform. These organizations include legal aid societies, ombudsmen, and proxy advocacy organizations. In addition, legislators have legitimized citizen intervention in the administrative process by approving it in advance. A key criticism of public intervenors has been that they do not really speak for the public interest. By designating certain groups as having a special claim as public spokespersons, elected officials have helped to pinpoint where the public interest lies. There is a kind of "halo effect" here. When citizens or their surrogates intervene in the administrative process, they now do so with the public blessing of elected officials. This encourages bureaucrats to listen.

2. *The Service.* There is a new kind of liturgy in the administrative process. Much of it is outlined in the federal Administrative Procedure Act (APA) and its state-level counterparts. Most of it is now accessible to the public thanks to the Government in the Sunshine Act, the Freedom of Information Act, and similar state statutes. There is also considerable lay participation. In addition, there is a good deal of pageantry reserved for special occasions. This includes candlelight vigils, colorful language and garments, and public displays of joy or grief. Services are more interactive, more open and more lively.

3. *The Petition.* The actual content of prayers has changed significantly in recent years. Petitions are no longer simple pleas but detailed documents—requests backed up by data. The wish lists of the past have given way to impressive statements replete with arguments, tables, and footnotes.

The accent is on persuasion, not expression. The hope is for relief, not a miracle. The claim is moral but rooted in reason, not faith.

Jawboning

In many policy settings, neither muscles nor prayers will work. Muscles may trigger unnecessary resentment, rigidity, and litigation; prayers may result in slow, fitful progress toward important social goals. Fortunately, the bureaucracy's sovereigns have other instruments at their disposal. These instruments may be thought of as hortatory controls. In effect, they rely upon a "jawboning" strategy to induce cooperation from a reluctant bureaucracy. Promises and threats are common, although the threats typically leave the bureaucracy some room to maneuver.

Jawboning frequently results in a protracted bargaining process, with bureaucrats and their overseers making concessions. This can be time-consuming and frustrating, but it avoids such side effects as sabotage, subversion, and defeatism. It encourages conflict resolution outside the courtroom. And it paves the way for cooperation in the future. When a quick fix is not absolutely necessary, jawboning constitutes a superior alternative to muscles.

Jawboning has become commonplace in intergovernmental relations, after a decade of experimentation with muscles (mandates) and prayers (general revenue-sharing). Intergovernmental jawboning has been strikingly successful when it has taken the form of partial preemptions. By delegating authority to state bureaucracies that agree to enforce federal standards, the federal government has saved money and preserved a degree of state discretion without sacrificing important national goals. Thanks to partial preemptions, we have made considerable progress in pursuing such goals as clean air, clean water, land reclamation, and occupational health and safety. Partial preemptions have succeeded because they have placed a premium on cooperation and mutual respect. They have also succeeded because relatively specific statutes have given federal bureaucracies considerable bargaining power in their dealings with the states.

Jawboning has been equally popular within the executive branch. Through jawboning, governors and presidents have pursued policy goals without exceeding their competence or undermining bureaucratic morale. By holding cabinet meetings and sub-cabinet meetings, governors have promoted greater coherence and integration in executive decision making. Thanks to the Senior Executive Service (SES), presidents have greater leverage over top career executives in the federal bureaucracy. In contrast to other more destructive controls (the politicization of the Office of Personnel Management, reductions in force, heavy-handed interventions by the Office of Management and Budget), the SES has the potential to promote trust and cooperation within the executive branch.

In the judiciary, jawboning has also yielded rich rewards. Federal judges have been able to secure prison reforms through skillful negotiations without actually taking over state facilities (Spiller, 1977). Federal judges have also improved conditions in state mental hospitals after working out the details with interested parties (Moss, 1984). In the judiciary as in other arenas there is a "slippery slope" that leads from hortatory controls to coercive controls. However, if judges and politicians are mindful of these dangers they can coax a reluctant bureaucracy to promote important social goals without sacrificing trust, flexibility, and cooperation.

Strategic Choices, Instrumental Choices

Reformers who seek to control the bureaucracy face two important decisions: the choice of strategies (muscles or prayers or jawboning) and the choice of instruments (public hearings or proxy advocacy, legislative vetoes or clear statutes, civil service reform or executive orders). In making such choices, reformers need to take both issue characteristics (e.g., complexity, conflict) and bureaucratic characteristics (e.g., skill, support) into account. Public hearings are likely to be very effective in environmental policy but fruitless in insurance regulation where issue visibility and constituency arousal are low. The hard look doctrine is likely to promote reasoned deliberation when an agency with understandable goals is neglected by politicians but may undermine reasoned deliberation and promote confusion when an agency with a complex mission is already receiving numerous instructions from political overseers. Intergovernmental mandates make more sense when a bureaucracy is infected with hatred or discrimination than when a bureaucracy is merely slow or strapped for funds.

The choice of instruments is especially important if we opt for coercive controls because of the extraordinary harm they can cause. For this reason, I have urged that coercive controls be characterized by legitimacy, selectivity, scalability, enforceability, and reversibility. Otherwise one set of bureaucratic pathologies will simply give way to another, with no net improvement in social welfare. Indeed the pathologies generated by excessive bureaucratic control are often more insidious than those that triggered the controls in the first place. That is because we often assume the legitimacy of political control without asking hard questions about the representativeness of an individual legislator or the clarity of an electoral mandate. Judges receive similar deference, except perhaps during confirmation hearings.

If strategic choices are so important we need to make them with greater care. At least three approaches are consistent with the themes of this book. First, when in doubt, we might choose the middle course (jawboning) as a way of hedging our bets. This way, we may be wrong, but we won't be far wrong. Second, we could begin with the least intrusive option (prayers) and then escalate if the need arises. This presumes that control is an iterative process with opportunities for revision. Third, we might try to get the match right in the first place. With so much at stake, we might seek to optimize when making strategic choices, while satisficing when making instrumental choices.

In chapter 1, I argued in favor of a matching strategy. By taking issue characteristics and bureaucratic characteristics into account, we ought to be able to design reforms appropriate to the situation at hand. This requires us to think carefully and shrewdly about issue characteristics and bureaucratic characteristics, viewing control in purposive rather than expressive terms. However, there are at least two circumstances under which matching is impractical. When issues are highly complex, uncertainty is likely to be high, and it becomes difficult to predict the consequences of a particular intervention. As we begin a matching exercise, we might discover that a single issue characteristic undermines the entire enterprise (i.e., if an issue is complex enough, we may be unable to determine whether the bureaucracy has the right skills for a particular job). A second situation can be equally exasperating. When a problem is highly urgent there is not enough time for a matching exercise that amounts to anything more than guesswork. Some decisions must be made almost immediately (whether to grant injunctive relief, whether to issue an executive order in an emergency). In short, there are circumstances in which a full-scale matching exercise is not feasible.

If there is not enough time or information for matching, we might simply choose the middle course (jawboning) and hope for the best. Although the middle course may eventually prove to be too strong or too weak for the problem, we won't be that far wrong and some fine-tuning may be possible down the road. Unfortunately, however, the middle course is the most time-consuming of all for the bureaucracy's overseers. Jawboning requires lengthy discussions and negotiations, rewards and sanctions, close monitoring and supervision, feedback and evaluations. Jawboning also requires exceptional leadership skills that many politicians, judges, and federal bureaucrats may lack. Indeed, the classic example of jawboning—John F. Kennedy's attempt to induce U.S. Steel to moderate its price increases—is widely acknowledged as a failure (Pious, 1979: 327–28). Thus, even if they have the patience for jawboning, the bureaucracy's overseers may lack the talent to make it succeed.

The final option is to begin with the least intrusive strategy (prayers) and to escalate pressure if necessary. This may not be the right strategy for all seasons because it may result in incrementalism or even backsliding when bureaucratic resistance is high. Moreover, the weakest remedy may be unacceptable when constitutional rights are at stake, as is the case with racial integration in the public schools (Hochschild, 1984). On the other hand, this approach has many advantages. In general, the least intrusive strategy is also the least time-consuming for judges, politicians, and federal bureaucrats who have other responsibilities besides overseeing the bureaucracy. In effect, they rely on citizens, citizen groups, or citizen surrogates to promote certain values they believe to be important. McCubbins et al. (1987) refer to this as "deck-stacking." Their deck-stacking is the rough equivalent of my blessing. Without the blessing, prayers would indeed go unanswered. With the blessing, prayers cannot be ignored. When the bureaucracy's overseers know which interests they want to promote but don't know which policies they ought to pursue, prayers make a lot of sense. An additional advantage of prayers is that they promote democracy between elections through direct citizen participation and interest representation beyond the level of a legislative district through proxy advocacy that transcends geographic boundaries. Thus, prayers may encourage self-actualization and discourage pork barrel politics. A final advantage is that prayers promote bureaucratic creativity, flexibility, innovation, and experimentation. In effect, they emphasize long-run goal attainment rather than short-run compliance with hastily crafted directives.

231

CHAPTER NINE

Nixonian Democracy

During the 1970s as confidence in government plummeted, we reached a remarkable consensus on our central political problem— a bureaucracy that had become too powerful and independent. This consensus ushered in a golden age of reform in which bureau-bashing became institutionalized at the federal level, at the state level, and in intergovernmental relations. The primary aim of reformers was to make the bureaucracy more accountable, more responsive, more efficient, and more effective. Reformers relied upon new forms of interest representation, due process, executive management, policy analysis, federalism, and oversight to achieve these goals.

Throughout this book, I have described the bureau-bashing impulse as essentially Madisonian in character. In effect, reformers applied the Madisonian theory of checks and balances to a fourth branch of government reluctantly acknowledged to be a permanent feature of our political system. A new set of auxiliary precautions was invented, with popular control of government taking a back seat to intragovernmental controls. Through these auxiliary controls, ambition would counteract ambition and the mischiefs of modern factions such as bureaucratic clientele groups would be curbed if not cured. All in all, it was a fitting prelude to our bicentennial celebration.

Yet if the logic of these reforms was Madisonian, the prime mover behind many of them was Richard Nixon. Nixon was the first modern president to make bureau-bashing a central tenet of his political philosophy. It was Nixon who created OMB—a leading symbol of bureau-bashing within the executive branch. It was Nixon who conceived of a daring strategy to seize control of the bureaucracy through creative use of appointments and transfers— the "administrative presidency." It was Nixon who concocted an equally daring strategy to bypass social service agencies in the federal bureaucracy—the New Federalism.

Some of Nixon's reforms were adopted; many were not. As is well known, Watergate disrupted Nixon's "game plan." But Nixon's legacy extended far beyond a particular set of reforms. With his street fighting instincts fully engaged, Nixon set the tone for intragovernmental checks on the bureaucracy for years to come. That tone was strident, relentless, agitated, and uncompromising. Ironically, public officials who regard Nixon with utter contempt have borrowed liberally from his manual of style in their own dealings with the bureaucracy. Bureau-bashing today helps to perpetuate a kind of Nixonian democracy in which people are transformed into grotesque, menacing characters who might have been sketched by Maurice Sendak. By now the hallmarks of Nixonian democracy are familiar to us all:

1. *Enemies.* Politics is not merely "partisan mutual adjustment" but warfare between mortal enemies. In such a world, trust is pointless and only coercion yields results. Conversations and negotiations make less sense than plots and "dirty tricks." The unctuous rhetoric that legislators use to soften disagreements with other legislators gives way to acerbic rhetoric that is deliberately spiteful and hyperbolic. In warfare, there is no place for weakness or accommodation.

2. *Crises.* In politics, there is no such thing as a small problem. Every disagreement is a crisis that must be resolved quickly before opponents can mobilize. This approach discourages patience and planning. It encourages sharp, sudden surges of attention, followed by rest, recovery, or collapse. By stressing the need for immediate results it generates quick fixes that substitute public relations triumphs for successful outcomes.

3. *The Denigrative Method.* Perhaps the essence of Nixonian democracy is what Wills (1971: 76–92) has called the "denigrative method." Through harsh criticism you put your opponent on the defensive and you continue to attack relentlessly. You question not just your opponent's judgment but his or her motives as well. You sink your teeth in and don't let go. By denigrating your opponent, you ensure that you are never put on the defensive yourself.

4. *Bureau-bashing.* Nixon's memoirs reveal contempt for many foes but especially for bureaucrats. The Family Assistance Plan was an effort to "cut down on red tape" (Nixon, 1978: 426). Administrative reorganization was an attempt to overcome "the combined and determined inertia of Congress and the bureaucracy" (Nixon, 1978: 761). The Pentagon Papers case was necessary to avoid sending "a signal to every disgruntled bureaucrat in the government that he could leak anything he pleased while the government simply stood by" (Nixon, 1978: 509). The New Federalism was

233

a stick of dynamite that would threaten "sections of the bureaucracy with obsolescence" (Nixon, 1978: 768). Bureau-bashing was not just an episode but a central theme of the Nixon presidency. Moreover, it is one that has had considerable staying power.

Nixonian Democracy owes a lot to Madison, but it is more than just checks and balances in a modern world. It is a strident, venomous application of Madisonian logic to the bureaucracy. It converts distrust into paranoia, disagreement into disloyalty, controversies into crises, critics into enemies. It abjures compromise and coalition-building in favor of combat. It emphasizes muscles rather than prayers. And it diminishes the bureaucracy's capacity to respond to policy problems with creativity, flexibility, and imagination. It is a legacy that warrants reexamination.

Books and Articles

Aberbach, Joel. 1979. "Changes in Congressional Oversight." *American Behavioral Scientist*, Vol. 22, No. 5 (May/June), pp. 493–515.

Aberbach, Joel, and Rockman, Bert. 1976. "Clashing Beliefs within the Executive Branch: The Nixon Administration." *American Political Science Review*, Vol. 70, No. 2 (June), pp. 456–68.

————. 1978. "Administrators' Beliefs about the Role of the Public: The Case of American Federal Executives." *Western Political Quarterly*, Vol. 33, No. 4 (December), pp. 502–22.

Abney, Glenn, and Lauth, Thomas. 1982. "Councilmanic Intervention in Municipal Administration." *Administration and Society*, Vol. 13, No. 4 (February), pp. 435–56.

————. 1985. "Interest Group Influences in City Policy-Making: The Views of Administrators." *Western Political Quarterly*, Vol. 38, No. 1 (March), pp. 148–61.

Ackerman, Bruce, and Hassler, William. 1981. *Clean Coal/Dirty Air*. New Haven, Conn.: Yale University Press.

Administration on Aging. U.S. Department of Health and Human Services. 1983. "National Summary of State Ombudsman Reports for U.S. FY 1982." Washington, D.C.

Administrative Conference of the U.S. 1980. "Recommendations: The Magnuson-Moss Act." *Federal Register*, Vol. 45, No. 135 (July), pp. 46771–73.

Alpert, Geoffrey; Crouch, Benjamin; and Huff, C. Ronald. 1984. "Prison Reform by Judicial Decree: The Unintended Consequences of Ruiz v. Estelle." *Justice System Journal*, Vol. 9, No. 3 (Winter), pp. 291–305.

Andrews, Richard. 1976. *Environmental Policy and Administrative Change*. Lexington, Mass.: D. C. Heath & Co.

————. 1982. "Cost-Benefit Analysis as Regulatory Reform." In *Cost-Benefit Analysis and Environmental Regulations: Politics, Ethics, and Methods*, edited by Daniel Swartzman et al. Washington, D.C.: The Conservation Foundation, pp. 107–35.

Archibald, Samuel. 1979. "The FOIA Revisited." *Public Administration Review*, Vol. 39, No. 4 (July/August), pp. 311–18.

Arnold, R. Douglas. 1979. *Congress and the Bureaucracy: A Theory of Influence*. New Haven, Conn.: Yale University Press.

Arnstein, Sherry. 1969. "A Ladder of Citizen Participation." *Journal of the American Institute of Planners*, Vol. 35, No. 4 (July), pp. 216–24.

REFERENCES

Bardach, Eugene. 1980. *The Implementation Game*. Cambridge, Mass.: MIT Press.

Bardach, Eugene, and Kagan, Robert. 1982. *Going by the Book: The Problem of Regulatory Unreasonableness*. Philadelphia: Temple University Press.

Bardach, Eugene, and Pugliaresi, Lucian. 1977. "The Environmental Impact Statement vs. the Real World." *The Public Interest*, No. 49 (Fall), pp. 22–38.

Baumer, Donald, and Van Horn, Carl. 1985. *The Politics of Unemployment*. Washington, D.C.: Congressional Quarterly Press.

Bernick, E. Lee. 1984. "Discovering a Governor's Power: The Executive Order." *State Government*, Vol. 57, No. 2 (Summer), pp. 97–101.

Bernstein, Blanche. 1982. *The Politics of Welfare: The New York Experience*. Cambridge: Abt Books.

Bernstein, Marver. 1955. *Regulating Business by Independent Commission*. Princeton, N.J.: Princeton University Press.

Black, Eric. 1985. "Why Regulators Need a Don't-Do-It-If-It's-Stupid Clause." *Washington Monthly*, Vol. 16, No. 12 (January), pp. 23–26.

Bodman, Lydia, and Garry, Daniel. 1982. "Innovations in State Cabinet Systems." *State Government*, Vol. 55, No. 3 (Summer), pp. 93–97.

Boffey, Philip. 1988. "Federal Agency, in Shift, to Back Artificial Heart." *New York Times*, 3 July, p. 1.

Boyer, Barry. 1981. "Funding Public Participation in Agency Proceedings: The Federal Trade Commission Experience." *Georgetown Law Journal*, Vol. 70, No. 1 (October), pp. 51–172.

Brickman, Howard. 1979. "Economic Impact Statements: A Trend in State Government." *State Government*, Vol. 29, No. 1 (Winter), pp. 19–23.

Brodkin, Evelyn, and Lipsky, Michael. 1983. "Quality Control in AFDC as an Administrative Strategy." *Social Service Review*, Vol. 157, No. 1 (March), pp. 1–34.

Bruff, Harold. 1984. "Legislative Formality, Administrative Rationality." *Texas Law Review*, Vol. 63, No. 2 (October), pp. 207–50.

Bruff, Harold, and Gellhorn, Ernest. 1977. "Congressional Control of Administrative Regulation." *Harvard Law Review*, Vol. 90, No. 7 (May), pp. 1369–1440.

Buenker, John. 1977. "Essay." In *Progressivism*, edited by John Buenker, John Burnham, and Robert Crunden. Cambridge, Mass.: Schenkman Publishing Co., pp. 31–69.

Byse, Clark. 1978. "Vermont Yankee and the Evolution of Administrative Procedure: A Somewhat Different View." *Harvard Law Review*, Vol. 91, No. 8 (June), pp. 1823–32.

Caldwell, Lynton K. 1975. *Man and His Environment: Policy and Administration*. New York: Harper & Row.

236

Caldwell, Lynton K. et al. 1976. *Citizens and the Environment*. Bloomington: Indiana University Press.

Cameron, David. 1985. "Does Government Cause Inflation? Taxes, Spending, and Deficits." In *The Politics of Inflation and Economic Stagnation*, edited by Leon Lindberg and Charles Maier. Washington, D.C.: The Brookings Institution, pp. 224–79.

Cameron, Juan. 1977. "Nader's Invaders Are Inside the Gates." *Fortune*, Vol. 96, No. 4 (October), pp. 252–62.

Campbell, Colin. 1986. *Managing the Presidency: Carter, Reagan, and the Search for Executive Harmony*. Pittsburgh, Pa.: University of Pittsburgh Press.

Carter, Jimmy. 1978. "CETA Extension." *Public Papers of the President of the U.S.* (February), pp. 39–392.

Causey, Mike. 1979. "U.S. Benefits Jump by 300 Percent since 1970." *Washington Post*, 16 September.

Chayes, Abram. 1976. "The Role of the Judge in Public Law Litigation." *Harvard Law Review*, Vol. 89, No. 7 (May), pp. 1281–1316.

Checkoway, Barry. 1981. "The Politics of Public Hearings." *Journal of Applied Behavioral Science*, Vol. 17, No. 4 (October–December), pp. 566–82.

Christenson, Arlen. 1985. "The Public Intervenor: Another Look." Paper presented at the Conference on the People's Counsel. Madison, Wis., 19 February.

Cilbulka, James. 1975. "School Decentralization in Chicago." *Education and Urban Society*, Vol. 7, No. 4 (August), pp. 412–38.

Clausen, Aage. 1973. *How Congressmen Decide: A Policy Focus*. New York: St. Martin's Press.

Cobb, Roger, and Elder, Charles. 1972. *Participation in American Politics: The Dynamics of Agenda-Building*. Boston: Allyn & Bacon.

Cohen, Marsha. 1983. "Regulatory Reform: Assessing the California Plan." *Duke Law Journal*, Vol. 1983, No. 2 (April), pp. 231–84.

Cohen, Michael. 1984. "Conflict and Complexity: Goal Diversity and Organizational Search Effectiveness." *American Political Science Review*, Vol. 78, No. 2 (June), pp. 435–51.

Cole, Richard, and Caputo, David. 1984. "The Public Hearing as an Effective Citizen Participation Mechanism: A Case Study of the GRS Program." *American Political Science Review*, Vol. 78, No. 2 (June), pp. 404–16.

Cooper, Joseph. 1985. "The Legislative Veto in the 1980's." In *Congress Reconsidered*, 3d ed., edited by Lawrence Dodd and Bruce Oppenheimer. Washington, D.C.: Congressional Quarterly Press, pp. 364–89.

Cooper, Laura. 1980. "Goldberg's Forgotten Footnote." *Minnesota Law Review*, Vol. 64, No. 6 (July), pp. 1107–79.

REFERENCES

Cooper, Phillip. 1986. "By Order of the President." *Administration and Society*, Vol. 18, No. 2 (August), pp. 233–62.

Council of State Governments. 1970. *The Book of the States, 1970–1971*. Lexington, Ky.: Council of State Governments.

———. 1978. *The Book of the States, 1978–1979*. Lexington, Ky.: Council of State Governments.

———. 1980. *The Book of the States, 1980–1981*. Lexington, Ky.: Council of State Governments.

Craig, Barbara. 1983. *The Legislative Veto: Congressional Control of Regulation*. Boulder, Colo.: Westview Press.

Cramton, Roger. 1972. "The Why, Where and How of Broadened Public Participation in the Administrative Process." *Georgetown Law Journal*, Vol. 60, No. 3 (February), pp. 525–46.

Crandall, Robert. 1983. *Controlling Industrial Pollution: The Economics and Politics of Clean Air*. Washington, D.C.: The Brookings Institution.

CRC Education and Human Development. 1981. "Technical Report: Task II of a Study to Evaluate Legal Services and Long-Term Care Ombudsman Services Funded under Title III of the Older Americans Act." Belmont, Mass.

Croke, Kevin, and Herlevsen, Niels. 1982. "Environmental Cost-Benefit Analysis: The Illinois Experience." In *Cost-Benefit Analysis and Environmental Regulations: Politics, Ethics, and Methods*, edited by Daniel Swartzman et al. Washington, D.C.: The Conservation Foundation, pp. 15–34.

Cushman, John, Jr. 1988. "Pentagon: Was Someone Asleep on Watch?" *New York Times*, 26 June.

Davis, Kenneth. 1978. *Administrative Law Treatise*. 5 vols. 2d ed. San Diego: K. C. Davis, Vol. 1.

Dean, Alan. 1981. "General Propositions of Organizational Design." In *Federal Reorganization: What Have We Learned?*, edited by Peter Szanton. Chatham, N.J.: Chatham House, pp. 131–54.

DeMuth, Christopher. 1980. "Constraining Regulatory Costs, Part I: The White House Review Program." *Regulation*, Vol. 4, No. 1 (January–February), pp. 13–26.

Derthick, Martha. 1970. *The Influence of Federal Grants*. Cambridge, Mass.: Harvard University Press.

———. 1987. "American Federalism: Madison's Middle Ground in the 1980s." *Public Administration Review*, Vol. 47, No. 1 (January–February), pp. 66–74.

Derthick, Martha, and Quirk, Paul. 1985. *The Politics of Deregulation*. Washington, D.C.: The Brookings Institution.

Diamond, S. J. 1987. "Telephone Bills Leave Customers Confused, Angry." *Milwaukee Journal*, 27 September.

DiIulio, John, Jr. 1987. "Prison Discipline and Prison Reform." *The Public Interest*, No. 89 (Fall), pp. 71–90.

Diver, Colin. 1981. "Policymaking Paradigms in Administrative Law." *Harvard Law Review*, Vol. 95, No. 2 (December), pp. 392–434.

Dodd, Lawrence, and Schott, Richard. 1979. *Congress and the Administrative State*. New York: John Wiley & Sons.

Dometrius, Nelson. 1979. "The Efficacy of a Governor's Formal Powers." *State Government*, Vol. 52, No. 3 (Summer), pp. 121–25.

———. 1979. "Measuring Gubernatorial Power." *Journal of Politics*, Vol. 41, No. 2 (May), pp. 589–610.

Edelman, Murray. 1964. *The Symbolic Uses of Politics*. Urbana: University of Illinois Press.

Eisendrath, John. 1986. "Watching the Watchdogs: Are They Barking up the Wrong Tree?" *Washington Monthly* 18 (July–August), pp. 17–22.

Elazar, Daniel. 1984. *American Federalism: A View from the States*. 3d ed. New York: Harper & Row Publishers.

Elling, Richard. 1979. "The Utility of State Legislative Casework as a Means of Oversight." *Legislative Studies Quarterly*, Vol. 4, No. 3 (August), pp. 353–79.

———. 1980. "State Legislative Casework and State Administrative Performance." *Administration and Society*, Vol. 12, No. 3 (November), pp. 327–56.

———. 1985. "Federal Dollars and Federal Clout in State Administration: A Test of 'Regulatory' and 'Picket Fence' Models of Intergovernmental Relations." Paper presented at the Midwest Political Science Association Meeting, Chicago, Ill., 17–20 April.

Engelberg, Stephen. 1986. "Lawmakers Want Answers on Iran." *New York Times*, 16 November.

Ethridge, Marcus. 1981. "Legislative-Administrative Interaction as 'Intrusive Access': An Empirical Analysis." *Journal of Politics*, Vol. 43, No. 2 (May), pp. 473–92.

———. 1984. "Consequences of Legislative Review of Agency Regulations in Three U.S. States." *Legislative Studies Quarterly*, Vol. 9, No. 1 (February), pp. 161–78.

Etzioni, Amitai. 1967. "Mixed-Scanning: A 'Third' Approach to Decision-Making." *Public Administrative Review*, Vol. 27, No. 5 (December), pp. 385–92.

———. 1986. "Mixed Scanning Revisited." *Public Administration Review*, Vol. 46, No. 1 (January–February), pp. 8–14.

Faith, Roger; Leavens, Donald; and Tollison, Robert. 1982. "Antitrust Pork Barrel." *Journal of Law and Economics*, Vol. 25, No. 2 (October), pp. 329–42.

Fairfax, Sally. 1978. "A Disaster in the Environmental Movement." *Science*, Vol. 199, No. 4330 (17 February), 743–48.

Ferejohn, John. 1974. *Pork Barrel Politics*. Stanford, Calif.: Stanford University Press.

Filene, Peter. 1970. "An Obituary for 'The Progressive Movement.'" *American Quarterly*, Vol. 22, No. 1 (Spring), pp. 20–34.

Fiorina, Morris. 1981. "Congressional Control of the Bureaucracy: A Mismatch of Incentives and Capabilities." In *Congress Reconsidered*, 2d ed., edited by Lawrence Dodd and Bruce Oppenheimer. Washington, D.C.: Congressional Quarterly Press, pp. 332–48.

Fortune. Editorial. 1977. "Congress Gets the Message." Vol. 96, No. 1 (July), p. 59.

Frank, Stephen. 1978. "State Supreme Courts and Administrative Agencies." *State Government*, Vol. 51, No. 2 (Spring), pp. 119–23.

Friendly, Henry. 1975. "Some Kind of Hearing." *University of Pennsylvania Law Review*, Vol. 123, No. 6 (June), pp. 1267–1317.

Friesema, H. Paul, and Culhane, Paul. 1976. "Social Impacts, Politics, and the Environmental Impact Statement Process." *Natural Resources Journal*, Vol. 16, No. 2 (April), pp. 330–56.

Frug, Gerald. 1978. "The Judicial Power of the Purse." *University of Pennsylvania Law Review*, Vol. 126, No. 4 (April), pp. 715–94.

———. 1984. "The Ideology of Bureaucracy in American Law." *Harvard Law Review*, Vol. 97, No. 6 (April), pp. 1277–1388.

Gardiner, John, and Lyman, Theodore. 1984. *The Fraud Control Game*. Bloomington: Indiana University Press.

Garland, Merrick. 1985. "Deregulation and Judicial Review." *Harvard Law Review*, Vol. 98, No. 3 (January), pp. 507–91.

Gellhorn, Ernest. 1972. "Public Participation in Administrative Proceedings." *Yale Law Journal*, Vol. 81, No. 3 (January), pp. 359–404.

Gilmour, Robert, and Sperry, Roger. 1986. "Pushing the String: Moving Central Management Reform in the Senate." *Public Administration Review*, Vol. 46, No. 5 (September–October), pp. 392–96.

Godschalk, David, and Stiftel, Bruce. 1981. "Making Waves: Public Participation in State Water Planning." *Journal of Applied Behavioral Science*, Vol. 17, No. 4 (October–December), pp. 597–614.

Goldenberg, Edie. 1985. "The Grace Commission and Civil Service Reform: Seeking a Common Understanding." In *The Unfinished Agenda for Civil Service Reform*, edited by Charles Levine. Washington, D.C.: The Brookings Institution, pp. 69–94.

Goldman, Eric. 1952. *Rendezvous with Destiny*. New York: Alfred A. Knopf.

Goodsell, Charles. 1983. *The Case for Bureaucracy*. Chatham, N.J.: Chatham House Publishers.

Gordon, Andrew, and Heinz, John, eds. 1979. *Public Access to Information*. New Brunswick, N.J.: Transaction Books.

Gormley, William, Jr. 1979. "A Test of the Revolving Door Hypothesis at the FCC." *American Journal of Political Science*, Vol. 23, No. 4 (November), pp. 665–83.

———. 1982. "Alternative Models of the Regulatory Process: Public Utility Regulation in the States." *Western Political Quarterly*, Vol. 35, No. 3 (September), pp. 297–317.

———. 1983. *The Politics of Public Utility Regulation*. Pittsburgh, Pa.: University of Pittsburgh Press.

———. 1986. "The Representation Revolution." *Administration and Society*, Vol. 18, No. 2 (August), pp. 179–96.

———. 1987. "Intergovernmental Conflict on Environmental Policy: The Attitudinal Connection." *Western Political Quarterly*, Vol. 40, No. 2 (June), pp. 285–303.

Greene, Kenneth. 1982. "Municipal Administrators' Receptivity to Citizens' and Elected Officials' Contacts." *Public Administration Review*, Vol. 42, No. 4 (July–August), pp. 346–53.

Gregson, Ronald. 1980. "Sunset in Colorado: The Second Round." *State Government*, Vol. 53, No. 2 (Spring), pp. 58–62.

Grubb, W. Norton; Whittington, Dale; and Humphries, Michael. 1984. "The Ambiguities of Benefit-Cost Analysis: An Evaluation of Regulatory Impact Analyses under Executive Order 12291." In *Environmental Policy under Reagan's Executive Order*, edited by V. Kerry Smith. Chapel Hill: University of North Carolina Press, pp. 121–64.

Gruber, Judith. 1987. *Controlling Bureaucracies: Dilemmas in Democratic Governance*. Berkeley and Los Angeles: University of California Press.

Gulick, Luther. 1937. "Science, Values and Public Administration." In *Papers on the Science of Administration*, edited by Luther Gulick and Lyndall Urwick. New York: Institute of Public Administration.

Halberstam, David. 1972. *The Best and the Brightest*. New York: Random House.

Halpern, Stephen. 1974. *Police Association and Department Leaders*. Lexington, Mass.: D. C. Heath & Co.

Hamilton, Alexander; Madison, James; and Jay, John. 1901. *The Federalist*. New York: M. Walter Dunne.

Hamilton, Gary, and Biggart, Nicole. 1984. *Governor Reagan, Governor Brown: A Sociology of Executive Power*. New York: Columbia University Press.

Hamm, Keith, and Robertson, Rory. 1981. "Factors Influencing the Adoption of New Methods of Legislative Oversight in the U.S. States." *Legislative Studies Quarterly*, Vol. 6, No. 1 (February), pp. 133–50.

Handler, Joel; Hollingsworth, Ellen; and Erlanger, Howard. 1978. *Lawyers and the Pursuit of Legal Rights*. New York: Academic Press.

Heclo, Hugh. 1977. *A Government of Strangers*. Washington, D.C.: The Brookings Institution.

Hill, Larry. 1983. "Must Implementation Studies Be Dismal? The Bureaucratic Impact of the Ombudsman's Reforms." Paper presented at the Annual Meeting of the American Political Science Association, Chicago, Ill., 1–4 September.

Hill, William, and Ortolano, Leonard. 1978. "NEPA's Effect on the Consideration of Alternatives: A Crucial Test." *Natural Resources Journal*, Vol. 18, No. 2 (April), pp. 285–311.

Hochschild, Jennifer. 1984. *The New American Dilemma: Liberal Democracy and School Desegregation.* New Haven, Conn.: Yale University Press.

Hofstadter, Richard. 1955. *The Age of Reform.* New York: Vintage Books.

Hollingsworth, Ellen. 1977. "Ten Years of Legal Services for the Poor." In *A Decade of Federal Antipoverty Programs*, edited by Robert Haveman. New York: Academic Press, pp. 285–314.

Hood, Christopher. 1983. *The Tools of Government.* Chatham, N.J.: Chatham House.

Hult, Karen. 1987. *Agency Merger and Bureaucratic Redesign.* Pittsburgh, Pa.: University of Pittsburgh Press.

Huntington, Samuel. 1952. "The Marasmus of the ICC: The Commission, the Railroads, and the Public Interest." *Yale Law Journal*, Vol. 61, No. 4 (April), pp. 467–509.

———. 1981. *American Politics: The Promise of Disharmony.* Cambridge, Mass.: The Belknap Press.

Ingram, Helen. 1985. "Policy Implementation through Bargaining: The Case of Federal Grants-in-Aid." In *American Intergovernmental Relations*, edited by Laurence O'Toole, Jr. Washington, D.C.: Congressional Quarterly Press, pp. 199–206.

Ingraham, Patricia, and Colby, Peter. 1982. "Political Reform and Government Management: The Case of the SES." *Policy Studies Journal*, Vol. 11, No. 2 (December), pp. 304–17.

Jacobs, James. 1977. *Stateville: The Penitentiary in Mass Society.* Chicago: University of Chicago Press.

Jacoby, Louis, and Steinbruner, John. 1973. "Salvaging the Federal Attempt to Control Auto Pollution." *Public Policy*, Vol. 21, No. 1 (Winter), pp. 1–48.

Jaffe, Louis. 1955. "Basic Issues: An Analysis." *New York University Law Review*, Vol. 30 (November), pp. 1273–96.

Johannes, John. 1979. "Casework as a Technique of U.S. Congressional Oversight." *Legislative Studies Quarterly*, Vol. 4, No. 3 (August), pp. 325–51.

Johnson, Earl. 1978. *Justice and Reform: The Formative Years of the American Legal Services Program.* New Brunswick, N.J.: Transaction Books.

Johnson, Loch. 1985. *A Season of Inquiry: The Senate Intelligence Investigation.* Lexington: The University Press of Kentucky.

Jones, Charles. 1975. *Clean Air: The Policies and Politics of Pollution Control.* Pittsburgh, Pa.: University of Pittsburgh Press.

Jones, Dick. 1987. "Making CUB Growl." *Milwaukee Journal Magazine*, 1 March.

Jones, Rich. 1982. "Legislative Review of Regulations: How Well Is It Working?" *State Legislatures*, Vol. 8, No. 8 (September), pp. 7–9.

Katzmann, Robert. 1986. *Institutional Disability* (Washington, D.C.: The Brookings Institution).

Kaufman, Herbert. 1956. "Emerging Conflicts in the Doctrine of Public Administration." *American Political Science Review*, Vol. 50, No. 4 (December), pp. 1057–73.

————. 1981. *The Administrative Behavior of Federal Bureau Chiefs*. Washington, D.C.: The Brookings Institution.

Kenski, Henry, and Kenski, Margaret. 1984. "Congress against the President: The Struggle over the Environment." In *Environmental Policy in the 1980s: Reagan's New Agenda*, edited by Norman Vig and Michael Kraft. Washington, D.C.: Congressional Quarterly Press, pp. 97–120.

Kessel, John. 1984. "The Structures of the Reagan White House." *American Journal of Political Science*, Vol. 28, No. 2 (May), pp. 231–58.

Kettl, Donald. 1980. *Managing Community Development in the New Federalism*. New York: Praeger Publishers.

————. 1983. *The Regulation of American Federalism*. Baton Rouge: Louisiana State University Press.

King, Susan. 1980. "Executive Orders of the Wisconsin Governor." *Wisconsin Law Review*, Vol. 1980, No. 2, pp. 333–69.

Kingdon, John. 1984. *Agendas, Alternatives and Public Policies*. Boston: Little, Brown & Co.

Koch, Edward. 1980. "The Mandate Millstone." *The Public Interest*, No. 61 (Fall), pp. 42–57.

Kole, John. 1986. "U.S. May Withhold Aid to Center for Retarded." *Milwaukee Journal*, 14 September.

Kopca, Justin. 1987. "Executive Orders in State Government." Unpublished manuscript. Madison, Wis.: La Follette Institute of Public Affairs.

Kraft, Ralph. 1981. "Successful Legislative Oversight: Lessons from State Legislatures." *Policy Studies Journal*, Vol. 10, No. 1 (September), pp. 161–71.

Krasnow, Erwin; Longley, Lawrence; and Terry, Herbert. 1982. *The Politics of Broadcast Regulation*. New York: St. Martin's Press.

LaFever, John. 1974. "Zero-Base Budgeting in New Mexico." *State Government*, Vol. 47, No. 2 (Spring), pp. 108–12.

Lanouette, William. 1982. "Inspectors General Say an Ounce of Prevention May Save Billions for Their Agencies." *National Journal*, 19 June.

Lardner, George, Jr. 1976. "Use, Abuse of FOIA." *Washington Post*, 27 July.

Lauth, Thomas. 1980. "Zero-Base Budgeting in Georgia State Government: Myth and Reality." In *Perspectives on Budgeting*, edited by Allen Schick. Washington, D.C.: American Society of Public Administration, pp. 114–32.

Lawrence, Christine. 1987. "Unrest at the Top of the Civil Services." *National Journal*, 11 April.

Lester, James et al. 1983. "A Comparative Perspective on State Hazardous Waste Regulation." In *The Politics of Hazardous Waste Management*, edited by James Lester and Ann Bowman. Durham, N.C.: Duke University Press, pp. 212–31.

Leventhal, Harold. 1974. "Environmental Decisionmaking and the Role of the Courts." *University of Pennsylvania Law Review*, Vol. 122, No. 3 (January), pp. 509–55.

Levine, Charles. 1986. "The Federal Government in the Year 2000: Administrative Legacies of the Reagan Years." *Public Administration Review*, Vol. 46, No. 2 (May–June), pp. 195–206.

Levinson, L. Harold. 1987. "The Decline of the Legislative Veto: Federal/State Comparisons and Interactions." *Publius*, Vol. 17, No. 1 (Winter), pp. 115–32.

Lindblom, Charles. 1977. *Politics and Markets*. New York: Basic Books.

Lipset, Seymour, and Schneider, William. 1983. *The Confidence Gap*. New York: The Free Press.

Lipsky, Michael. 1980. *Street-Level Bureaucracy: Dilemmas of the Individual in Public Services*. New York: Russell Sage Foundation.

Liroff, Richard. 1976. *A National Policy for the Environment: NEPA and Its Aftermath*. Bloomington: Indiana University Press.

———. 1981. "NEPA Litigation in the 1970s: A Deluge or a Dribble?" *Natural Resources Journal*, Vol. 21, No. 2 (April), pp. 315–30.

Litan, Robert, and Nordhaus, William. 1983. *Reforming Federal Regulation*. New Haven, Conn.: Yale University Press.

Lovell, Catherine, and Tobin, Charles. 1981. "The Mandate Issue." *Public Administration Review*, Vol. 41, No. 3 (May–June), pp. 318–31.

Lowi, Theodore. 1969. *The End of Liberalism*. New York: W. W. Norton.

———. 1979. *The End of Liberalism*. 2d ed. New York: W. W. Norton.

Lukas, J. Anthony. 1985. *Common Ground*. New York: Alfred A. Knopf.

Lufler, Henry, Jr. 1982. "The Supreme Court Goes to School: *Goss v. Lopez* and Student Suspensions." Ph.D. diss., University of Wisconsin.

Lundqvist, Lennart. 1980. *The Hare and the Tortoise: Clean Air Policies in the U.S. and Sweden*. Ann Arbor: University of Michigan Press.

Lynch, Mark. 1977. "Oversight of the FOIA." Testimony at hearings before the Subcommittee on Administrative Practice and Procedure of the Committee on the Judiciary, U.S. Senate, 95th Cong., 1st Sess., 16 September, pp. 111–22.

Lynn, Laurence. 1981. *Managing the Public's Business: The Job of the Government Executive*. New York: Basic Books.

———. 1984. "The Reagan Administration and the Renitent Bureaucracy." In *The Reagan Presidency and the Governing of America*, edited by Lester Salamon and Michael Lund. Washington, D.C.: The Urban Institute Press, pp. 339–70.

————. 1987. *Managing Public Policy*. Boston: Little, Brown.

Madison, James. 1953. "Letter to W. T. Barry, 4 August 1822." In *The Complete Madison*, edited by Saul Padover. New York: Harper & Row.

March, James, and Olson, Johan. 1983. "What Administrative Reorganization Tells Us about Governing." *American Political Science Review*, Vol. 77, No. 2 (June), pp. 281–96.

Marcus, Alfred. 1980. *Promise and Performance: Choosing and Implementing an Environmental Policy*. Westport, Conn.: Greenwood Press.

Mashaw, Jerry. 1974. "The Management Side of Due Process." *Cornell Law Review*, Vol. 59, No. 4 (April), pp. 772–824.

————. 1985. *Due Process in the Administrative State*. New Haven, Conn.: Yale University Press.

————. 1983. *Bureaucratic Justice: Managing Social Security Disability Claims*. New Haven, Conn.: Yale University Press.

Mayer, Robert, and Scammon, Debra. 1983. "Intervenor Funding at the FTC: Biopsy or Autopsy?" *Policy Studies Review*, Vol. 2, No. 3 (February), pp. 506–15.

Mazmanian, Daniel, and Nienaber, Jeane. 1979. *Can Organizations Change? Environmental Protection, Citizen Participation, and the Corps of Engineers*. Washington, D.C.: The Brookings Institution.

Mazmanian, Daniel, and Sabatier, Paul. 1980. "A Multivariate Model of Public Policy Making." *American Journal of Political Science*, Vol. 24, No. 3 (August), pp. 439–68.

McConnell, Grant. 1966. *Private Power and American Democracy*. New York: Alfred A. Knopf.

McCubbins, Mathew; Noll, Roger; and Weingast, Barry. 1987. "Administrative Procedures as Instruments of Political Control." Working papers in political science, the Hoover Institution, Stanford University.

McCubbins, Mathew, and Schwartz, Thomas. 1984. "Congressional Oversight Overlooked: Police Patrols versus Fire Alarms." *American Journal of Political Science*, Vol. 28, No. 1 (February), pp. 165–79.

McFarland, Andrew. 1984. *Common Cause: Lobbying in the Public Interest*. Chatham, N.J.: Chatham House Publishers.

Meier, Kenneth. 1980. "Executive Reorganization of Government: Impact on Employment and Expenditures." *American Journal of Political Science*, Vol. 24, No. 3 (August), pp. 396–412.

————. 1987. *Politics and the Bureaucracy*. 2d ed. Monterey, Calif.: Brooks/Cole Publishing Co.

Melnick, R. Shep. 1983. *Regulation and the Courts: The Case of the Clean Air Act*. Washington, D.C.: The Brookings Institution.

Monk, Abraham; Kaye, Lenard; and Litwin, Howard. 1982. "National Comparative Analysis of Long Term Care Programs for the Aged."

New York: Brookdale Institute on Aging and Adult Human Development and Columbia University School of Social Work.

Moore, John. 1973. "Honolulu's Office of Information and Complaint." In *Executive Ombudsmen in the U.S.*, edited by Alan Wyner. Berkeley, Calif.: Institute of Governmental Studies, pp. 45–69.

Morone, Joseph. 1981. "Models of Representation: Consumers and the HSAs." In *Health Planning in the U.S.* Vol. 2. Washington, D.C.: National Academy Press, pp. 225–56.

Morone, Joseph, and Marmor, Theodore. 1981. "Representing Consumer Interests: The Case of American Health Planning." *Ethics*, Vol. 91, No. 3 (April), pp. 431–50.

Mosher, Frederick. 1979. *The GAO: The Quest for Accountability in American Government*. Boulder, Colo.: Westview Press.

———. 1984. *A Tale of Two Agencies: A Comparative Analysis of the GAO and the OMB*. Baton Rouge: Louisiana University Press.

Mosher, Lawrence. 1982. "Who's Afraid of Hazardous Waste Dumps? Not Us, Says the Reagan Administration." *National Journal*, 29 May.

Moss, Kathryn. 1984. "Institutional Reform through Litigation." *Social Service Review*, Vol. 58, No. 3 (September), pp. 421–33.

Moynihan, Daniel. 1969. *Maximum Feasible Misunderstanding*. New York: The Free Press.

Nader, Ralph. 1981. Statement before Subcommittee on Government Operations, U.S. House of Representatives, 97th Cong., lst Sess., 14–16 June, pp. 315–22.

Nathan, Richard. 1983. *The Administrative Presidency*. New York: John Wiley & Sons.

Newland, Chester. 1984. "Executive Office Policy Apparatus: Enforcing the Reagan Agenda." In *The Reagan Presidency and the Governing of America*, edited by Lester Salamon and Michael Lund. Washington, D.C.: The Urban Institute Press, pp. 339–70.

Niskanen, William. 1971. *Bureaucracy and Representative Government*. Chicago: Aldine.

Nixon, Richard. 1972. "State and Local Fiscal Assistance." *Weekly Compilation of Presidential Documents*, 23 October, pp. 1534–36.

———. 1978. *RN: The Memoirs of Richard Nixon*. New York: Grosset and Dunlap.

Nonet, Philippe. 1980. "The Legitimation of Purposive Decisions." *California Law Review*, Vol. 68, No. 2 (March), pp. 263–300.

Nordlinger, Eric. 1973. "Boston's Little City Halls: Citizens or Clients." In *Executive Ombudsmen in the U.S.*, edited by Alan Wyner. Berkeley, Calif.: Institute of Governmental Studies, pp. 71–110.

Note, 1979. "Due Process and Ex Parte Contacts in Informal Rulemaking." *Yale Law Journal*, Vol. 89, No. 1 (November), pp. 194–212.

Note, 1979. " 'Mastering' Intervention in Prisons." *Yale Law Journal*, Vol. 88, No. 5 (April), pp. 1062–91.

Note, 1979. "State Economic Substantive Due Process: A Proposed Approach." *Yale Law Journal*, Vol. 88, No. 7 (June), pp. 1487–1510.

Ogul, Morris. 1976. *Congress Oversees the Bureaucracy*. Pittsburgh, Pa.: University of Pittsburgh Press.

Olson, Mancur. 1965. *The Logic of Collective Action*. Cambridge, Mass.: Harvard University Press.

Parsons, Talcott. 1960. "Pattern Variables Revisited: A Response to Robert Dubin." *American Sociological Review*, Vol. 25, No. 4 (August), pp. 467–83.

Pasztor, Andy. 1984. "Interior Prepares to Crack Down on States with Deficient Strip-Mining Programs." *Wall Street Journal*, 14 February.

Pearlman, Kenneth. 1977. "State Environmental Policy Acts: Local Decision Making and Land Use Planning." *Journal of the American Institute of Planners*, Vol. 43, No. 1 (January), pp. 42–53.

Pertschuk, Michael. 1979. "Listening to the Little Guy." *Washington Post*, 26 June.

———. 1982. *Revolt against Regulation: The Rise and Pause of the Consumer Movement*. Berkeley and Los Angeles: University of California Press.

Peters, B. Guy. 1985. "Administrative Change and the Grace Commission." In *The Unfinished Agenda for Civil Service Reform*, edited by Charles Levine. Washington, D.C.: The Brookings Institution, pp. 19–39.

Peterson, Paul. 1970. "Forms of Representation: Participation of the Poor in the Community Action Program." *American Political Science Review*, Vol. 64, No. 2 (June), pp. 491–507.

———. 1976. *School Politics Chicago Style*. Chicago: University of Chicago Press.

Peterson, Paul, and Greenstone, J. David. 1977. "Racial Change and Citizen Participation: The Mobilization of Low-Income Communities through Community Action." In *A Decade of Federal Antipoverty Programs*, edited by Robert Haveman. New York: Academic Press, pp. 241–78.

Peterson, Paul; Rabe, Barry; and Wong, Kenneth. 1986. *When Federalism Works*. Washington, D.C.: The Brookings Institution.

Pious, Richard. 1979. *The American Presidency*. New York: Basic Books.

Piven, Frances Fox, and Cloward, Richard. 1971. *Regulating the Poor: The Functions of Public Welfare*. New York: Pantheon Books.

———. 1977. *Poor People's Movements: Why They Succeed, How They Fail*. New York: Pantheon Books.

Polsby, Nelson. 1984. *Political Innovation in America: The Politics of Policy Initiation*. New Haven, Conn.: Yale University Press.

Portney, Paul. 1984. "The Benefits and Costs of Regulatory Analysis." In *Environmental Policy under Reagan's Executive Order*, edited by

V. Kerry Smith. Chapel Hill: University of North Carolina Press, pp. 226–40.

Press, Aric. 1986. "Inside America's Toughest Prison." *Newsweek*, 6 October.

Price, David. 1978. "Policy Making in Congressional Committees." *American Political Science Review*, Vol. 72, No. 2 (June), pp. 548–74.

Quirk, Paul. 1981. *Industry Influence in Federal Regulatory Agencies*. Princeton, N.J.: Princeton University Press.

Rabin, Robert. 1976. "Job Security and Due Process: Monitoring Administration Discretion through a Reasons Requirement." *University of Chicago Law Review*, Vol. 44, No. 1 (Fall), pp. 60–93.

Reagan, Michael. 1987. *Regulation: The Politics of Policy*. Boston: Little, Brown & Co.

Reagan, Michael, and Sanzone, John. 1981. *The New Federalism*. 2d ed. New York: Oxford University Press.

Reich, Charles. 1964. "The New Property." *Yale Law Journal*, Vol. 73, No. 5 (April), pp. 733–87.

———. 1965. "Individual Rights and Social Welfare: The Emerging Legal Issues." *Yale Law Journal*, Vol. 74, No. 6 (May), pp. 1245–57.

Relyea, Harold. 1981. "The Administration and Operation of the FOIA: A Capsule Overview, 1966–1980." In Freedom of Information Act oversight hearings before a subcommittee of the Committee on Government Operations, House of Representatives, 97th Cong., 1st Sess., 14–16 July 1981. Washington, D.C.: U.S. Government Printing Office, pp. 945–74.

Renfrow, Patty; West, William; and Houston, David. 1985. "Rulemaking Provisions in State Administrative Procedure Acts." Paper presented at the Annual Meeting of the Midwest Political Science Association, Chicago, Ill., The Palmer House, 17–19 April.

Rich, Spencer. 1987. "On the Front Line with Inspector General Kusserow." *Washington Post National Weekly Edition*, 6 July.

Ripley, Randall, and Franklin, Grace. 1984. *Congress, the Bureaucracy, and Public Policy*. 3d ed. Homewood, Ill.: The Dorsey Press.

Robbin, Alice. 1984. "A Phenomenology of Decisionmaking: Implementing Information Policy in State Health and Welfare Agencies." Ph.D. diss., University of Wisconsin, pp. 196–205.

Rockman, Bert. 1985. "Legislative-Executive Relations and Legislative Oversight." In *Handbook of Legislative Research*, edited by Gerhard Loewenberg et al. Cambridge, Mass.: Harvard University Press, pp. 519–72.

Rodgers, Harrell, and Bullock, Charles III. 1976. *Coercion to Compliance*. Lexington, Mass.: D. C. Heath & Co.

Roederer, Doug, and Palmer, Patsy. 1981. *Sunset: Expectation and Experience*. Lexington, Ky.: Council of State Governments, June.

Rose, Richard. 1980. "Implementation and Evaportation: The Case of

MBO." In *Perspectives on Budgeting*, edited by Allen Schick. Washington, D.C.: American Society for Public Administration, pp. 103–13.

Rosenbaum, Nelson. 1980. "Statutory Structure and Policy Implementation: The Case of Wetlands Regulation." *Policy Studies Journal* (special issue), pp. 575–96.

Rosenbaum, W. Anthony. 1978. "Public Involvement as Reform and Ritual: The Development of Federal Participation Programs." In *Citizen Participation in America*, edited by Stuart Langton. Lexington, Mass.: D. C. Heath & Co., pp. 81–96.

———. 1985. *Environmental Politics and Policy*. Washington, D.C.: Congressional Quarterly Press.

———. 1987. *Energy, Politics, and Public Policy*. 2d ed. Washington, D.C.: Congressional Quarterly Press.

Rosener, Judy. 1982. "Making Bureaucracies Responsive: A Study of the Impact of Citizen Participation and Staff Recommendations on Regulatory Decision Making." *Public Administration Review*, Vol. 42, No. 4 (July–August), pp. 339–45.

Rosenthal, A. M. 1986. "Learning on the Job." *New York Times Magazine*, 14 December.

Rosenthal, Alan. 1981. *Legislative Life*. New York: Harper & Row.

———. 1983. "Legislative Oversight and the Balance of Power in State Government." *State Government*, Vol. 56, No. 3, pp. 90–98.

Rothman, David, and Rothman, Sheila. 1984. *The Willowbrook Wars*. New York: Harper & Row.

Rubin, Irene. 1985. *Shrinking the Federal Government: The Effect of Cutbacks in Five Federal Agencies*. New York: Longman.

Sabato, Larry. 1983. *Goodbye to Good-time Charlie*. 2d ed. Washington, D.C.: Congressional Quarterly Press.

Salamon, Lester. 1981. "The Question of Goals." In *Federal Reorganization: What Have We Learned?*, edited by Peter Szanton. Chatham, N.J.: Chatham House, pp. 58–84.

Saloma, John. 1969. *Congress and the New Politics*. Boston: Little, Brown.

Scalia, Antonin. 1982. "The FOIA Has No Clothes." *Regulation*, Vol. 6, No. 2 (March–April), pp. 14–19.

Schattschneider, E. E. 1960. *The Semisovereign People*. New York: Holt, Rinehart and Winston.

Schick, Allen. 1973. "A Death in the Bureaucracy: The Demise of Federal PPB." *Public Administration Review*, Vol. 33, No. 2 (March–April), pp. 146–156.

———. 1976. "Congress and the Details of Administration." *Public Administration Review*, Vol. 36, No. 5 (September–October), pp. 516–28.

———. 1981. "The Coordination Option." In *Federal Reorganization: What Have We Learned?*, edited by Peter Szanton. Chatham, N.J.: Chatham House, pp. 85–113.

REFERENCES

Schick, Allen. 1980. *Congress and Money: Budgeting, Spending and Taxing*, Washington, D.C.: The Urban Institute.

———. 1983. "Politics through Law: Congressional Limitations on Executive Discretion." In *Both Ends of the Avenue*, edited by Anthony King. Washington, D.C.: American Enterprise Institute, pp. 154–84.

Schmidt, Warren, and Posner, Barry. 1986. "Values and Expectations of Federal Service Executives." *Public Administration Review*, Vol. 46, No. 5 (September–October), pp. 447–54.

Schneider, Andrew, and Flaherty, Mary Pat. 1986. "U.S. Investigation Details Loose Controls, Profiteering." *Pittsburgh Press*, 13 July.

Schutz, Howard. 1983. "Effects of Increased Citizen Membership on Occupational Licensing Boards in California." *Policy Studies Journal*, Vol. 2, No. 3 (March), pp. 504–16.

Schwarz, John. 1983. *America's Hidden Success: A Reassessment of Twenty Years of Public Policy*. New York: W. W. Norton.

Shabecoff, Philip. 1982. "Environmental Agency Won't Relax Rules on Lead Levels in Gasoline." *New York Times*, 30 March.

Shapiro, Martin. 1983. "Administrative Discretion: The Next Stage." *Yale Law Journal*, Vol. 92, No. 8 (July), pp. 1487–1522.

Sharkansky, Ira. 1971. "Agency Requests, Gubernatorial Support and Budget Success in State Legislatures." In *State and Urban Politics*, edited by Richard Hofferbert and Ira Sharkansky. Boston: Little, Brown & Co., pp. 323–42.

Sherick, L. G. 1978. *How to Use the Freedom of Information Act*. New York: Arco Publishing Co.

Shribman, David. 1983. "Judge Blocks Watt from Selling Rights to Mine U.S. Coal." *New York Times*, 29 September.

Spiller, Dudley, Jr. 1977. "A Case Study of Holt v. Sarver." In *After Decision: Implementation of Judicial Decrees in Correctional Settings*, edited by M. Kay Harris and Dudley Spiller, Jr. Washington, D.C.: National Institute of Law Enforcement and Criminal Justice (October), pp. 31–142.

Stein, Jane. 1982. "Warning from Health Experts: Federal Anti-Lead Drive Is Running out of Gas." *National Journal*, 5 June.

Stewart, Richard. 1975. "The Reformation of American Administrative Law." *Harvard Law Review*, Vol. 88, No. 8 (June), pp. 1669–1813.

Sundquist, James. 1981. *The Decline and Resurgence of Congress*. Washington, D.C.: The Brookings Institution.

———. 1983. "The Legislative Veto: A Bounced Check." *The Brookings Review*, Vol. 2, No. 1 (Fall), pp. 13–16.

Sundquist, James, with Davis, David. 1969. *Making Federalism Work: A Study of Program Coordination at the Community Level*. Washington, D.C.: The Brookings Institution.

Sunstein, Cass. 1984. "Deregulation and the Hard-Look Doctrine." In *The*

Supreme Court Review, 1983, edited by Philip Kurland et al. Chicago: University of Chicago Press, pp. 177–213.

Taylor, Serge. 1984. *Making Bureaucracies Think: The Environmental Impact Statement Strategy of Administrative Reform*. Palo Alto, Calif.: Stanford University Press.

Thain, Gerald, and Haydock, Kenneth. 1983. "A Working Paper: How Public and Other Members of Regulation and Licensing Boards Differ: The Results of a Wisconsin Survey." Madison, Wis.: Center for Public Representation.

Thayer, Frederick. 1981. "Civil Service Reform and Performance Appraisal: A Policy Disaster." *Public Personnel Management Journal*, Vol. 10, No. 1, pp. 20–28.

———. 1984. "The President's Management 'Reforms': Theory X Triumphant." In *Legislating Bureaucratic Change: The Civil Service Reform Act of 1978*, edited by Patricia Ingraham and Carolyn Ban. Albany: State University of New York Press, pp. 29–41.

Thompson, Frank, and Scicchitano, Michael. 1985. "State Implementation Effort and Federal Regulatory Policy: The Case of Occupational Safety and Health." *Journal of Politics*, Vol. 47, No. 2 (May), pp. 686–703.

Thompson, James. 1967. *Organizations in Action*. New York: McGraw-Hill.

Tolchin, Martin. 1983. "In Spite of the Court, the Legislative Veto Lives On." *New York Times*, 21 December.

Trubek, Louise, and Hickey, Margaret. 1985. "Intervenor Financing at the Wisconsin Public Service Commission: A Program in Search of a Model." Paper presented at Conference on the People's Counsel, Madison, Wis., 18 February.

U.S. General Accounting Office. 1980. "Federal-State Environmental Programs—The State Perspective." Washington, D.C., U.S. Government Printing Office. August.

———. 1981. *Annual Report 1980*. Washington, D.C.: U.S. Government Printing Office.

———. 1986. "Food Stamp Program: Refinements Needed to Improve Accuracy of Quality Control Error Rates." Washington, D.C. September.

———. 1986. "Managing Welfare: Issues and Alternatives for Reforming Quality Control Systems." Washington, D.C. August.

U.S. Senate. Committee on Governmental Affairs. 1977. "Public Participation in Regulatory Agency Proceedings." July.

U.S. Senate. Subcommittee on Administrative Practice and Procedure. Committee on the Judiciary. 1980. "Staff Report on Oversight Hearings, Agency Implementation of the 1974 Amendments to the FOIA." March.

"U.S. Won't Cut Funds for Southern Center." 1987. *Milwaukee Journal*, 31 January.

REFERENCES

Van Alstyne, William. 1977. "Cracks in 'The New Property': Adjudicative Due Process in the Administrative State." *Cornell Law Review*, Vol. 62, No. 3 (March), pp. 445–93.

Van Horn, Carl. 1979. *Policy Implementation in the Federal System*. Lexington, Mass.: D. C. Heath.

Van Riper, Paul. 1958. *History of the U.S. Civil Service*. Evanston, Ill.: Row, Peterson & Co.

Verkuil, Paul. 1978. "The Emerging Concept of Administrative Procedure." *Columbia Law Review*, Vol. 78, No. 2 (March), pp. 258–329.

Vernon, Charles III. 1977. "The Inflation Impact Statement Program: An Assessment of the First Two Years." *American University Law Review*, Vol. 26, pp. 1138–68.

Vogel, David. 1983. "Cooperative Regulation: Environmental Protection in Great Britain." *The Public Interest*, No. 72 (Summer), pp. 88–106.

Walcott, Charles, and Hult, Karen. 1986. "Organizational Design as Public Policy." Paper presented at the annual conference of the Association for Public Policy Analysis and Management. Austin, Tex., 31 October.

Warner, Gary. 1986. "Despite Ruling, Future of Liquor Stores up in Air." *Pittsburgh Press*, 30 December.

Washington Post. Editorial. 1977. "The GAO's Tour of the Smithsonian." 25 September.

Wattenberg, Ben. 1987. "MacNeil/Lehrer News Hour," 4 August.

Weaver, Warren. 1977. "U.S. Information Act: Difficulties Despite Successes." *New York Times*, 8 August.

Weiss, Janet. 1982. "Coping with Complexity: An Experimental Study of Public Policy Decision-Making." *Journal of Policy Analysis and Public Management*, Vol. 2, No. 1 (Fall), pp. 66–87.

Welborn, David; Lyons, William; and Thomas, Larry. 1984. "Implementation and Effects of the Federal Government in the Sunshine Act." Final report for the Administrative Conference of the U.S., Washington, D.C. June.

Wenner, Lettie. 1982. *The Environmental Decade in Court*. Bloomington: Indiana University Press.

Wholey, Joseph. 1978. *Zero-Base Budgeting and Program Evaluation*. Lexington, Mass.: D. C. Heath & Co.

Wildavsky, Aaron. 1966. "The Political Economy of Efficiency: Cost-Benefit Analysis, Systems Analysis, and Program Budgeting." *Public Administration Review*, Vol. 26, No. 4 (December), pp. 292–310.

———. 1979. *Speaking Truth to Power: The Art and Craft of Policy Analysis*. Boston: Little, Brown & Co.

———. 1984. *The Politics of the Budgetary Process*. 4th ed. Boston: Little, Brown & Co.

Williams, Lena. 1986. "Reagan Drug Testing Plan to Start Despite Court Rulings Opposing It." *New York Times*, 29 November.

Williams, Stephen. 1975. " 'Hybrid Rulemaking' under the APA: A Legal and Empirical Analysis." *University of Chicago Law Review*, Vol. 42, No. 3 (Spring), pp. 401–56.

Willoughby, W. F. 1923. *The Reorganization of the Administrative Branch of the National Government*. Baltimore: Johns Hopkins University Press.

Wills, Garry. 1971. *Nixon Agonistes*. New York: Signet Books.

Wilson, James Q. 1974. "The Politics of Regulation." In *Social Responsibility and the Business Predicament*, edited by James McKie. Washington, D.C.: The Brookings Institution, pp. 135–68.

———. 1978. *The Investigators: Managing FBI and Narcotics Agents*. New York: Basic Books.

———. 1978. "The Rise of the Bureaucratic State." In *Bureaucratic Power in National Politics*, 3d ed., edited by Francis Rourke. Boston: Little, Brown & Co., pp. 54–78.

———, ed. 1980. *The Politics of Regulation*. New York: Basic Books.

Wilson, Woodrow. 1887. "The Study of Administration," *Political Science Quarterly*, Vol. 2 (June), pp. 197–222.

Wright, J. Skelly. 1974. "The Courts and the Rulemaking Process: The Limits of Judicial Review." *Cornell Law Review*, Vol. 59, No. 3 (March), pp. 375–97.

Yarbrough, Tinsley. 1982. "The Judge as Manager: The Case of Judge Frank Johnson." *Journal of Policy Analysis and Management*, Vol. 1, No. 3 (Spring), pp. 386–400.

———. 1981. *Judge Frank Johnson and Human Rights in Alabama*. University: University of Alabama Press.

Yates, Douglas. 1982. *Bureaucratic Democracy: The Search for Democracy and Efficiency in American Government*. Cambridge, Mass.: Harvard University Press.

Court Cases

Action for Children's Television v. FCC, 564 F. 2d 458 (D.C. Cir., 1977).

American Textile Manufacturers Institute v. Donovan, 452 U.S. 490 (1981).

Appalachian Power Co. v. EPA, 477 F. 2d 495 (4th Cir., 1973).

Appalachian Power Co. v. Ruckelshaus, 477 F. 2d 495 (4th Cir., 1973).

Arnett v. Kennedy, 416 U.S. 134 (1974).

Bell v. Burson, 402 U.S. 535 (1971).

Bishop v. Wood, 426 U.S. 341 (1976).

Board of Curators of University of Missouri v. Horowitz, 435 U.S. 78 (1978).

Board of Regents v. Roth, 408 U.S. 564 (1972).

Citizens to Preserve Overton Park v. Volpe, 401 U.S. 402 (1971).

Columbia Gas Transmission Corp. v. FERC, 628 F. 2d 578 (D.C. Cir., 1979).

Dames & Moore v. Regan, 453 U.S. 654 (1981).

Dixon v. Love, 431 U.S. 105 (1977).

Equal Employment Opportunity Commission v. Wyoming, 460 U.S. 226 (1983).

Federal Energy Regulatory Commission v. Mississippi, 456 U.S. 742 (1982).

Finney v. Arkansas Board of Corrections, 505 F. 2d 194 (8th Cir., 1974).

Finney v. Hutto, 410 F. Supp. 251 (E.D. Ark., 1976).

Gagnon v. Scarpelli, 411 U.S. 778 (1973).

Garcia v. San Antonio Metropolitan Transit Authority, 105 S. Ct. 1005 (1985).

Goldberg v. Kelly, 397 U.S. 254 (1970).

Goss v. Lopez, 419 U.S. 565 (1975).

Greater Boston TV Corp. v. FCC, 444 F. 2d 841 (D.C. Cir., 1970).

Gulf South Insulation v. CPSC, 701 F. 2d 1137 (5th Cir., 1983).

H&H Tire Co. v. DOT, 471 F. 2d 350 (7th Cir., 1972).

Halderman v. Pennhurst State School and Hospital, 446 F. Supp. 1295 (E.D. Pa., 1977).

Hodel v. Virginia Surface Mining and Reclamation Association, 452 U.S. 264 (1981).

Holt v. Hutto, 363 F. Supp. 194 (E.D. Ark., 1973).

Holt v. Sarver, 300 F. Supp. 825 (E.D. Ark., 1969).

Holt v. Sarver, 309 F. Supp. 362 (E.D. Ark., 1970).

Home Box Office v. FCC, 567 F. 2d 9 (D.C. Cir., 1977).

Humphrey's Executor v. U.S., 295 U.S. 602 (1935).

Immigration and Naturalization Service v. Chadha, 462 U.S. 919 (1983).

Industrial Union Dept. v. American Petroleum Institute, 448 U.S. 607 (1980).

Ingraham v. Wright, 430 U.S. 651 (1977).

International Harvester Co. v. Ruckelshaus, 478 F. 2d 615 (D.C. Cir., 1973).

James v. Wallace, 406 F. Supp. 318 (M.D., Ala., 1976).

Mathews v. Eldridge, 424 U.S. 319 (1976).

Meachum v. Fano, 427 U.S. 215 (1976).

Mobil Oil Corp. v. FPC, 483 F. 2d 1238 (D.C. Cir., 1973).

Morales v. Turman, 364 F. Supp. 166 (E.D. Tex., 1973).

Morales v. Turman, 383 F. Supp. 53 (E.D. Tex., 1974).

Morrissey v. Brewer, 408 U.S. 471 (1972).

Motor Vehicle Manufacturers Assn. of U.S., Inc. v. State Farm Mutual Automobile Insurance Co., 103 S. Ct. 2856 (1983).

National League of Cities v. Usery, 426 U.S. 833 (1976).

Natural Resources Defense Council v. U.S. Nuclear Regulatory Commission, 547 F. 2d 633 (D.C. Cir., 1976).

Newman v. Alabama, 349 F. Supp. 278 (M.D., Ala., 1972).

Newman v. Alabama, 559 F. 2d 283 (5th Cir., 1977).

New York State Association for Retarded Children v. Carey, 393 F. Supp. 715 (E.D. N.Y., 1975).

New York State Association for Retarded Children v. Rockefeller, 357 F. Supp. 752 (E.D. N.Y., 1973).

Pacific Gas and Electric v. P.U.C. of California, 106 S. Ct. 903 (1986).

Palmigiano v. Garrahy, 443 F. Supp. 956 (D.R.I., 1977).

Paul v. Davis, 424 U.S. 693 (1976).

Pennhurst State School and Hospital v. Halderman, 101 S. Ct. 1531 (1981).

Perry v. Sindermann, 408 U.S. 593 (1972).

Pikes Peak Broadcasting Co. v. FCC, 422 F. 2d 671 (D.C. Cir., 1969).

Portland Cement Association v. Ruckelshaus, 486 F. 2d 375 (D.C. Cir., 1973).

Public Citizen Health Research Group v. Rowland, 796 F. 2d 1479 (D.C. Cir., 1986).

Pugh v. Locke, 406 F. Supp. 318 (M.D., Ala., 1976).

Torres v. New York State Department of Labor, 405 U.S. 949 (1972).

U.S. v. Nova Scotia Food Products Corp, 568 F. 2d 240 (2d Circuit, 1977).

United Transportation Union v. Long Island Railroad Company, 102 S. Ct. 1349 (1982).

Vermont Yankee Nuclear Power Corp. v. Natural Resources Defense Council, 435 U.S. 519 (1978).

WAIT Radio v. FCC, 418 F. 2d 1153 (D.C. Cir., 1969).

Walter Holm and Co. v. Hardin, 449 F. 2d 1009 (D.C. Cir., 1971).

Welsch v. Dirkswager, No. 4–72 Civ. 451 (D. Minn. Dec. 7., 1977).

Welsch v. Likins, 373 F. Supp. 487 (D. Minn., 1974).

Wisconsin v. Constantineau, 400 U.S. 433 (1971).

Wolff v. McDonnell, 418 U.S. 539 (1974).

Wuori v. Zitnay, No. 75-80-SD (D. Me. July 14, 1978).

Wyatt v. Aderholt, 503 F. 2d 1305 (5th Cir., 1974).

Wyatt v. Stickney, 325 F. Supp. 781 (M.D. Ala., 1971).

Wyatt v. Stickney, 344 F. Supp. 373 (M.D. Ala., 1972).

Yee-Litt v. Richardson, 412 U.S. 924 (1973).

Youngberg v. Romeo, 102 S. Ct. 2452 (1982).